JOB

Published by
The Bible Reading Fellowship
First Floor, Elsfield Hall
15–17 Elsfield Way, Oxford OX2 8FG
ISBN 1 84101 094 4

First published 2002
10 9 8 7 6 5 4 3 2 1 0

Acknowledgments
Unless otherwise stated, scripture quotations are taken from
The New Revised Standard Version of the Bible, Anglicized
Edition, copyright © 1989, 1995 by the Division of Christian
Education of the National Council of the Churches of Christ in
the United States of America, and are used by permission. All
rights reserved.

A catalogue record for this book is
available from the British Library

Printed and bound in Great Britain
by Bookmarque, Croydon

JOB

THE PEOPLE'S
BIBLE COMMENTARY

KATHARINE
DELL *of St Catharine's College Cambridge*

A BIBLE COMMENTARY FOR EVERY DAY

ACKNOWLEDGMENTS

I would like to thank Naomi Starkey of BRF for commissioning me to do this work, which I have found very enjoyable. It has taken me back to the subject of my doctoral research and I am always amazed by the way the text speaks afresh every time I read it. I would like to dedicate this book to my husband Douglas Hamilton, who has patiently read and commented upon various works of mine on Job. Having mentioned one of my cats in my last book, I would like to mention the other two in this—Tobias and Keren-Happuch, the latter named, appropriately for the subject of this book, after the third daughter of Job!

Introducing the
People's Bible Commentary
SERIES

Congratulations! You are embarking on a voyage of discovery—or rediscovery. You may feel you know the Bible very well; you may never have turned its pages before. You may be looking for a fresh way of approaching daily Bible study; you may be searching for useful insights to share in a study group or from a pulpit.

The People's Bible Commentary (PBC) series is designed for all those who want to study the scriptures in a way that will warm the heart as well as instructing the mind. To help you, the series distils the best of scholarly insights into the straightforward language and devotional emphasis of Bible reading notes. Explanation of background material, and discussion of the original Greek and Hebrew, will always aim to be brief.

- If you have never really studied the Bible before, the series offers a serious yet accessible way in.

- If you help to lead a church study group, or are otherwise involved in regular preaching and teaching, you can find invaluable 'snapshots' of a Bible passage through the PBC approach.

- If you are a church worker or minister, burned out on the Bible, this series could help you recover the wonder of scripture.

Using a People's Bible Commentary

The series is designed for use alongside any version of the Bible. You may have your own favourite translation, but you might like to consider trying a different one in order to gain fresh perspectives on familiar passages.

Many Bible translations come in a range of editions, including study and reference editions that have concordances, various kinds of special index, maps and marginal notes. These can all prove helpful in studying the relevant passage. The Notes section at the back of each PBC volume provides space for you to write personal reflections, points to follow up, questions and comments.

Each People's Bible Commentary can be used on a daily basis, instead of Bible reading notes. Alternatively, it can be read straight through, or used as a resource book for insight into particular verses of the biblical book.

If you have enjoyed using this commentary and would like to progress further in Bible study, you will find details of other volumes in the series listed at the back, together with information about a special offer from BRF.

While it is important to deepen understanding of a given passage, this series always aims to engage both heart and mind in the study of the Bible. The scriptures point to our Lord himself and our task is to use them to build our relationship with him. When we read, let us do so prayerfully, slowly, reverently, expecting him to speak to our hearts.

Contents

PBC JOB: INTRODUCTION

Job, a story for today

The book of Job is in many ways one of the most relevant books of the Bible. This has no doubt been true for many generations and it is no less so today. The book of Job airs the problem of undeserved suffering and, although it presents the specific case of a man called Job who was pious and God-fearing but was struck by calamity, anyone in a situation of suffering can relate to at least some of the sentiments found within its pages.

The book opens in storylike fashion, telling us of this extremely pious man called Job who was so anxious that he and his family should please God that he did good deeds on behalf of his children as well as himself. A series of calamities falls upon him—he loses his property and his children and, on seeing the devastation, his wife advises him to give up on God. He does no such thing and at first sight he appears to respond to the calamities with remarkable acceptance. The other part of the story, about which Job knows nothing, is the heavenly debate which takes the form of a wager in heaven between God and Satan on the very question of Job's motivation for his piety. Is he being pious only because of the material and spiritual rewards that he hopes to gain? What would happen if his prosperity was taken away? How would we feel if a string of catastrophes happened to us? Would we lose our faith and trust in God? How would we rationalize the situation?

Three friends come to visit Job in his distress and at the end of the prologue (2:13) they sit in companionable silence alongside Job. The storyline is then broken in chapter 3 by the beginning of a long dialogue section, which comprises the main body of the book and attempts to answer such questions. Here we encounter a rather different Job from the patient and accepting one. Job now offers a tirade of laments and protests about his situation.

Scholars have generally thought that an author took an older tale that had been circulating about this patient man called Job and said to himself, 'People don't really respond in this pious manner to suffering.' He then wrote the dialogue, perhaps based on his own experience of suffering, which brings Job to life as a character. Job in the dialogue is no longer accepting: he mounts a protest against his suffering, against the orthodoxy as represented by his three friends (who now become rather verbose) that tells him he must have sinned to be suffering this fate, and even against God himself.

In the 27 chapters of dialogue between Job and the friends, both sides present their arguments, indulge in a little banter and criticism and gradually become more hardened in their positions. The main question revolves around whether Job deserves this punishment. Job maintains that he does not, and that something has gone seriously wrong. Maybe God is not just after all; maybe he is not listening; maybe the usual doctrine that right is rewarded and wickedness is punished is all wrong: all these options crowd Job's mind. The friends maintain that he does deserve the punishment he is receiving because God does reward right and punish wrongdoing, and that he is blinded by pride so that he cannot recognize his own sin.

In chapter 28 we find a separate hymn to Wisdom that is in the mouth of Job but probably has a separate origin, and in chapters 29—31 there is a final and heart-rending lament by Job. Then, ironically, a fourth friend appears—an angry young man who, in deference to his elders and betters, had been afraid to speak before, but now decides to have his say. He speaks along the same lines as the other friends but puts more emphasis on the justice and might of God. The very thought that God might not be just is abhorrent to Elihu, who speaks of the mighty and lofty works of God in creation. This section is a little repetitive of what has gone before and anticipates what comes after. It doesn't add much to the plot and some scholars have considered it to have been added to the book later than the main dialogue. However, we will consider it as a full part of the book, in the interests of considering the book as a whole and as a text that was read as a unity for many centuries before the rise of critical scholarship in the late 19th century.

Once Elihu has had his say, it is the turn of God—and this is the real climax of the book. Throughout the dialogue, Job gradually realizes that it is with God that he is having an argument. He leaves the arguments of the friends behind and finds them to be 'worthless comforters'. He even asks for a mediator to appear between himself and God: God is the judge who appears to have become his enemy too, and that is no good for impartiality in the system of justice. Part of Job's complaint was that God appeared to be absent or not listening. Once God responds, he is partly satisfied: at least there is some communion with God, although God doesn't really answer Job's questions directly. He speaks, as Elihu did, of his great work in creation, of his might and power and of the natural order that he set up which runs according to principles that vary from human ways of looking at things. He overwhelms Job by a display of his power, and the inference is that human ways of looking at the problem of suffering and at the nature of God himself are far too limited. Job is certainly put in his place and he responds with humility and an attitude of repentance.

The ending of the book returns us to the story. We are told that Job passed the piety test and God restored him. We are also told that Job was vindicated by God over against the friends, who were seen to have spoken falsely. What we have here may be the original ending to a story about a pious man who suffered, accepted it in a simple manner on its own terms and then was restored to an even greater prosperity than ever. However, in the context of the dialogue section and all that has gone before—that is, in the context of the overall book as we have it—the epilogue comes across as a highly ironic postscript.

What sort of book is Job?

The book of Job is quite unlike other books of the Old Testament. It is not part of the Pentateuch or *Torah* (the books from Genesis to Deuteronomy), nor does it number among the prophetic books. Rather, it forms part of a more disparate collection of writings which includes narrative literature, apocalyptic works, psalms and wisdom. Job is generally counted among the wisdom writings of the Old Testament, a successor to the book of Proverbs and companion to the book of Ecclesiastes. The book takes for granted the wisdom worldview that those who are righteous in their behaviour are rewarded by God and those who are wicked are punished. Of course we all know that there are shades of righteousness and wickedness—few people are completely one or the other at any time. Yet the world is presented in this rather black-and-white way in order to make plain that life is full of choices and moral decisions, and that it is good to make the right choices wherever possible, and bad to take a series of choices that lead down the path of ruin and despair. The proverbial material is made up mainly of maxims that express truths about human behaviour and relationships as well as some instructional material aimed at educating young men.

The book of Job is rather different in genre from Proverbs in that it mainly consists of narrative and dialogue, and yet its presuppositions are the same, for it shares the same wisdom worldview. The friends of Job, in the dialogue section, maintain the standard position as found in Proverbs, that the righteous are rewarded while the wicked are punished. Job is clearly being punished, they say, and so he must have sinned against God. Job, on the other hand, although he had also espoused the wisdom worldview in that he had acted piously in everything in order to guarantee that he was walking along the path of righteousness, now finds his experience showing that the simple equation of righteousness with reward and wickedness with punishment does not work. He has done nothing wrong—he is sinless—and yet he is being punished. He is an innocent man, so what has happened? The book of Job is thus a challenge to the traditional wisdom position and in that sense is a kind of 'wisdom in revolt'.

Another point to make about genre is that, although Job fits in with the wisdom debates and is in that broad sense a wisdom book, it also draws on genres from a wider world. In the dialogue in particular, Job uses lament forms, more familiar to us from the psalms (for example, Psalm 49, which provides a close parallel to Job) than the wisdom literature, and he also uses legal terminology as he tries to clarify his case against God, the supreme arbiter. This suggests that the book is not to be classified narrowly as wisdom literature, but is part of a wider intellectual tradition in which the author was able to draw on other thought-worlds. He did so in a clever manner, too, in that not only did he use other genres, but he also subverted them, almost parodying the tradition at times. So, for example, instead of presenting us, as the psalms might, with a list of God's good actions in his creation of the world, the author of Job points out the bad actions; and instead of having Job praise God for his continual presence and care, he has Job wishing that God would go away and not hedge him in. The book of Job thus provides a critique of the status quo and in that sense is close in sentiment to another wisdom book in the Old Testament canon, Ecclesiastes.

The author of Ecclesiastes also deeply questions the tradition of 'just deserts' and also raises serious doubts about the possibility of real meaning in life, in relationships and with reference to God. That book is more deeply pessimistic than Job: Job is still wrestling with the problems and having a good argument with God, while the author of Ecclesiastes is much more resigned.

The wisdom tradition is, then, a rich and varied one, a tradition that speaks very much to us today in its emphasis on universal human experience and on trying to forge a moral path through the maze of choices on offer, trying to understand the bad times alongside the good.

Who wrote it—where, when and why?

I have already indicated the widespread scholarly opinion that we see in the book of Job the hand of a main author who recognized the potential of a rather simplistic prose tale and added the dialogue and God's speeches to turn it into a much more profound book. The actual prose tale that is contained in the prologue and epilogue to the book may have formed an existing narrative in which Job was the victim of trials and responded in a pious fashion. There is further question as to whether the scenes in heaven and the wager are part of the original story. One argument against this is that the prologue and epilogue are generally very well balanced: for example, the number of camels and other animals lost in the prologue is exactly doubled in the epilogue. However, there is no such parallel with the mention of God and Satan. Satan is omitted entirely from the epilogue and not one word is said about the restoration of Job's health (although it is presupposed that he was cured of the disease which had been inflicted by Satan in the prologue). It is possible, then, that the reference to the wager with Satan was a later editor's attempt to take some of the blame for Job's plight away from God. It is also the case that the idea of Satan or 'the Satan' (the adversary) as it appears in Job is not widespread in the Old Testament and may have appeared as an idea with the influence of Persian religion on Judaism in the post-exilic period. This might suggest that it did not form a part of the story of an earlier folktale.

There is an interesting witness to an early tale of some kind in the prophet Ezekiel, who reveals in 14:14, 20 that he knew of a particularly righteous person called Job. The prophet mentions him alongside Noah and Daniel as a righteous man. The gist of what Ezekiel is saying to the exiles in Babylon is that even if these super-righteous people were here, they would not save the rest of that generation by a kind of overspill of righteousness; rather, each person is responsible for his or her own behaviour. This reference does indicate that the story of Job in some form was known before the exile. However, the balance of probability lies in favour of the book of Job, as written by the main author, coming after the exile, perhaps between the sixth and fourth centuries BC. The issue of punishment for sin had come very much to the fore at the exile: did Israel as a nation deserve their punishment? The response of the prophets was generally that Israel did deserve it. However, as Ezekiel mentions, this raised the question of individuals and their rewards and punishments, and Job is a kind of test case of an innocent person who nevertheless is seemingly punished by God. The earlier presuppositions of Proverbs were ripe for challenge: life was not as simple as the straightforward maxims of the wisdom literature made out. There were genuine cases of un-deserved suffering, but how were these to be understood within the existing worldview?

Wisdom literature is international in its scope. There was wisdom literature in Egypt and Mesopotamia, and we can find parallel texts especially from Mesopotamia where there was a tradition of lament and questioning similar to the biblical book of Job. The international flavour of wisdom literature makes the book difficult to date, except in very general terms. The author also hides behind his characters. While we might say that this author was clearly educated, well versed in wisdom techniques and worldview, possibly even a wise man himself (although one who was prepared to criticize the status quo), we cannot know much more than that. He must have suffered him-self to be able to give us such profound thoughts about the nature of suffering. The use of Edomite names for the three friends might suggest some context in Edom, south-east of Jerusalem in part of today's Jordan. Job is not presented as an Israelite, which is interest-ing given that the debate is certainly of concern to Israelites, but one of the factors about the wisdom literature is that it is not bound to Israel in any kind of nationalistic way. The history of Israel and its main characters are not mentioned. There is an international and uni-versal flavour to the book, making Job a character to whom more than just Israelites or Jews can relate.

Whoever did write the book of Job created a masterpiece of world literature that continues to speak to people in situations of suffering today. It is one of the most profound books in the Bible in that it airs a difficult and extremely important issue—that of innocent suffering

—with sensitivity and depth of insight. It also provided a challenge to the orthodoxies of its own day, and even to the orthodoxies of our own day. Have you not come across people who still believe that if you are ill with a terminal disease, or if you have fallen on bad times, the judgment of God is in there somewhere?

How did it reach its final form?

The main author of the book of Job probably composed the dialogue section and God's speeches, including Job's replies, setting them within a prose narrative that either already existed or that he wrote himself, based on an oral tradition. It is likely that he put chapter 28 in its present position, although this could originally have pre-dated the book as it has the nature of a separate hymn to Wisdom. Alternatively, a clever editor could have added this chapter later on, as the book was reaching its final form. Some scholars believe that the second God-speech was also added by editors. Many think that the Elihu speeches were added later and some believe that the Satan passages in the prologue were also an addition.

These kinds of opinions are largely out of vogue today, with scholars preferring not to carve up the text but to read the book as a whole, as it has been read by centuries of Bible readers. I have some sympathy with this view and will of course in this commentary be looking at the text in its entirety. However, some understanding of the work of editors does enable us to get a sense of the development of the text and of the changing priorities of those who added sections. If the Elihu speeches, hymn to Wisdom and other parts have been added, why would that be? Why was the book felt to be incomplete? I suggest that the additions reveal an early stage of 'orthodoxization' of the book. The main author wrote something daring and revolutionary: he had Job challenging God himself. Possibly this was shocking to an increasingly pious audience, who wished to affirm Job's right to protest on the one hand but to bolster the traditional position, as held by the friends, on the other. Hence the appearance of a fourth friend who has another 'go' at Job and of the hymn to Wisdom which reinforces the 'wisdom' nature of the book.

The second of God's speeches might be part of this process—an extra piece, reaffirming God's power not just over ordinary animals (as in the first speech) but over extraordinary ones too. The wager between God and Satan also might have been added to take some of the blame off God and to moderate the baldness of Job's protest against God himself (for nowhere in the dialogue does Job blame Satan—he is not even mentioned). This kind of reconstruction is necessarily speculative, but it does have some support in the way that the 'tradition' read Job.

We find in both Jewish and Christian circles an interest in the character of Job and an emphasis on his more pious responses rather than on his more protesting ones. Because most people did not have access to a 'written text'—only a few copies would have existed, and only among the learned—the 'story' of Job was all that was known. Even when Job was used in the Christian liturgy in medieval times, it was very much an abbreviated version of the sentiments that people knew. The protest of Job was lost in the focus on the prose section—the 'story'—and in the interest shown in the character of Job. This is famously illustrated by the reference in the epistle of James to 'the steadfastness/patience of Job' (James 5:11), a phrase that has entered the English language as a reference to an extremely patient person. It is ironic that the tradition remembers Job thus, when what we actually find in the main body of the book is a highly protesting and angry figure. Scholars sometimes wonder how Job even got into the canon of scripture, such is its protesting nature, but if people were reading the book in this pious manner from early times, perhaps it is hardly surprising that no questions were asked about its inclusion.

The author's protest, too, is cleverly concealed in his parodying of the tradition, a subtlety that not all readers would have appreciated. There is also some scribal dislocation of the third round of speeches, which has the effect of causing the speakers to change their viewpoints. Perhaps this too was a deliberate part of the 'orthodoxization' process which enabled Job to be read in rather more traditional ways than we might choose to read it today. There is a surprising message for us here: God allows us to protest against unfairness, not just at the unfairness of others or of life, but even at his apparent unfairness towards us. It is all right for us to pray to him in our need, in our anger, in our suffering and in our despair.

What are its main themes?

The main theme of the book of Job is the problem of suffering. However, this is presented differently in the various parts of the book. The opening prologue seems to focus on the motives of humans to do good. Why should we do good things? The answer is because we expect to be rewarded by God in this life. Or is it? This is the question posed by Satan: does Job love God because of the hope of reward or is it simply because he loves God? This is a difficult question because clearly the God-fearer does hope that God will keep an eye on him or her: do we not pray to God to help us and protect us? We might draw the line at asking God to make us rich, but there is always a niggling hope when the lottery numbers are called or the horse race is run! Job is promised not only material reward but also long life, a large family, happiness and prosperity according to the 'just deserts' scheme whereby God rewards those who follow the path of righteousness and punishes those who choose to reject it. Job seemingly passes the test of his motives in chapter 2 when he says, acceptingly, that good and bad come alike from God and that we have to receive whatever is dealt out to us. However, the Job of the dialogue is not so accepting and is prepared to wage an attack on God for not keeping to the strict system of reward that was expected by all who followed him.

Another theme that comes out of the book (but this time more from the dialogue) is the acceptance that human beings tend towards sin and that they are justly punished for it. The friends adopt the position that this simple worldview is alive and well and that if Job is being punished then he must have committed some sin, of which perhaps even he is unaware. The propensity to sin is a presupposition that had been around since Adam and Eve—they fell into sin fairly quickly. This idea is countered by Job, notably the conclusion that when humans suffer it must mean that they are sinful. In today's world, the accusation of sinful or wicked deeds is still sometimes made to those who seem to be suffering: he has cancer because he led a selfish and greedy life, living for himself and lining his own pockets, one hears people say. People want to justify a calamity, and it is much more problematic when someone suffers who appears to have been a paragon of virtue. Then the suffering is much harder to understand: here we are back at the Job situation.

Another answer to suffering is that God is 'in his heaven' and is not to be limited by human ideas of his justice. This is to raise the more profound question of how human beings and God interrelate. Clearly God has sought a relationship with human beings and given us some guidelines as to how he wants us to behave, how he wants us to worship him and relate to him and so on. Yet in his speeches, God appears as a mighty 'other' who acts according to his own rules. Elihu maintains that God is just at all costs—but God's speeches make one wonder if that is necessarily so, certainly according to human standards of conduct. The friends are rightly rebuked for having tried to limit God by thinking that they always know the reasons for misfortune. Job perhaps comes a little nearer to appreciating the contradictions of human experience by trying to relate to a God who seems to have his own agenda.

The answer seems to be that God does what he likes and that the world is not simply created for human benefit: look at creation, look at nature and the animals! And yet how satisfactory is that solution for a person who is attempting to please God, to lead a pious life and to be in a rewarding relationship with God? Perhaps the answer is that we have to hope for the best—that God will be on our side—but we have to reckon with the possibility of calamity for no apparent reason and not give up our faith because of it, in the knowledge that God's purposes are greater than ours. This is a possible answer to suffering, one of a number that the author seems to throw up in the discussion and leave for us to reflect upon. The final answer that the author leaves us with is the one given in the epilogue—that if you 'hang in there' as Job does, you too will be rewarded with twice the number of camels that you had before, and a new set of children to replace the old! Is this a satisfactory answer—or is the author having a little fun at our expense?

Outline

1:1—2:13	Opening prologue
3:1–26	Job's opening lament
4:1—14:22	The first round of speeches: Job/the friends
15:1—21:34	The second round of speeches: Job/the friends
22:1—27:23	The third round of speeches (dislocated): Job/the friends
28:1–28	The hymn to Wisdom
29:1—31:40	Job's final lament
32:1—37:24	Elihu's speeches
38:1—40:2	God's first speech
40:3–5	Job's first response

40:6—41:34   God's second speech
42:1–6   Job's second response
42:7–17   Closing epilogue

FURTHER READING

Scholarly books

Katharine J. Dell, *The Book of Job as Sceptical Literature*, BZAW 197,
Walter de Gruyter, 1991
R. Gordis, *The Book of God and Man*, University of Chicago Press, 1965
B. Zuckerman, *Job the Silent*, Oxford University Press, 1991

Commentaries

D.J.A. Clines, *Job 1—20*, Word Bible Commentary, 1989
H.H. Rowley, *Job*, New Century Bible Commentary, 1983
R. Gordis, *The Book of Job: Commentary*, Jewish Theological Seminary
of America, 1978

Devotional books

Katharine J. Dell, *Shaking a Fist at God: Understanding Suffering through
the Book of Job*, Fount Paperbacks, 1995
H.S. Kushner, *When Bad Things Happen to Good People*, Pan Books,
1981
C. Wright and S. Haines, *Suffering: 'Why Silent God, Why?'*, Lion
Publishing, 1991

BLAMELESS & UPRIGHT

We are introduced to Job, a man who lived in the land of Uz, and the first detail we are given about his character is that he is 'blameless and upright' (v. 1). On this fact the entire story rests: Job is an innocent man who has done all he can to lead a pious life. He does not deserve the calamity that is about to fall upon him. The next thing we are told is that Job 'feared God and turned away from evil'. The fear of God is a mainspring of the Wisdom quest, as is adopting the path of right-eousness rather than that of evil. Being blameless and upright are also ideals of Wisdom (Proverbs 2:21). In other words, Job is the perfect wise person.

We all strive in our lives to live up to some of these ideals and we don't always achieve our goals. We make the decision that we are not going to go around murdering people or thieving, or that we are not going to drink to excess or take drugs, but leading an overall 'blameless and upright life' is more difficult. Job, we are told, took his duties seriously. He was a God-fearing man too, and so he could expect, as appears to be the case, that piety would equal prosperity.

The location of Uz isn't of great importance—it is probably part of Edom, an area south-east of Israel, but it could equally well be a legendary, folktale land.

Many possessions

The inevitable consequence of doing 'right' according to the system of just deserts, as promoted by the Wisdom worldview, is prosperity, first in the blessing of children and then in goods. So, in the next breath we are told that Job was the proud father of seven sons and three daughters (v. 2), about the right ratio in a culture that valued male children over female ones. Clearly these are regarded as the first and most important of Job's 'possessions', which are then enumer-ated—7000 sheep, 3000 camels, 500 yoke of oxen, 500 donkeys (in fact, she-asses—more versatile than male donkeys!) and many ser-vants. It is interesting that the servants come last, after the animals: it has been suggested that they were the servants tending the flocks rather than being a generic term for all Job's servants. The numbers of the possessions have a slightly stylized feel to them: the 'seven' and 'three' of sons and daughters is paralleled by the 7000 sheep and 3000 camels. The story is set in patriarchal times when wealth was measured in such things—an indication that it is an ancient tale.

Then we are given an evaluation of Job: this man was a great one, greater than others. He was pious, well-to-do, blessed and rich. That could be the end of the story—a man who did right and was rewarded—but we have 42 chapters to go!

Job's children

We are now introduced properly to Job's children. We are told that Job's sons used to hold feasts in each other's houses in turn (v. 4). We are also told that they invited their sisters to come along. No mention is made of any spouses, which would be an unusual omission in this culture in the case of adult children. The nature of their feasting is uncertain. Were they celebrating birthdays, so that the 'in turn' would refer to the particular day of the year on which a certain child's birthday fell, or were they feasting on every day of the week? Or were they celebrating national feast days? Maybe they were over-indulging—the literal meaning of 'feasts' is 'drinking bouts'. Verse 5 talks of the 'feast days', suggesting that these celebrations lasted for more than one day.

Job was aware of his children's activity and made a point of sanctifying them at the end of the feasting, offering a sacrifice for each. Job was anxious that his children might have sinned and so did this on their behalf. We get the impression that the feasting was legitimate and that Job was being perhaps over-scrupulous in interfering. The purpose of including this detail is not, it seems, simply to tell us about the activities of the children, but rather to highlight this over-scrupulous aspect of Job's character. He was not only blameless and upright himself, he sought to eradicate any trace of sin from the lives of his children too. He was super-pious: if his children had cursed God in their hearts he wanted to absolve it.

PRAYER

Lord, help us to set standards of behaviour for ourselves
and to do all in our power to live up to our own expectations
before we criticize others.

The SCENE IN HEAVEN

We now have a rather dramatic scene change from earth to heaven, giving the reader a peek behind the scenes at the reason for Job's coming suffering. It is a wager between God and Satan that Job is being 'upright' only because of what he can gain—that is, out of self-interest. Of course, Job knows nothing of this heavenly discussion and so, when suffering strikes, there is no apparent reason for it, as is the case in our own experience when we suffer. Satan argues his case that Job is only 'in it for what he can get out of it', against God who maintains that Job's motives are pure. In the first two verses, however, there is no mention of Job. Rather, we are being introduced to the heavenly scene (v. 6) in which God presides in council over heavenly beings. These beings are thought to be either angels or lesser gods—literally 'sons of God' in the Hebrew, recalling Psalm 82 where God takes his seat at the head of a heavenly council consisting of lesser gods.

It is interesting that Satan is mentioned separately from the other divinities. He is 'the Satan', 'the adversary', and the inference is that he has a different role from the others. He was probably once one of the 'sons of God' but has become detached from them. He appears to have a legitimate messenger-type role, going to earth to report on what is happening, a role perhaps shared by other lesser divinities. The idea of 'the Satan' may spring from Persian religion in which good and evil were embodied as deities within a two-tiered view of the universe.

The action is advanced as God asks Satan a question: 'Where have you come from?' (v. 7). This suggests, curiously, that God does not know what Satan gets up to. Does this imply some kind of limitation on God? Maybe it is just a stylistic device to get Satan replying to God and setting the action in motion. Satan's reply is somewhat evasive: 'From going to and fro on the earth…' (v. 7). Satan has been out stirring up trouble, no doubt!

Consider Job's case

God's next question relates to the specific case of Job: has Satan considered Job, God's model servant? (v. 8). The phrase 'no one like him' is usually reserved for God, and so its use as a description of Job is a great honour. God then repeats what we heard in the opening lines—that Job is a rare commodity, blameless and upright, fearing God and turning away from evil. God is simply affirming what we knew already. It is Satan who questions Job's motives. Satan accuses God (vv. 9–10) of putting a fence of protection around Job and his family so that he knows that if he continues being pious, he will prosper. What would happen if that fence was taken away? Satan describes how God has blessed everything that Job has ever done and how he has had nothing but prosperity. Job doesn't know what suffering is. Satan's premise is that Job has chosen the path of uprightness because he knows that it will lead to reward (v. 11). This, Satan holds, is Job's reason for continuing to fear God. Take everything away and he won't be God's model servant any more.

The first test

Satan effectively challenges God to strike Job down: 'Stretch out your hand now and touch all that he has,' he says. The right hand was regarded as the hand of power, and this is presumably what is meant here, although it is not specified. Then, Satan argues, Job will curse God because he will see that piety is not a guarantee of reward and that God is not to be trusted. God quickly agrees to this test and passes the execution of the task of destruction to Satan—but the destruction is to have one proviso, not to touch Job himself. With this commission, Satan leaves the presence of God.

We might ask ourselves what kind of God submits his faithful servants to such a test. The reality here is that Job is an innocent victim, used by God to prove a point in a contest with Satan. We might be reminded of the testing of Abraham in Genesis 22, where a trusting servant is driven to the limits of his obedience to God by being asked to sacrifice his son. Yet in both instances, it is in fact an expression of God's trust in his servant that leads him to allow each of them to go through such a test, and so perhaps we can see the testing in a more positive light.

PRAYER

Lord, you understand our motives for doing things.
Help us to trust you for who you are and not for what
we hope to gain from the relationship.

3

BACK ON EARTH

The scene reverts to the picture of domestic harmony and feasting that we saw before the first heavenly interlude (v. 13). On one of the days on which the eating and drinking was taking place, this time at the house of the eldest brother, a messenger appears with bad news for Job. This is the first of four messages received by Job: four disasters strike from different directions, two natural and two human, showing perhaps the different forms of disaster that can strike unexpectedly, as we find nowadays too. The first disaster (v. 14) is that the oxen and donkeys were attacked by the Sabeans, who took them and killed the servants tending them. Calamity has fallen—the word 'falls' is used repeatedly in this description. Here the Sabeans 'fall' upon the animals. The reference to the servants being killed does indicate that they were especially employed to tend those animals. The second disaster, news of which is brought by a second messenger, is lightning (fire from heaven, as it was regarded in those days) which burned up the sheep and the servants tending them. In this natural disaster, the fire 'fell' from heaven: the word 'fell' again conveys the suddenness of the disaster (v. 16). People often remark that accidents or disasters happen in an instant and can affect you for the rest of your lives, like a car accident, for example, or falling and breaking a limb.

The third messenger brings news of another human disaster (v. 17). This time the Chaldeans raided the camels and carried them off, again killing the servants. It is noticeable that we are running through the animals that make up Job's possessions, as described at the start of the book. This raises a question in our mind as to his other blessing, his children. The fourth messenger answers this question in that a natural disaster has occurred (v. 19). A great desert wind (possibly a tornado) blew across and struck the four corners of the house in which the youngsters were feasting. The house 'fell' upon them and killed them all. This is the greatest of the four tragedies.

'I alone have escaped to tell you'

As a kind of refrain at the end of each of the disasters, the messenger says, 'I alone have escaped to tell you.' This conveys the overwhelming nature of each disaster. The theft and slaughter in disasters one and three are wholesale, and the natural disasters of two and four are so fierce that there is no chance of anyone surviving—except the messenger. We might ask who the Sabeans and the Chaldeans were. The Sabeans might be the inhabitants of Sheba in south-west Arabia, although they are nowhere else in the Old Testament referred to as plunderers. They may be more local enemies or a nomadic group. The Chaldeans were probably northern nomads who conducted raids.

Job's grief and pious response

We are now waiting with bated breath to hear Job's response, and he does so in a somewhat public way with the use of traditional mourning actions. He tears his robe, shaves his head and falls on the ground (v. 20). Tearing the garments is representative of the sudden pain that comes with calamity (compare Genesis 37:29) and shaving the head may be an act of identification with the dead. Job falls to the ground probably to denote his submission in the face of God. Then, surprisingly perhaps, we are told that he worships God. This is our first hint that Job has not lost his faith as a result of these calamities. Instead he says, somewhat resignedly, that he came into this world with nothing and he will die with nothing. God gives and God takes away and for that he is to be blessed (v. 21). It could be an existing liturgical formula that Job is uttering here.

We may be surprised at this pious response. Would we, after all that had happened, be so stoical? The point is reiterated at the end: Job's piety is without limit and he has not sinned (v. 22). He did not charge God with wrongdoing, that is, he did not blame him. This latter point is made to establish his innocence and his fidelity to God, things which will be severely questioned by the three friends. The message here is that Job has survived the first test as set up by God and Satan. Job's piety is still intact.

PRAYER

Lord, preserve us from sudden calamity or accident by your saving power, but if we find ourselves their victims, give us fortitude and courage in the face of difficulty or despair.

REPEAT ACTION IN HEAVEN

Now the scene returns to heaven for round two of the debate between God and Satan. We are returned to the scene as we left it (v. 1), with a divine council assembling as before and Satan coming among them, rather than being one of them, to present himself before God. We have the repetition, in folktale style, of the question, 'Where have you come from?' with the same answer from Satan (v. 2). The technique of repetition has the effect of heightening the drama.

This is the second of only two scenes in heaven, until we come to the actual appearance of God towards the end of the book. We should take note at this stage that there is no scene in the epilogue where Satan is seen to capitulate. Rather, God is in control of all the action to restore Job to his fortunes.

Job—still the test case

We now have the same test case presented by God to Satan: has he considered Job? (v. 3). There is an enumeration of Job's qualities as before, but perhaps in slightly gloating vein, with the addition of one sentence telling us that God is aware of Job's response to calamity. The sentence concerns the fact that Job has persisted in his integrity despite the disasters that Satan persuaded God to bring upon Job 'without cause'. The last phrase is very important because it again confirms Job's innocence of any sin and indicates that God had no reason to punish him.

A loathsome disease

Satan, however, has a clever answer in store. He replies that of course Job maintains his integrity while he is untouched in his person. Possessions and even offspring are one thing, but strike him down with an illness and it will break him. Satan says, 'Skin for skin' (v. 4). He maintains that when one's own life is under threat, one will give up anything to preserve it. So he challenges God to stretch out his hand again but this time to touch Job's bone and flesh, breaking the proviso in the first test that Job's person would not be touched. This will make Job curse God, Satan maintains (v. 5), and then he will have won his wager. God agrees to Satan inflicting an unpleasant disease on Job but is careful to add that Job must not die (v. 6).

So it is done, and Job is inflicted with sores from head to toe. We are not sure what kind of a disease this is, and many options have been suggested. The most likely suggestion is leprosy, but other possibilities include elephantiasis, a disease producing swollen limbs and blackened skin, chronic eczema, smallpox, ulcerous boils, syphilis, scurvy or vitamin deficiency. Take your pick—they all sound unpleasant! Presumably the sores are running ones that itch, and so Job needs to scratch them. He takes a potsherd (a piece of broken pottery) with which to scrape himself—scraping out the pus, perhaps—and sits among ashes. The ashes may be a part of his mourning ritual, signifying his debasement, but 'ashes' probably refers to the burnt remains of a dungheap outside the town wall, a place where lepers and other outcasts from the city congregated. He would be treated by now as a leper and thus unable to mix with the people within the city.

So Job's fate is sealed: he has now become a pathetic figure. He has gone from being a man of wealth, power and respect to an outcast, despised and rejected by all. We all know people who have metaphorically fallen from a great height, those who have become ill or elderly or infirm when previously they were in good health, energetic and so on. Let us remember not to despise their misfortune or to feel secretly glad that it isn't we who have had to suffer. We need to help each other and not to treat people as outcasts or as modern-day lepers.

PRAYER

Lord, we pray for all who are the victims of long-term illness and disease. Give them strength and fortitude to bear the pain and send the power of your healing love into their lives.

CURSE GOD

Uttering curses is blasphemous according to the Bible, whether it be a curse against another person or, even more reprehensible, a curse against God. It was believed that if you uttered a curse against someone, it was a powerful weapon and it really could have some effect upon their well-being. In this context, we meet Job's wife. Interestingly, she was not mentioned earlier in the story as one of Job's blessings. It should be remembered that her children and possessions were also taken away in the calamities described in 1:13–19, and yet no mention is made of her loss or her feelings. Her role is a minor one and she doesn't even have a name. Nor does she reappear in the epilogue.

It is odd that Job's wife was not taken away from Job as part of his loss of family: maybe the irony is that it adds to Job's suffering to have her around and to hear her reaction! We are reminded, perhaps, of the warnings about nagging wives in the book of Proverbs! Her function here is to criticize Job for holding on to his integrity, as when she advises him to 'curse God and die' (v. 9). She can see that God has put Job in the wrong, but she, like him, does not know the real reason for the disasters. For her, there is no point being pious any more—all is lost. Her reaction, then, is a hostile and blaming one. Cursing God was the ultimate crime and indicated a desire for complete severance from him. If one did this, death would normally follow.

Job's response

Job will do no such thing! He accuses his wife of speaking as foolish women would talk (v. 10). Perhaps this comment is a slight on womankind in general, or perhaps Job is referring to a specific group that he knew, or simply to the antitheses of wise women. This is where Job's most pious response comes in: 'Shall we receive the good at the hand of God, and not receive the bad?' It echoes his earlier response that God gives and God takes away, but it is expressed in terms of good and evil. Good things come from God, and these things Job and his wife have enjoyed. Now that bad times are here, they need to accept those too. Again Job shows a strong spirit of acceptance, with no wavering in his faith, that many of us might find incredible in the face of such calamity. The message is reiterated that in all this Job did not sin—an important point to notice as his friends make their appearance.

Enter the friends

Three new characters now appear (v. 11)—these are the three friends of Job who have heard of his troubles and have come from their own lands to comfort him. Their names suggest Edomite connections, but it is not clear exactly who they are or where they are from. Interestingly, we are told that they met together first before going to console Job. Were they not confident enough to come separately? We assume from this, anyway, that they know each other too. As they come along and see Job from a distance—sitting on his dungheap, perhaps—they do not recognize him. It is not clear whether they didn't recognize him because they saw him from far away or because he was so changed in appearance (v. 12). They too indulge in traditional mourning rituals on seeing him: they do what is expected of them, as they will go on to do all along. They raise their voices and weep aloud, probably the traditional wailing that often accompanies mourning. They also tear their clothes as Job did and they throw dust on their heads, an act of self-identification with the dead.

The friends are very considerate at this stage, sitting on the ground with Job for seven days and nights in consoling silence. No one speaks to him, out of respect for the intensity of his suffering. When we suffer a significant calamity in our lives, we often need 'space' to think it through and come to terms with it. There is a period in which we cannot think about anything else because we cannot get thoughts of the calamity out of our minds. We don't always hear if people talk consolingly, and, although at some stage it is helpful to 'talk things through', sometimes the opinions of others are unwelcome as we seek to come to terms with a very personal issue. Yet the presence of others is often very comforting, especially if they don't attempt to offer advice or opinions for a while. This is what the friends do while Job is in this early, shocked state of grief.

PRAYER

Lord, help us to know when to speak and when to be silent, when to support and when to leave alone, when to laugh and when to cry, when to rejoice and when to mourn.

6   JOB 3:1–10

CURSING *the* DAY *of* HIS BIRTH

Having heard that Job will on no account curse God, we now find him cursing the day of his birth. A sudden change seems to come over him. His unquestioning piety turns to protest. Here we are introduced to the Job of the dialogue who is not prepared to take his suffering lying down. It is a powerful thing to curse the day of one's birth—meaning to wish oneself into non-existence (v. 3). He also curses the night in which he was conceived. These are, of course, both events over which Job himself had no control. He wishes that the day of his birth had not been 'sought out' by God. If only he had never existed, he would never have endured this suffering. All memory of him would then be gone from the world.

These are dark, disturbing thoughts from deep down within him. His wife had advised him to 'curse God and die': he has not in fact done this, because he has cursed the day of his birth instead, but it comes remarkably close to her advice nevertheless. We might compare this passage to Jeremiah's curse on the day of his birth (Jeremiah 20:14–18) and with lament psalms, which have a similar pattern. In these verses, then, a very different Job appears—he is no longer patient, he is profoundly distraught.

And the night...

The night is personified as speaking the news of Job's birth (v. 3), presumably referring indirectly to whoever brought the news of the birth of a male to people at the time, although the way the passage reads is as if the night had knowledge of the sex of the child. Job wishes that he could make the day into darkness like the night—light being a sign of blessing and night of evil (v. 6). He wants to remove the day from the calendar so that he is not reminded of it annually. This is in sharp contrast to his children's celebration of their birthdays in the prologue. Job wants the night that conceived him to be barren so that no conception might take place in it. No joyful cries are to be heard on that blackest of nights—a reference possibly to the joy of sexual union experienced by his parents and leading to his conception (v. 7). The adjectives used to describe day and night communicate the sense of despair that Job feels.

The sea monster

Those who curse this 'day' are the powers of darkness, those with power even to raise the sea monster Leviathan. NRSV refers to cursing the 'Sea', an emendation that has occurred to fit in with the subsequent reference to the sea monster, but in fact the Hebrew text reads 'day' and some scholars question whether this change is necessary. The reference to Leviathan is to the creative act in which God put down the sea monster (v. 8; compare Psalm 104:26). Job thus calls upon evil powers that can evoke the chaos monster which was overcome at creation by God. In a reversal of creation itself he longs for darkness rather than light.

Job's further wish is for even the stars of the dawn of the day after his conception—a different day from that of his birth—to be dark (v. 9). This is a reference to the disappearance of the night stars at the dawn as they see the light approaching: let light not appear, he says, and let the sleepy morning not open its eyes. The use of the word 'Let' echoes the words of creation in Genesis 1:3, as spoken by God, suggesting again the wish for a reversal of creative acts. Job wishes that he had never been born. Why weren't the doors shut on his mother's womb so that she could not give birth? Then, the argument goes, he would not have been here to suffer. It is interesting that all thought of his former prosperity is quickly gone. The same sentiment regarding a mother's womb is found in Jeremiah, who, overburdened by the responsibility of his prophetic task, argues that dying in the womb would have been a better fate than being born (Jeremiah 20:17b).

We find here in the book of Job, then, a really agonized, suffering figure—in many ways a more real character than the pious Job of the prologue. This might speak to us more deeply as we ask our questions about suffering today. Many suffering profoundly might think of suicide as an option (interestingly, not a course of action that Job ever considers). Depression and misfortune can mix into a deadly concoction at times. Yet there is always another side to the coin, and even when life does not seem to be all good, there are often good elements that can be reflected upon. Even bad relationships or bad memories can sometimes be worked through to make life more bearable.

PRAYER

Lord, let us never feel so low that we wish for non-existence.
Let us rejoice in the life that we have been given, even if, at times,
it does not seem to be all good.

DYING *at* BIRTH

Job continues to wish that he had died at birth: perhaps he could have died during the process of childbirth (v. 12). He asks why his mother's knees received him, why her breasts were there to give him milk. If everything had not been so straightforward and normal, he would have died and he would not be bearing this excruciating pain now. Some scholars have seen the knees as a reference to the father's knees—his acknowledging of the child as his own—but the mother's knees are more likely. Job longs for the peacefulness of death in contrast to the torment of his life.

In this section we ostensibly have a straightforward lament, but it is actually a parody of the lament form. We find laments in many psalms and they usually involve a sufferer who is making a plea to God. Usually the supplicant is in some distress and is wanting God to help find a way out of present distress. Appeal is often made to God to hear the prayer, to act on the supplicant's behalf and so on, and God is reminded of mighty deeds done in the past on behalf of either an individual or, more likely, the whole people. Usually the supplicant longs for life over death. This is what is surprising here in Job—Job asks for death instead of life! This passage, then, parodies passages in the psalms in particular in which death is regarded as undesirable (for example, Psalm 88:4–5), a technique employed by this author many times during the dialogue, as we shall go on to see.

At rest with the mighty

Job's thoughts move on to the idea of being at rest, that is, of being dead. He thinks of death as a long sleep and sees himself lying down quietly (v. 13). He thinks of kings and rulers who have died. He thinks of their lives spent rebuilding ruins for themselves, presumably a reference to refurbishing palaces. This is a process that continues with each generation, for the buildings that these kings refurbished are no doubt ruins now (v. 14). There is an overtone of the futility of life here: death is the great equalizer and relativizes all activity as futile (compare similar sentiments in Ecclesiastes, for example, 9:2, 10). Job thinks of rich princes accumulating gold and silver all their lives. The unspoken inference is that the accumulation of wealth is a futile activity. There could be a suggestion here that Job is recalling what he had possessed, both in terms of status and material goods.

Oh for some peace...

Job returns to the idea of dying at birth. Being a stillborn child is an attractive option, which could refer to being born dead, or to a miscarriage or even an abortion. Once again, he is wishing for what did not happen, although trying to change the past seems somewhat futile. He thinks of infants that have never experienced life, and wishes he was one of them—upside-down sentiments as compared to the usual gratitude one might feel at having had a chance at life. He uses the imagery of light and darkness again, a keynote of this passage, and thinks of the realm of the dead as a peaceful place where there is no trouble from the wicked, and where the weary are at rest. Prisoners are at ease together, with no prison warden telling them to get on with their hard labour. All are equal in death whether they be small and great. In death, no slaves are subject to masters and all hierarchies are gone: death is the great leveller.

These are pessimistic thoughts. Of course, when people suffer terribly, death can be a great release, and yet we must never forget the gift of life that we have all been given. To wish oneself out of existence is a profoundly negative approach. It is helpful for us to see that others have trodden the path of despair before us and to be able to understand the depths of human pathos, as in this passage from Job. Maybe in some curious way it will help us to regain some sense of balance in our own lives. Sometimes people look at the misfortunes of others and realize that their own misfortunes, which may have loomed large at times, are small by comparison. This in turn may lead to a more positive approach to sorting life out, rather than the futile approach that Job takes in wishing that he had never been born.

PRAYER

Lord, for many, death is a release from pain and suffering,
and for that we must be grateful; but let us not forget
the greatness of the gift of life that you have given to us
and let us not fail to rejoice in it.

WHY LIGHT?

Job now asks why he is alive at all. Sometimes we all wonder why we are alive, but it is usually with a note of thanks in our mind that we have been given this great opportunity to experience the world, whatever life throws at us. However, when life becomes oppressive and miserable, people look for a way out. Here Job is bitter in his complaint and longs for death, although he never considers dying by his own hand. Job longs for death but it doesn't come on request (v. 21a). He uses the analogy of digging for death more than for hidden treasures; and there are overtones here of Job 28, a hymn in which men dig for treasures but can never find the elusive creative principle of wisdom. For one who longs for death, the grave is a welcome friend: it is often said that, for those suffering great pain, death is what they long for because it will be a release from all pain. The joy of receiving what you have tried to gain—such as the joy of those finding hidden gemstones—is expressed by Job in relation to finding death (vv. 21b–22).

Job repeats the refrain, 'Why is light given?' (v. 23; compare v. 20). Light contrasts with darkness as goodness with badness and pleasure with pain. The light here indicates life as opposed to death, but this light is not appreciated by those who wish to end their suffering. Job feels that he has lost his way. In wisdom literature, the wise man knew that if he trod the path of wisdom all would be well. Now those certainties have been taken away and Job can no longer see the way ahead.

We all plan our way to a certain extent. Of course many things happen outside our control, but most people have a sense of what they intend to do today, this week, next month, with a career plan for the next ten years—or even a whole life plan. Job feels that he can no longer plan because of his miserable state. When people suffer long-term illness there is that same feeling of not being able to plan ahead. Job feels that he has been 'fenced in' by God (v. 23). In the prologue he was described by the Satan as 'hedged in' (1:10), but then it was a hedge of protection. Now Job feels God's protective hedge to be an oppression.

Sighing and groaning

Such is Job's pain now that he can do nothing but sigh and groan. He describes his sighings as coming like his bread and his groanings as poured out like water (v. 24). Bread and water are the essentials of life, so this imagery is showing how integral Job's sighings and groanings now are to his character. Sighing a great deal is a sign of stress, and groaning represents pain. Job's worst fears have been realized (v. 25): his dread has overtaken him in the events that have occurred. He has lost his inner confidence and has become insecure, fearing what might lie around every corner. After a shocking experience, people often say that they cannot go out at night, or that they feel nervous at every strange sound. This is a similar sign of insecurity in the face of a loss of confidence. We might see Job's anger as masking an underlying fear: people who feel threatened can become aggressive, trying to display an outer confidence that they don't really feel. Job longs for rest because that is the one thing that is denied him as his fear overtakes him. God is no longer the anchor of his life and he feels exposed and forsaken.

No rest

All Job wants is rest, which is denied to him by the pain that he endures, both physically and mentally. He has no inner peace, he is hyperactive and he cannot rest for thinking of the next trouble facing him.

In this opening lament—thought by most scholars to be a unity— Job is bewailing his lot in the face of God's treatment of him, but it is not a direct address to God. It is rather a kind of monologue based on his own experience, setting the scene for the dialogue that is to follow. His experience has turned everything upside-down. His old certainties have gone and he cannot rest in his mind for worrying about his situation and about the collapse of his world.

The author relays this torment in Job's mind by filling traditional lament forms with an unusual content. Normally a lament expresses a longing for God and a recognition of the benefits that he can endow. Job, by contrast, complains about the light and life that he has been given because they are the opposite of the darkness and death that he desires. Job calls into question his own purpose for being in the world. He also uses the opportunity to muse on the fate of humanity as a whole and on the nature and desirability of death. He is in a gloomy mood!

PRAYER

Lord, let us rejoice in the life and light that we enjoy
and let us try to comfort those who have lost sight of that light
and need our help and guidance.

FINDING *the* RIGHT WORDS

Words have great power. As the proverb reminds us, 'Pleasant words are like a honeycomb, sweetness to the soul and health to the body' (Proverbs 16:24) and, of course, the opposite is true—words spoken in anger or bitterness can be hurtful and are not easily forgotten. Words have the power to excite, to wound, to persuade, to undermine. The power of words is a favourite theme of wisdom literature and here we find Eliphaz, a representative of the wise, trying to find the right word with which to approach the despairing Job. He is cautious, even slightly timid as he wonders whether speaking to Job will offend him. He begins his speech with a tentative question, but then he feels a compulsion to speak welling up within him (v. 2). Sometimes, even when we are afraid to speak up, we have to grit our teeth and do so. The friends sat in consoling silence with Job at first, but now the time is ripe to say something. As friends, they cannot just stand by and let Job feel such despair without trying to help. Their friendship leads them to feel a compulsion to speak—a natural desire arising out of concern for the person. Ironically, their words, although well meant, will probably simply add to Job's present burdens.

We all feel the dilemma at times of whether to speak out or whether to keep a guarded silence. It is all very well having your say, but are your words being heard, are they doing more harm than good and are you jeopardizing the friendship by being outspoken? And so begins what is known as the dialogue section of Job, although we might wonder at times whether 'dialogue' is the right word to use. Often, as we shall see, Job and the friends seem to be talking past each other. Because the friends' words are generally unwelcome, Job often appears to ignore them, but then at times he turns on them in anger, accusing them of 'windy words' (16:3). How difficult it is to be a friend to someone in this state of mind!

Appeal to the past

Eliphaz reminds Job that before his troubles came upon him it was he who always had the right word to say to people (v. 3). He taught people and gave a moral lead. He was a respected elder of the community. He was kind to weaker members of society, giving encouragement and support. Images of weak hands and knees are used for those having difficulty walking along life's path. Their slack hands are hanging by their side; their knees are bent under the weight of their burdens (v. 4). In other words, they have lost morale and sunk into depression. For such as these, Job had the right word to lift their spirits and pull them out of despair. Their path seemed to be strewn with hazards that led them to stumble until Job, with a kind or timely word or deed, helped them back on their feet. Eliphaz is hoping that his words now will have the same effect on Job and that his recalling of Job's former life might restore Job's confidence and hope. He is acting out of good intentions and out of genuine concern, just as Job once did to others.

When the tables are turned...

It is easy, perhaps, to be kind to someone less fortunate than ourselves in the knowledge that we are secure. But what happens when the tables are turned? What happens when you are the one suffering illness or when you have lost family or property in a wave of misfortune, as Job has? Eliphaz is pointing out to Job that now he is in the grip of misfortune he seems to have lost his ability to react with patience and with the right words. He has become as helpless as those he formerly helped. Eliphaz expresses surprise that misfortune has made Job lose his sense of perspective, forgetting the grounding of his beliefs—his fear of God and personal integrity.

Eliphaz cuts to the heart of the problem in a tactful, sympathetic and yet effective manner. Having started cautiously, he then recalls Job's own past actions and comes round to challenging Job for his present attitude which seems to be out of keeping with what went before. He ends with an appeal to belief in God and in right moral action by which Job formerly lived. This touches on a common human experience, that when any one of us is very much changed by despair, it is hard for friends to understand. They knew us as we were before and they want to see us restored. They seek to persuade us out of our grief, all with the best intentions, although it may not be what we want to hear at the time.

PRAYER

Lord, help us to find the right words at the right times,
and give us the courage to speak out in your name, to spread
your living and life-giving word.

10   JOB 4:7-11

JUST DESERTS

How simple life would be if it was fair! If good actions were always rewarded by prosperity, many offspring, many friends and good health, there would be no question about the right path to follow. If bad deeds were always punished by a difficult and painful path through life, would crime not disappear completely? Sadly, life does not always match such a simple pattern, as Job found out, although of course this doesn't nullify the attempt to pursue good rather than wickedness. Many people who are good, upright citizens, helping others and being generous in spirit, do in fact lead happy and prosperous lives. It often seems that the principle of just deserts is alive and well, and that is what Eliphaz is maintaining here. His opening statement is a rhetorical question: 'Who that was innocent ever perished?' (v. 7). In other words, do you know someone who has been punished for being good? It is important to Eliphaz to maintain the principle of justice, because without it his world starts to fall apart. He is asking Job to cite a specific case of goodness being punished. Of course Job could easily point to himself—'Look at me, I have led an upright life, been good to others and I am being unjustly punished'. Eliphaz, however, has his own opinion about that. It emerges later on that, along with the other friends, he thinks that Job must have performed some wicked deed that is being punished according to the established principle of just deserts. This is his logic: the upright are not cut off in their prime and there is not an unprincipled system of justice at work in the universe. Rather, God rewards and punishes according to the rules of retribution. It is of prime importance to Eliphaz to maintain this principle in the face of Job's questioning.

God's wrath

The Old Testament often gets a bad press for portraying God as angry and powerful. Of course, this is not the only picture of God in the Old Testament. We only need to turn to Isaiah to find some profound statements about the love of God and his concern for humankind (for example, Isaiah 40:1–2). However, here Eliphaz makes use of the image of God as being able to strike down the wicked in a moment, with but one blast of his anger—bringing natural disaster, perhaps, or disease. These calamities are things that all people dread, and they have recently happened to Job. The 'breath of God' (v. 9) may refer to the hot wind of the desert rising up and destroying the harvest in an instant, recalling perhaps the wind that caused the demise of Job's children in 1:19, hinting that even they might have been sinful. Perhaps by this hint Eliphaz is underlining Job's supposed guilt, although he has not come out and explicitly said so. Eliphaz is deliberately asserting God's power here, perhaps with the aim of frightening Job. This has often been the approach taken by religious leaders, using language about God to frighten people into belief and submission: we only have to think of images of hell, and of the threats that such terrors might happen to you if you are wicked. Although we might find such imagery unpalatable today, we do perhaps need reminding from time to time of the need to pursue the good rather than the bad, and of the unpleasant consequences both to ourselves and to other people that can arise from unnatural, immoral and antisocial behaviour. If we are to live in a moral world, we need to inspire belief in good and in the importance of right actions. Maybe, then, instilling a little fear of the consequences of wickedness is not such a bad thing...

The lion

Eliphaz goes on to use the imagery of the lion, the most powerful animal in the world (v. 10). He likens the anger of God to the roar of the lion. Such is the power of its roar that the teeth of the young lions are broken. We might think here of breaking glass—such is the power of the sound that it shatters all around it. I think too of Concorde, breaking the sound barrier. The imagery of the lion is continued in a slight digression from the point, almost as if the author, once he thought of lion imagery, got rather carried away with it! Verse 11 may have been an independently circulating proverb, which the author saw fit to add in here. It is a truism that a lion will perish from lack of prey to feed both himself and his family. Once he perishes, the lion cubs will be left to fend for themselves, which probably means death, as another lion moves in to take over the lioness and breed cubs of his own.

PRAYER

God, help us to affirm your power and your love and yet also your right to be angry and to punish. Help us to acknowledge our own limited understanding of your purposes and avoid being dogmatic to others about what we can and cannot do.

A VISION

In this passage we have the unusual description of a visionary experience given by God to Eliphaz. Normally the wisdom literature is seen as the more 'rational' part of the Old Testament—it is the prophets who have visions. Here, however, we have an appeal to a vision from God, a kind of personal revelation, which gives authority to what Eliphaz wishes to say. He claims to have had truth revealed to him at dead of night. It is interesting that the content of the vision is described as a 'word' spoken to him—he is claiming a new revelation beyond usual wisdom ideas. The experience of the presence of God caused his hair to stand up and his bones to shake (v. 14). His mind was agitated and he suddenly felt great terror. He experienced a breath or cold wind passing before his face. He then dimly saw before him in the half light a figure, who uttered words to him.

Can mortals be righteous?

The message revealed by this voice—presumably a manifestation of the presence of God—is part of the argument used by all the friends. We can compare verses 17–19 with later words from Eliphaz in 15:14–16 and with Bildad's words in 25:4–6. The sentiments are also echoed by Job, for example in 9:2. The crux of the issue here is whether a person can be righteous before God. What kind of righteousness do human beings think they have by comparison with God? In the first part of his speech, Eliphaz has established that God does not punish the innocent person. But now he is saying that, in fact, no person can be innocent and pure. It is in the nature of human beings to err. It is part of being created to be imperfect. Even the angels are not pure. We may perceive someone as just, but God's standards of purity are beyond ours. Only God is truly righteous, so all humans are less than perfect and must expect some suffering, as designed for all the unrighteous. This is not the usual wisdom line of argument, which stresses rewards for the righteous and punishment for the wicked, but it does echo traditional sentiments about God alone holding the key to true Wisdom (see, for example, Proverbs 20:24). The idea here, however, is that all fall short of God's standards and so Job's suffering is part of the human condition. Job's claim that he is innocent and does not deserve such suffering is refuted on these grounds.

Earth-creatures

Being earth-creatures, dwelling in 'houses of clay', humans are by nature fragile and lowly (v. 19). They die easily, just like moths: we have a picture in verse 20 of the swatting of insects in great numbers, indicating the scale of the 'turnover' of human life. Eliphaz is musing here on the transience and futility of life. The end of human life is compared to the collapse of a tent as soon as the cord holding it in place is ripped up (vv. 20–21). Eliphaz adds the point that people die without wisdom—a dig at Job, perhaps, for not having perceived what he, Eliphaz, has already understood as a result of his vision. This is a very hierarchical view of the world which tends to denigrate human beings. We might have problems with this portrayal of humans as inherently sinful and so unable to do anything good, but Genesis 1—11 seems to reinforce the idea that we are fallen beings, fallen from an ideal to which we once aspired but, because of our human nature, were destined to lose.

As we shall see in chapter 9, Job is unhappy with this picture. He refuses to see himself (and the rest of humanity) as inherently sinful. In answer to the question, 'How can a man be just before God?' he will argue that God's justice cannot be understood, because it is on a different plane from ours. How, then, can human beings ever hope to know where they stand or how to argue with him? He will stress the impossibility of talking about the justice or otherwise of God, and the need to hold on to our own integrity because that is all we have got. So Job holds on to the knowledge that he has not sinned.

PRAYER

We are but dust and to dust we shall return—help us to be aware,
Lord, of our mortality and to try to live to the full
the life that you have given us.

NOWHERE *to* TURN

Sometimes we get the feeling that the whole world is against us, that no one understands and that we have nowhere to turn. Even friendships on which we had previously relied for a comforting word at the right time can sour and the friends seem to have turned against us. Job must have felt like this while being harangued by his so-called friend, Eliphaz, who taunts him with having no one to support his case (v. 1). He asks Job rhetorically if anyone will answer him. Does he have any heavenly witnesses? This links up with Job's later sentiments about the need for a heavenly mediator to judge between him and God (9:33) because of the unfairness of the fact that God is both judge and prosecution for the defence. Eliphaz is, of course, expecting the answer 'No' to his questions. There is no one who will plead Job's case for him because it is fundamentally wrong. Of this he is sure as he launches into the second part of his diatribe against Job.

Moments of doubt

When we are constructing an argument, we are usually quite good at putting forward all the points that will be in our favour and omitting the arguments against us. We leave those to our opponent to point out! Just occasionally, however, we find ourselves bringing in the wrong point, undermining what we are trying to say. Moments of doubt in our own position are thus revealed. A point of weakness in an argument is often revealed by the use of the word 'surely'. When we start saying, 'Surely, you can see that' or 'Surely, good things happen to good people', we are beginning to sound rather less sure. Here we find Eliphaz saying, 'Surely vexation kills the fool' (v. 2). It is an established fact that too much worry and anxiety will rebound on the worrier, as will jealousy shown by one to another: we only have to think of Shakespeare's Othello, eaten up by jealousy and ruining all his relationships in the process. Or is this fact so established, after all? For a moment, we get a sense of Eliphaz's doubt. He owns up to the fact that he has actually seen fools appearing to prosper (v. 3). But he quickly dismisses the thought, in a hasty redressing of the balance that seemed just for a moment to be out of kilter. Surely their households will be cursed suddenly—or will they?

Hammering the point home

One of the main characteristics of the speeches of the friends is a certain amount of repetition. It is a keynote of the dialogue form used by the author. There is a sense that a point worth making is worth making more than once! Here we find Eliphaz expanding on the successful point he has just made that of course the wicked will be punished. How could he have entertained the thought that it might be otherwise? It is almost as if he is angry with himself at having allowed a moment of doubt, and so he has decided to hammer the point home. He speaks of the danger posed to the children of the foolish: no one is there to protect them and so they are 'crushed' (v. 4) before they have grown to maturity and before they have the right to sit with the elders at the city gate. He describes the foolish as being weak before others: their harvest will be eaten by others. People will snatch food away from those who do not act wisely and from those who have more wealth than they know what to do with.

Eliphaz then goes into a more philosophical mode with the thought that human beings are born to trouble—an established fact, just as it is a fact that sparks fly upwards rather than down (v. 7). It is not the earth that contains trouble; nor does trouble shoot up from the ground (v. 6). Wickedness and foolishness are human attributes, not natural ones. This is an interesting reflection on the goodness of God's created world and the badness that human beings are capable of bringing into it—a point, again, to which the friends will no doubt return.

We might not think of ourselves as 'wicked' or 'foolish', or even at all 'bad'. In fact, it would be difficult to think of anyone as entirely wicked, given that most people have some redeeming qualities. We might reflect, even so, on how we might have been less than thoughtful or kind to someone, or on how we might inadvertently have caused 'trouble' to someone else. Even in the small things, we can work on making lives better, so that one step at a time the world can start to look less 'troubled' than human beings have a tendency to make it.

PRAYER

Lord Jesus, be there for us in our moments of doubt and in our moments of feeling that the world is against us. Help us to reflect on helping others and trying to make the world a less troubled place.

13   JOB 5:8–16

LEADING *by* EXAMPLE

In the last section, Eliphaz was talking, at least indirectly, to Job. Now he changes his tack and expresses what he thinks to be the best course of action: seek God and commit one's cause to him (v. 8). It is often the case that telling others what to do, or even jibing at them, does no less than strengthen their resolve to continue on their own course. Simply stating what one is going to do oneself, or just doing it without saying anything, can be much more powerful. We tend to admire those who do things that we wish we could do. We all model ourselves on others to some degree, and so leading by example can often be the most effective line of persuasion. 'This is what I would do in this situation,' says the concerned friend, rather than, 'This is what I think you ought to do.' Maybe Eliphaz would have been well-advised to have started with this kind of approach, rather than leaving it towards the end of his speech. In its present position it sounds like bragging—trust in God, he is saying, and all will be straightforward. This is, of course, what Job had previously done. However, now that he is beginning to question God's justice, it is less easy for him blindly to accept all that God does on trust, as Eliphaz recommends.

God, the creator

Much of the wisdom literature speaks of God as creator, as do many of the psalms (for example, Psalm 104). God's action in creation is a great source of praise in the Old Testament. The created world demonstrates his wonder and his greatness, beyond human under-standing. His provision of rain is mentioned here (v. 10), recalling part of his original work of creation. The provision of water is a generous, life-giving act, and reveals an order in creation which can be translated into the social order that pervades God's treatment of human beings. Just as he gives rain out of his bounty, so he raises up the lowly and comforts those who mourn (v. 11).

The appeal to God as creator is being used, then, as the backdrop to Eliphaz's argument about God's justice. Not only does God mete out exact justice according to the doctrine of retribution, but he also goes the extra mile to help the needy. In verse 11, and then in verses 15–16, God raises up the underdog, he saves the needy from those who are more powerful and he gives hope to the poor in the face of injustice. We find a clever use of body imagery here: the mouth is used to characterize the power of the mighty, to communicate the idea that by their clever words alone they persecute the needy. The hand is representative of power too: we think of the hand that holds the sword or the hand that strikes a blow. Alternatively, we might recall the hand that holds or the hand that caresses.

Countering craftiness

Human beings often have a rather inflated sense of their own cleverness—especially clever people! In verses 12–13, Eliphaz speaks of God's awareness of the wily schemes and craftiness of humans and of his action against such people. This is part of Eliphaz's argument for God's control over humans and his just judgment of them. God is said here to 'frustrate the devices of the crafty' (v. 12)—we find hand imagery again in the thought that the work of their hands does not lead to success. Hands are often used as a symbol for work: as the popular English proverb says, 'Many hands make light work.' Eliphaz speaks of the craftiness of the wise (v. 13). Isn't it often the case that intelligent people try to run rings around others, confusing them with highbrow arguments and making them say things they do not mean? We are reminded, perhaps, of the clever barrister or politician, for whom words are great power and argument is everything. God, says Eliphaz, will bring such wiliness and scheming to nothing. The end of the wicked will be sudden; they will roam around in the dark like those struck blind; their punishment will be quick and resounding. We are back to the God of judgment, and a certain amount of chilling language is used by Eliphaz just to remind us that bad behaviour—even simple scheming—can lead to devastating consequences from a God who is on the side of justice and whose preference is for the poor and the lowly.

PRAYER

Creator God, your hands have formed and made us. Help us to be aware of your guiding hand in our lives. Help us to keep our hands busy with your work and to be ready to lend a helping hand to others in need.

A DISCIPLINARY GOD

We find in this passage a number of different views of God. We have already learned in the earlier parts of Eliphaz's speech of the God of justice, the God of creation, the God who takes the side of the poor and who slays the wicked. We now meet the God who disciplines. It is often said that discipline is necessary to give children a sense of right and wrong and to enable them to learn right behaviour. Although discipline may seem unfair at the time and cause temporary grief, the long-term effects are beneficial. Here we find Eliphaz revealing his view that suffering can be sent by God as a discipline (v. 17)—unpleasant, but temporary. The inference is that Job's suffering is going to be temporary, a brief period of reproof before the reason for it becomes clear and the relationship moves on. Don't therefore despise God's discipline, Eliphaz warns. He tries to reassure Job that reproof is beneficial and that despite present anguish, God will bind up the wounds and his hands will heal where blows have been struck. Eliphaz believes that God's intention is always to enact justice, even when that justice is not clear to the one suffering (vv. 18–19). He uses a technique known as numerical heightening here: 'God will deliver you from six troubles; in seven…' It is rather like a riddle-me-ree, 'My first is in x, my second in y': the numbering has a cumulative effect. Here the idea is that in trouble after trouble, God will be there to deliver Job in the end—of that he can be sure.

A redeeming God

The thought of redemption and deliverance leads Eliphaz to explore the theme a little further. There is no mention in the wisdom literature of the story of God's great redemption of the people of Israel at the time of the Exodus. This is one of the factors that makes the wisdom literature rather different from the rest of the Old Testament. However, God is described as rescuing all who trust in him from famine and war, from the criticisms of others and from destruction in general. There is talk of laughing in the face of disaster, such is one's trust in God. We might raise some problems with this viewpoint: is it right, for example, to say that God protects all who trust in him in situations of famine and war? Do we not regularly find examples of good people struck down in such conflicts? God does not prevent natural disasters, nor does he pick out a few righteous people from under the rubble of the buildings destroyed by an earthquake. He can be alongside those suffering, those bereaved and those rescued, but is there a pattern to it all? These are hard questions, which we all face at some time or other. But we might just add that Eliphaz's answer here, while simple, does not really begin to address the reality of such situations. He believes in a mechanistic system of reward which means that life is entirely predictable. It is this system that Job is questioning in his anguish, as many in situations of suffering might do today. The questioning does not nullify the idea of God as redeemer, however. We can still believe that God's ultimate purpose for us is a good one, that he redeems us by his love and that he grieves alongside us in situations of sudden calamity and death.

A protecting God

God not only redeems; he also protects. Once again, Eliphaz's slightly simplistic view of the world leads him to say that of course you should not fear wild animals, you should be assured that your tents and flocks are safe (vv. 23–24). God is on your side. Again, we all know that while we might fervently believe that God is on our side, this belief does not entirely protect us from harm. God may desire harmony, but he has created a world that is not harmonious, where animals attack each other and where sometimes human beings themselves do evil.

Of course we could argue that this is not the ideal world that God created—it is a result of human sin. Yet it is the world we have, and unless we can change that world for the better, we have to survive in it. We cannot naïvely proclaim that God will prevent all unpleasantness in our lives. We can hope and pray that it may be so, but ultimately we need a more pragmatic view than Eliphaz's speech allows, and we shall see how Job feels this way too. The speech ends on a note of the blessings that will come to the person who is wise (vv. 25–26)—descendants and longevity. These are traditionally signs of blessing in Jewish thought. Eliphaz finishes with a challenge to Job: this is what the friends understand to be true, and Job needs to realize it too.

PRAYER

God, help us to accept your discipline, to praise your redeeming purpose for us and to know your protection in an unsafe world. Help us to do all we can do to make this world a better place, and help us to spread word of your redeeming love.

15

TASTELESS FOOD

One of the first outward signs of stress is a loss of appetite. Here we find Job suffering from just such a reaction. His anguish is real and deep-seated. If one could weigh it on a pair of scales, he says, it would be heavier than the sands of the sea (vv. 2–3). That's pretty heavy! Of course, in Job's day little would have been known of the world outside the small geographical area that we call today the Middle East, but even the sands of the Mediterranean on Israel's shores would weigh heavily enough for the friends to get the point Job is making. They are simply the heaviest thing he can imagine— impossible, in fact, to weigh. Similarly, his suffering is so great that it falls off the scales. Job seems not to be responding to Eliphaz's points at this stage, but rather dwelling with self-pity on his own situation. In fact, he is justifying his angry words: his anguish is his excuse. The burden of it is so intolerable that it leads him to violent speech. How often this can be the case with those who are ill or in despair. They cannot look outside themselves; they become introverted and sorry for themselves and angry with all around them.

God has turned nasty

It becomes clear here, for the first time in the book, that Job's complaint is entirely against God. God is the one to blame for Job's misfortunes, and this is stressed by Job from the start of his speech (v. 4). He admits to a certain rashness in his words—not apologetically, but because of the huge quantity of suffering he is trying to bear. He then goes on to describe the onslaught that he has received from God's hand. God is portrayed as an archer, the one who has fired poisoned arrows into Job, which have, according to Job, sapped his spirit and made him afraid. This is powerful imagery, making God appear malevolent and vindictive (compare the same image in the lament of the psalmist in Psalm 7:12–13). God is also portrayed as lining up terrifying experiences as one might line up a hostile army, ready to strike on all sides. Again, we have to remember that it is Job's perspective that has so radically changed. Once God was his friend who could do no wrong; now God has, for him, turned nasty. Job is alluding here partly to the misfortune that has come upon him—his illness is the poison eating up his spirit—but he is also painting God in a negative light because of what has happened to him. How often are we also tempted to blame God and be angry at him? We may have just cause—God gives no promises to be nice to us all the time—although we might ask ourselves how far our anger is helping us to feel better, rather than being the attitude we really ought to adopt towards God.

The need for salt

Verses 5–7 need some unpacking. Here we find analogies from the animal world used to illustrate a point, and the wisdom writings abound with such imagery. Job is asking rhetorical questions expecting the answer 'No'. This is another favourite technique of the 'wise': it has the clever effect of hitting the point home. And the point being made here (v. 5) is that wild asses don't bray when they have grass, because that is what they enjoy eating. Nor does an ox low over its fodder, for the same reason. No animal complains when it has the food it normally eats.

These questions lead on to a further question more pertinent to Job's own situation: 'Can that which is tasteless be eaten without salt?' (v. 6). Again the answer is 'No'. Obviously, if food is bland, it needs salt added to make it palatable. Likewise, it seems that mallow juice is equally tasteless, although what precisely is being referred to here is unclear. It may be a vegetable with a very slimy texture or a tasteless jelly from a plant; the white of an egg has been suggested, or even the slime from soft cheese. Whatever it is precisely, the point being made is clear: it is something completely inedible.

The questions in verse 6 are the opposite of those in verse 5, which said that there is no need to complain when one has what one wants. Here, by contrast, there is plenty of reason to complain if your food doesn't have flavour, if it doesn't have the salt you need. God is, for Job, the salt that makes food tasty, but all God is offering at present is tasteless food. Without the right food on offer, Job cannot eat. Food has become repulsive to him.

PRAYER

Lord Jesus, you called us the salt of the earth (Matthew 5:13).
Help us to live up to that reputation and to savour your gifts.

16

A PLEA TO GOD

In a plea that comes from the depths of his despair, Job asks God to grant his request (v. 8). Normally, in the psalms, for example, that request would be for deliverance from present suffering, but Job here turns the usual sentiment on its head and asks God to crush him and cut him off (v. 9). As we have seen already, this is a common feeling among those suffering great pain or distress: they wish that they could die in order to be freed from the pain. It is this kind of thought-process that leads to suicide, although there is never any hint of this in Job's thought. Rather, he sees his life as being in God's hand, for God to do as he will with it. He has already suffered such hardship with the loss of family, property and status and then with the inflic-tion of disease upon his person that he has little left to live for. His continued existence in this state of anguish is nothing but a burden to him. He wishes he could just be finished off by God, who could let go of his hand and cut him off.

We have the image of the hand again here—the hand of God holding the hand of Job. The loosening of the hand is an image of dis-owning and of letting go. Job begs for this release and says that this alone would be his consolation. He would be able to bear even more pain in the knowledge that it was all about to end. He could die content that he had not denied God; rather, in the placing of his life in God's hands, he is abandoning himself to God's will. This is the difference between suicide and allowing life to take its own course: suicide represents a taking of one's life into one's own hands and has traditionally been seen as a wrongful act in religious circles. The placing of one's life in God's hands involves more of a risk, but if one believes in God's guidance and ultimate purposes for us, then it is the only option to take. This does not stop us from asking God to change things, and we would normally seek a change for the better, but it is credible that in Job's present state, he can only think in somewhat radical and negative terms of the desirability of his own destruction.

Here Job's sentiments are bold and daring—outside what we would normally expect from laments and pleas to God, and indica-tors of his anguish and despair. They are a parody of lament forms that long for safety as offered by God, such as Psalm 55:6–8. Here Job longs not for safety, but for personal destruction by God.

No energy left

Having pleaded with God, Job now attempts to rationalize his plea. What is the point of going on when he has no strength? (v. 11). Again it is a common feeling among those suffering illness that they have no energy left with which to fight, and just wish for release from the pain. Also, among those suffering from stress and despair, the energy spent worrying and the lack of sleep at night leaves them feeling weak and tired. Job is suffering the stress of bereavement and loss of property combined with illness—it is no wonder that he is feeling like this. Why should he wait, why should he be patient? People often tell us when we are ill to be patient and the illness will run its course, but often it can be such a slow process that we become impatient and want the waiting to end. This is true of waiting for anything: waiting cannot be a permanent state, otherwise it will itself drive us to despair.

Job asks a rhetorical question expecting the answer 'No'. Does he have the strength of stones, or is his flesh bronze? (v. 12). He thinks of two hard commodities to which to compare his lack of energy. Anyone would think, as he goes on suffering, that he is expected to be as strong as the strongest objects he can find, but he is the opposite: he is weak. He is so lacking in energy that he feels that he cannot help himself (v. 13). His inner resources have all disappeared as a result of his suffering. It is often said that strength of inner will is essential to help us to overcome disease: attitude of mind is crucial. We are increasingly learning about the power of the mind over the body and of the need to try to reduce stressful situations. Here, both Job's mind and his body are affected by a deep misery, and he is turning to God to release him from the pain and acknowledge his weakness.

PRAYER

Lord, be near us when we are suffering or in pain and help us to pray for others in distress or despair. Give us and them the strength to fight, the wisdom to trust in your guidance and a sense of inner peace.

CRUEL FRIENDS

Job now turns to the friends with whom he is supposed to be in dialogue, although that dialogue might have been forgotten in the course of his continuing conversation with God. He uses strong language to accuse them of having turned cruel (v. 14), quoting what sounds like a proverb accusing those who withhold kindness from a friend of not fearing God. This may have been a proverb that they all knew, which circulated orally in families and tribes and was part of the collected wisdom of the time. While the proverb is no doubt something they would all agree on, it hardly seems fair to the friends to accuse them of withholding kindness, when they have sat with Job in comforting silence and are trying to offer advice. There is perhaps an element of 'cruel to be kind' in the friends' words. They are trying different lines of approach on Job in an attempt to shake him out of his present mood, but it seems to be to no avail. Job is behaving badly towards them in this passage. They may be misguided, but they have come to him with good intentions. His curse on the friends parodies passages in the psalms which would be used to curse one's enemies, such as Psalm 31:11–13; 38:11 and 41:9. Job accuses his friends of failing to provide the support that he so badly needs.

Imagery of melting ice

Job uses a rich image of a fast-flowing river and melting ice to describe the way his friends have changed in their attitude towards him (vv. 15–16). It is as if their friendship has melted away only to become a river full of rapids, the melted ice infusing the river with a rush of fresh water (known as a freshet). The author might be thinking of a wadi in a desert, a channel in the sand that fills up very rapidly with dangerously fast water, which can vanish as quickly as it came as the heat of the desert dries it up. The next image (vv. 17–18) is of dryness that causes the marker of the river to disappear, making it unclear where the routes across the desert are and disappointing thirsty travellers who come to drink. Caravans from Tema and Sheba, ancient trading nations, hope to find their way but get lost. So have the friends become to Job: they are as dangerous as fast water, they have dried up when the heat has become too much and they no longer provide Job with any meaningful direction or advice. Job was expecting more from them than they appear to be able to give.

Accusations

Having used a more general image, Job now makes it clear that he is addressing the friends directly (vv. 21–23). He accuses them of being afraid of the trouble that has fallen upon him. This might be a natural reaction of friends—they sympathize with us in our distress, but when that distress is extremely great they are almost afraid. They feel genuinely sorry for us, and yet do not wish to patronize; they wish to behave naturally with us, but know that it will not be easy to do so; they want to talk to us about the problem, but do not want to depress us. Friends are often in a difficult position and, in this case, Job does not make it any easier for his friends. He fires off a series of accusations (vv. 22–23). Has he asked them for anything? Has he taken advantage of their wealth or asked them to save him from opponents? These are, of course, rhetorical questions expecting the answer 'No'. He has asked nothing of them—no money and no favours—and yet they are to him worthless comforters, adding to his suffering rather than detracting from it. They have no grounds on which to hold any grievance against him and so he thinks that they should have treated him rather better.

There is no ceremony on Job's part now, no pretence. There is also no tact and no appreciation of the fact that his friends are there. Many friends might at this point have vanished from sight but, as we will see, despite the taunts and jibes these friends stick it out and continue to try to persuade Job of their view. They have certainly got persistence! Maybe one of the good things about real friendship is that true friends will be there for you in the bad times and will even put up with some taunts and jibes, knowing that in better times you might not really mean them. It is the bad times that are the real test of friendship. Those people who disappear when things get 'hot' were not worth having as friends in the first place.

PRAYER

Lord God, help us to value our friends and to be ready to offer real friendship to others. Help us to be strong for others and not to fall at the first hurdle during the hard times.

The NEED *for* HONESTY

The best course of action in most situations is to be honest and to tell the truth. If only everyone did that all of the time, the world would be a better place—although it might become rather uninteresting too! Job is calling on his friends to be honest with him. He wants real teaching from them. It is unclear whether he is simply asking them to say what he wants to hear or whether he is genuinely interested in what they have to say. There is an indication in verse 24 that he may be owning up to having done something wrong, although this is probably a reference more to his understanding than to his actions, since it has been stressed from the start that Job is innocent of any misdeed. Job expresses the sentiment here that honest words are powerful.

There is a strong theme in wisdom literature concerning communication and the power of words. Words uttered in curses were thought to have real power to channel evil, and words of blessing were believed to channel good. In verses 25–26 Job is upholding the power of honest words, contrasting them with the words of reproof that he is getting from his friends. He asks them what is the point of telling off someone as desperate as Job is, and treating him as if his words were worthless. Refusing to listen to the words of others and treating them as mere babbling, as he feels they have done with his words, is inexcusable and unsympathetic.

Unscrupulous behaviour

Job now likens the reproving words of the others to casting lots over an orphan or bargaining over a friend (v. 27). These are unnatural acts: to cast lots is to trivialize the life of someone needing a home, to bargain over a friend is to devalue what friendship means and, likewise, to scold someone who is at the end of his tether is heartless. Job is in fact matching the friends' reproof with an equally stern one of his own, hoping to teach them the error of their ways just as they are trying to teach him the error of his. To accuse friends of unscrupulous behaviour is to insult and taunt them, as Job has already done before in this speech (6:14–23).

Look at me!

In verse 28, Job changes his approach slightly, and we get the feeling in these speeches that lines of argument are almost as important as what is actually being said. Job is trying to win the friends around, just as they tried to do to him. Job now asks them to look at him, in the knowledge that he will not lie to their face. It is often the case that lying to someone on the telephone or in writing is easier than actually lying to their face, because we might give ourselves away by blushing or perhaps by the look in our eyes, which are said to be the windows to our souls. To look someone in the face and lie to them is somehow a worse crime, and it is not something that anyone would recommend. Job is saying here that if his friends would actually look at him, they would see that he is not lying (v. 28). They have turned away from him, refraining from looking directly upon his calamity as a mark of respect, but he is asking them to turn back, to look at him and thus not to wrong him any further. This would be a means of his vindication: if they look, they will see the innocence written on his face.

Once again picking up on the imagery of words and speech that we have found here, Job asks rhetorically, 'Is there any wrong on my tongue?' (v. 30). Of course, he expects the answer 'No'. He does not think that he has spoken out of turn as his friends have accused him of doing. He would surely have known if there had been something wrong, just as we know that rotten food is bad when we taste it. He is issuing a challenge to his friends to confound his innocence when it is written on his face and when his words confirm it. His mood is more placatory here and less hostile, and we might reflect on the fact that mood-changes often characterize a person who is suffering greatly. Or maybe Job realizes that he has crossed a few boundaries in the words that he has previously uttered, and is trying to draw back from them with a more conciliatory approach.

PRAYER

Lord, help us to listen to the advice of others and be open to change. Help us to be honest with you and with one another.

Life Is Hard

Job now moves from his criticism of the friends to more general musings about the human lot. Human life is seen to be characterized by hard work and little pleasure (v. 1). He is getting into one of his more pessimistic moods here! He compares human hardship to a slave who longs for the shadow of evening—the end of the working day (v. 2). Presumably the inference is that a slave has nothing to strive for, unlike a labourer who has money to earn. Yet even that is seen as an empty thing in that the man who has nothing but a pay packet to look forward to is one whose life is narrowed down to an unbearable extent. Job is starting to sound like his wisdom counterpart, the author of Ecclesiastes, who speaks of the futility of life and its hardship and toil (for example, Ecclesiastes 3:9–13). Perhaps we all feel sometimes that human life is hard and that there are only moments of happiness in an otherwise arduous existence. But such pessimistic moods are usually short-lived and we have only to think of more pleasurable moments in our lives, and of our friends and families, to feel that our lot is not quite so hard.

Sleepless nights

Reflection on the hardship of life leads Job to describe his own feelings of emptiness and pointlessness. He feels that his life has become entirely miserable. Time is hanging heavily upon him so that he is wishing it away. He has to endure months of emptiness and nights of misery (v. 3). We have all known the misery of sleepness nights and most of us, thankfully, do not have to endure them too often. We can identify with the way time seems to stand still while our feverish thoughts flow all too quickly. However, for Job, nights of misery have become the norm. As soon as he lies down, he wonders when it is time to get up. He describes a sleepless night: the night is long, seemingly endless, and he is tossing and turning. Furthermore, his stress, his depression and his illness are exacerbating the situation. We learn more and more nowadays about how psychological stress affects the sound working of the body. His illness is more than simply a skin disease: his mental anguish is leading to a psychological state of mind that is in turn affecting his health and possibly his reasoning too.

An unpleasant affliction

In this section of Job's speech, he starts to describe his physical ailment. His flesh is clothed with worms and dirt and his skin hardens and then breaks open again (v. 5). As mentioned in reading 4 (p. 29), there have been many discussions among scholars over what precisely Job's disease might have been. Leprosy has been suggested, which would fit in with his being cast outside the city walls as any unclean person would have been. However, it might be a kind of skin disease in which sores appear, seem to heal and then break out afresh, with pus oozing out. The reference to worms may simply indicate his general state of uncleanness.

From having described the length of his nights, Job goes on to describe the brevity of his days—swifter than a weaver's shuttle, which, of course, moves very fast once the weaver gets going (v. 6). His days are also hopeless, with no meaning or purpose. This distorted sense of time accompanies his affliction and leads to a melancholia that leads Job himself to the point of despair. He sees himself as on a path towards inevitable death. We see here another change of direction in this first speech of Job, from criticizing his comforters to reflecting on the hardships of human life and of his own afflicted state.

PRAYER

Lord, let us pray for those whose days rush by and whose nights are sleepless. Give them the reassurance of your peace, for the sake of your only Son, our Lord, Amen.

The BREVITY *of* LIFE

Having complained about the speed with which the days slip by, Job now moves on to the idea that his life is but a breath (v. 7). So often we hear older people say that their lives seem to have passed all too quickly, and also that they feel that they are the same person 'underneath', even though their outward appearance has changed. I suppose that we are so busy for much of the time that the years seem almost to merge one into another, or disappear completely. Another common saying is that time flies when you are enjoying yourself, so maybe the rapid pace of life indicates that we are enjoying it to the full. In addition, it is true that, on the grand scale of God and the universe and even in relation to human civilization, an individual life is a short period of time.

Job calls on God to 'remember' (v. 7), not in a mood of appeal, as is usual in psalms of lament, but in a mood of reproach. Job goes on to muse on the fact that he is so close to death that his eye will 'never again see good': he will not have the chance to continue his life and experience good things or see goodness around him. Since his life has been made a mockery and a misery, he sees nothing but the bad side of it. There is some truth in the thought that happiness and goodwill breed positive feelings, but pessimism and darkness close one's eyes to the goodness in life itself and in other people.

Now you see me, now you don't

Continuing the imagery of the eye, Job now considers not his own eye but the eyes of others, who will shortly not see him any more because he will be dead (v. 8). When someone dies, it is strange to think that one moment you are accustomed to seeing that person regularly and then suddenly you will never see them again. We often expect just to turn a corner and see the person in a place where we have usually found them. Visiting familiar places and knowing that that person is absent can be a painful experience for those left behind. Job moves on to this thought in the next few verses: the dead do not return to their houses or to familiar places. We find a good deal of 'eye' imagery in Job—the eye darkened with grief is another example. Job goes on to the thought that even as he is being watched by others, he may disappear, such is his feeling of closeness to death: now you see me, now you don't.

Sheol

Job likens his coming fate to a cloud disappearing. As you watch it, it disappears, never to return in exactly that formation (v. 9). So, he says, those who die never reappear. It would be a shock if they did! The Hebrew idea of death is found here in the reference to Sheol. Sheol was the land of the dead, a shadowy place, perceived as being downwards—a kind of underworld—but not to be equated with hell. It was a state of nothingness where one was out of communion with God and with the living, and a place of no return. Job is bewailing the fact that he will shortly be dead and that presumably this implies no further contact with those around him or even with God. Those who go down never come up again. Their houses are empty, the places that they frequented no longer see them there, and so they are gradually forgotten (v. 10).

One might mention here the idea of remembrance. It is part of our culture to remember people—those who gave their lives in war, for example—on plaques and on particular days. It is helpful to those grieving to keep the anniversary of a loved one's death, giving up time to remembrance. This is some kind of counter to the feelings that one will be forgotten, although the idea is a reality that we must all face and one that Job is facing squarely as he feels himself to be at death's door.

PRAYER

Lord, help us to make the most of every day and to enjoy the interchange with the people we meet and the places we visit. Let us feast on life with our eyes open, rather than closing them and shutting the world out.

SPEAKING OUT

In verse 11, Job's mood suddenly seems to change—it swings from despair to anger. In the light of his feeling so close to death, Job now decides that there is no time to lose and that he must speak out. It is important for all of us to know when to speak out, and occasionally to take that opportunity. Sometimes we do not speak our minds, and are sorry later on when the moment has gone. Words have great power to change situations and the writers of the wisdom literature recognized that fact. The book of Proverbs contains many maxims about the importance of speech and of a carefully chosen word at the right time. See, for example, Proverbs 12:25, 'Anxiety weighs down the human heart, but a good word cheers it up.' Job has decided to speak out despite his anguish, or perhaps because of it. He will not take suffering lying down. He is angry and determined to protest. Gone is the meek Job of the prologue who receives good and evil alike from the hand of God. He is uttering a protest both at his friends and at God. In what follows, he openly accuses God of being his tormentor.

No respite

In the next few verses Job voices his fury at God. He accuses him of watching him constantly, a pressure that he finds unbearable. God's constant attention, once a source of joy, is now oppressive to him. He asks rhetorically, expecting the answer 'No', 'Am I the Sea, or the Dragon, that you set a guard over me?' (v. 12). Job is recalling the ancient myth of a sea dragon that seems to have circulated in the ancient Near East and found its way into Israelite literature. God is thought to have conquered the sea dragon at creation, but has to keep constant watch that it does not rise up again to challenge him. The dragon is usually known as Leviathan. Job feels like the dragon here, in that he feels watched by God. He looks for respite in bed, but then can get no peace, as he experiences nightmares (v. 14). So frightening are his dreams that he would prefer strangulation or death rather than suffering as he does. He expresses loathing of his life and the thought that he would not wish to live for ever, even if that gift were on offer. This recalls another myth of the quest for immortality which was a favourite theme in the ancient Near East. The Epic of Gilgamesh, a famous parallel to the biblical flood story, has Gilgamesh on a quest for immortality, and there are hints of such a myth in the Genesis creation story when the way is guarded to the tree of life so that the man and the woman may not eat of it and learn the secret of immortality (Genesis 3:24). While many people would crave for immortality, it is not something that Job wants. He simply wants to be left alone to live whatever is left of his short life.

Leave me alone

Job now expands on the theme of God's constant protection of him, which is oppressive. Usually God's care and concern are considered worthy of praise. We think of Psalm 8:4, 'What are human beings that you are mindful of them?'—a similarly phrased question but with a very different intention, that of praising the fact that God, the great creator, troubles to take notice of mere mortals. Job parodies this kind of sentiment, asking instead why God makes so much of human beings, why he thinks about them, visits them, tests them. He just wants to be left alone. He asks God to look away (v. 19). There is a tradition in the Old Testament of God hiding his face, often mentioned when God does not seem to be providing the care that is expected, and one way of explaining suffering is that things might have happened when God's back was turned (see, for example, Psalm 13). Here, however, Job wants God to look away. He can't even swallow his spittle without feeling that God is watching. He calls God a 'watcher of humanity'. Why should his sinning even matter to God, why is he the target, and why has he lost favour, why is he not forgiven if indeed he has sinned?

These questions tumble out of Job's mouth in the turmoil of his condition—'Why me?' And he ends his speech with the thought that he won't receive answers because he will soon be dead. God will seek him, but it will be too late because there will be no contact with God in Sheol.

PRAYER

Lord God, let us be glad that you have made us the recipients of your concern, and learn to appreciate your protection. In moments of gloom, let us not lose sight of your love and your will for us.

22   JOB 8:1–7

BILDAD'S REPLY

We now meet the second of Job's friends, Bildad, who is free with his advice to Job. He insists on the justice of God, and first accuses Job of speaking false words. Unlike Eliphaz, who acknowledged Job's exemplary character at the beginning of his speech, Bildad stands on no such ceremony. He is somewhat blunt in his manner and his opening words are critical, indicating that he is already convinced of Job's guilt. In verse 2, Bildad picks up Job's own phrase, 'How long?' (7:19) to mock Job, perhaps, or at least to show that he has been listening. He uses the imagery of the wind, suggesting the worthlessness and emptiness of what Job is saying. He scolds Job for such talk and picks up on the emphasis on correct speech that we often find in the wisdom literature, for example, in proverbs expressing the idea that a word spoken correctly has great power, but bad words lead to bad influences (see Proverbs 15:1, 'A soft answer turns away wrath, but a harsh word stirs up anger'). A great wind is powerful as well as empty, and so there is a hint here of the violence of Job's words.

Questions about God

Bildad also asks a question—a rhetorical one, expecting the answer 'No'. 'Does God pervert justice?' (v. 3). No, of course he does not. Bildad maintains that what has happened to Job cannot be unjust because it comes from the Almighty God, who is a God of justice. He argues that Job's children must have sinned and this is why they have died, as a just punishment for their sin (v. 4). Bildad maintains the traditional doctrine of just deserts: to the good come good things, while the wicked are punished. Thus, if Job is suffering, as he clearly is, he must have done bad things. If he is righteous he will be restored to greater well-being than he had before. Bildad firmly believes that God acts according to these fixed principles, as do the other friends. Job perhaps used to believe it, but his experience has told him otherwise. Bildad seems more dogmatic here than Eliphaz was, and he is certainly more directive towards Job in having no hesitation in offering him the benefits of his wisdom. How many people do we know like that, who have no hesitation in telling us what we ought to do in this or that situation?

The answer is in communion

Bildad suggests to Job that he seek God. Ironically this is what Job spent his whole time doing, if we are to believe the prologue, and yet Bildad clearly thinks that Job has fallen away from upright behaviour (vv. 5–6). There are many injunctions in the wisdom literature to 'seek God and live', which forms an antithesis to the words of Job's wife, 'Curse God and die' (2:9). If one will put oneself in God's hand and do all to follow the path of righteousness, Bildad says, 'life' in its fullest sense should be the reward. In fact, Bildad even suggests that Job's latter days could be better than his former ones, hard though that is to believe at this point.

Although 'seeking God' in the context of wisdom literature refers to ethical choices, it could also have overtones of seeking communion with God. The quest for God and the recognition that we are in contact with God can often be a profound experience. Of course, Bildad sees seeking God in the rather narrow sense of expecting good things from him, but we might extend the range of such an expectation. Communion with God can help during the bad times just as much as during the good. Bildad thinks that if Job makes supplication to God and he is in fact innocent, then God will rouse himself. Maybe God has been lazy in reference to Job and will now redress the wrong. It is ironic that Bildad suggests here that God might act when he realizes Job's plight, while Job in his last speech complained that God was too active!

PRAYER

Lord, help us not to see the world in too narrow a perspective, and help us to have a real and lasting communion with you throughout our lives.

ANCESTORS

Bildad appeals to the past. Learn from the wisdom of old, he says, for our lifespan is short. We need to rely on the accumulated experience of past generations (v. 8). He has a good point here: the wisdom literature, by its relevance to us today, shows that human experience has remained very much the same for thousands of years. Human nature is still as it is described in Job, and that is why we can still relate to the book in a profound way. Many of us would react to misfortune in just the way that Job has done in the dialogue. And yet there is a further lesson here. While we may learn from the wisdom of the past, we should also learn from its mistakes. Not everything from the past is good. There is a place for fresh thought and new ideas, and, while much will not turn out to be new after all (recalling Ecclesiastes' repeated sentiment that 'there is nothing new under the sun'), it is important to guard against the inability to think outside a traditional framework. This is what the friends suffer from. They have a fixed idea of how God deals with humans. It is an easy way of seeing life, but it is an oversimplification and does not allow them to grow in their understanding of the divine. Perhaps we should look at ourselves and ask whether we are too confined within our own traditional ways of thinking in the manner of the friends of Job.

The fleetingness of life

The appeal to the wisdom of the past is not, this time, to personal experience but to the accumulated intelligence of different generations. This highlights the fleeting nature of each individual life within that context. We all need to rely on the cumulative wisdom of many generations so that our generation can take knowledge and insight a step further. Bildad's comments echo Job's complaints about the brevity of life, but not on such a personal experiential level. People nowadays live a longer life than ever our ancestors did. In biblical times you were lucky if you reached 30, and 40 was quite a ripe old age, despite what it says in the book of Genesis about the grand old ages of the ancestors. And yet, despite our longer lifespan, we still hanker after longevity and after staying young and healthy for as long as possible. It is as if we have an unquenchable desire for life, and hence an accompanying fear of death.

Teaching

The idea put forward in these verses is that the ancestors of old might 'teach' the present generation, and we certainly do learn from our forebears and from the great men and women who have trodden this earth before us. Bildad phrases it as a rhetorical question with the effect of jibing at Job: the inference is that he is not paying proper respect to the wisdom that he has learnt over the years. Theirs was a culture in which respect for the past and for the aged was very strong, so maybe Job is crossing another line of acceptability here. The teaching motif is strong in the wisdom literature and these words of Bildad's echo traditional wisdom sentiments.

We might reflect briefly on our own culture, which glorifies youth and diminishes old age. We are always looking for new experiences, new ideas and new 'toys' to buy, and we tend to forget that we can sometimes learn just as much from the experiences of others. We often find that seemingly new ideas are simply old ones in different dress. And we need to preserve the past, its artefacts as well as its memories, so as to give us a proper sense of identity today. Life is short and we all need reminding from time to time that we should value and respect the elderly and the experienced much more than we tend to do.

PRAYER

Lord, we know that we are but a shadow that passes across the face of the earth for a brief moment in time. Help us to make the most of our short lives and experience real happiness in them.

WITHERING REEDS

We find an image of papyrus and reeds in verses 11 and 12. Both plants are very plentiful in the right conditions—we have all seen reeds by rivers and in marshy areas. The point being made here is that even quite common plants such as these thrive only in marshy ground and are known to dry up more quickly even than other grasses if there is no water to sustain them. The image is phrased in the form of a rhetorical question expecting the answer 'No': of course these plants will not grow where there is no moisture. There is an underlying order to life that can be known. To this is likened God's treatment of those who neglect or forget him. Just as reeds will wither without water, so will the godless shrivel up. This is the message Bildad wants to drive home—that the punishment of the wicked is as inevitable as the water of life being taken away from everyday plants. There is a hidden note of warning to Job contained in this image and in the other illustrations that Bildad uses.

Fleeting and meaningless lives

Bildad's description of the wicked continues with the point that there is nothing enduring about them (v. 14). Their confidence is false: they are like gossamer and like a spider's 'house' (presumably its web). Each looks substantial from a distance, but in reality will break like a thread. Images from nature are used here, as is common in the wisdom tradition of the Old Testament. We might be reminded of Jesus' parable of the house built on the sand (Matthew 7:26). Here instead we have the image of leaning against something unstable (v. 15). The house of the godless (like the spider's 'house') will not stand up if you lean against it—it will fall like a pack of cards. What the godless have to offer is not enduring; it is impossible to take hold of it for any length of time. This is the characteristic of the path of wickedness: the godless have no hope, their lives are fleeting and meaningless. Bildad gives us an imaginative and penetrating description of the transience and lack of substance of those who do not follow the path of God.

Seeming prosperity

The other side of the coin is the apparent prosperity of the wicked. Taking up the plant imagery again, Bildad describes the way the wicked seem to thrive (v. 16). Plenty of sunshine makes their shoots spread out in abundance. This passage evokes the idea of a creeper that covers the whole garden and enters into hidden places under rocks (v. 17). This is how the wicked take root: they go into places where they are not welcome and choke the occupants. Yet, despite this seeming infiltration, if they are removed, and if the roots taken out one by one, the place will forget them—another image of transience. The wicked make so little impression that they are quickly forgotten. Yet they go on springing up regardless of the consequences. Bildad is putting forward the point that the wicked need to be recognized for what they are. They are unreliable and untrustworthy and their seeming prosperity is illusory. There may be a time-delay in their punishment, but it will happen eventually.

All will be fair in the end

At the end of his speech we find a strong affirmation by Bildad of the doctrine of just deserts: 'God will not reject a blameless person' (v. 20). There is justice in the universe—of that he is sure. God will not support wickedness—that is against the order of things. Job just has to be patient and wait for the deserved happiness that will be just around the corner. Bildad ends his speech on an upbeat note: you will laugh again, he tells Job, you will feel joyful (v. 21). There will be nothing but shame for those who oppose Job; shame will be as much a part of them as their clothes. Furthermore, the seeming reign of wickedness will be at an end (v. 22).

We often feel in life that we want to put everything right for people. In a situation of despair, when there really is no cure, we want to be able to wave a magic wand and make it all better. We want to see the one in pain being able to laugh and be joyful again and we want a better life for them. This is a similar moment of affirmation by Bildad. He assures his friend that all is well with the doctrine that seems to have gone so badly wrong. He wants to be affirming and positive. He ends his speech with a reference to the wicked being 'no more', possibly an overtone of Job's desire for non-existence at the end of his last speech.

PRAYER

Lord God, make us not envious of others and help us to prioritize what is important in life before we dwell on matters of more fleeting concern. Help us to assist each other in good faith and with good intentions.

25

JOB'S REPLY

Job immediately picks up on Bildad's point about the doctrine of retribution, saying that he knows that it is so (v. 1). This is a doctrine in which Job himself believed. This was the mainspring of his life and dictated all his actions. He does not need to be told what he used to believe—he knows it! There are times when we are all told things that we already know and we impatiently say, 'Oh I know that, but…'. We all had beliefs drummed into us when we were younger which perhaps we have learnt to question, or at least to modify. This is a similarly impatient rebuff: 'I know all this,' says Job, 'but…'.

We might well come to question certain beliefs on the basis of a conflicting experience. We are taught one thing but then we experience another, and experience has a great power of its own. It is often said that people don't fully understand suffering, for example, until it actually happens to them. This mismatch between what he believed and what he now experiences is what has happened to Job: he knew all about the doctrine of retribution, but he has questions now.

Questioning God's justice

The question that concerns Job in this passage is, 'How can a mortal be just before God?' (v. 1). The idea here is that God is great and, in a sense, holds all the trump cards, so what is human justice in comparison? It is all very well believing that right will triumph, but what is God's idea of justice? Is it the same as ours? We may be trying to limit God by making him behave according to our own neat ideas of what good and bad behaviour are. Maybe he isn't always constrained in the way that we would like him to be. It is possible that his principles of justice are rather different from ours.

God holds all the trump cards

This sentiment is expanded in what follows. Job realizes that there is no contest between human beings and God because God has all the answers (v. 3). One cannot argue with him, and his understanding is so far above human powers of understanding that he would have all the answers anyway. Job affirms God's wisdom and strength, but instead of proclaiming them in the context of prayer, he is using them as reasons why no one can offer up any kind of resistance to God. Again Job's words reverse usual expectations. Instead of simply praising God for his wisdom and strength, he sees God's power as frightening (v. 4)—an ironic anticipation, perhaps, of the speeches at the end of Job in which God does have all the answers and in which the display of his power is overwhelming. Job asks rhetorically, 'Who has resisted him, and succeeded?' Of course, the expected answer is 'No one', because God is so great and mighty that he cannot be held in check or held responsible. We are arriving at a theme that Job goes on to expand in more legal terms: God is both prosecutor and judge and thus Job has no hope of finding justice, as we understand it, from him. If God has decided that he is going to punish Job, he can do it. There are no constraints on his actions and he does not have to justify them to anyone. He holds all the trump cards.

PRAYER

Let us be aware of your wisdom and power and might, Lord, and may they may be used beneficially for us in all we do. Let us not, however, take that for granted, or belittle your greatness; let us learn to trust in your wisdom which is greater than ours.

26

The ALL-POWERFUL GOD

This passage contains a description of the all-powerful acts of God—with a difference. Here Job turns usual descriptions of this kind on their head. In parodic style he reproaches God for his overwhelming might. Normally, hymns praise the unknowability of God and the marvels of creation (for example, Psalm 104), but this passage actually turns out to be about the unpredictability of God in nature. It is not sounding a note of praise about the orderliness of the universe; rather it is a critique of God. Job's tone is an accusing one: God removes mountains and nobody knows about it (v. 5). He has *carte blanche* to do what he likes. This follows on from the previous sentiment about God's accountability. The point is that he is not accountable to anyone but himself, and although we may look for the order in things, and particularly in nature, God is not constrained by that order. His anger could lead to unpredictability. There is a sense of God's power and terribleness—his unpredictability is frightening.

The unpredictability of anger

We have probably all experienced someone (even ourselves) losing their temper. Anger is something that can spiral out of control when it becomes too intense. The wisdom writers were all too well aware of this. Here we have a picture of God's anger and its accompanying unpredictability. The image continues with a description of the earth being shaken out of its place (v. 6)—probably a reference to an earthquake. Thunder was often seen as a manifestation of God's anger, as were earthquakes, wind, storms and fire. In a world that had more primitive understandings than ours, all the extremes of nature that the earth experiences from time to time were seen as emotions of God. His control is absolute: he can command the sun not to rise; he can stop the stars from shining (v. 7). He is God the creator and although he created according to a pattern, such is his power that it can be undone. After all, didn't he stretch out the heavens and overcome the sea dragon? Didn't he create the stars? (v. 9).

Job in a sense anticipates what God himself will say later in the book—that is, how can you expect to understand all the wonders of my action in creation; how can you try to limit me? Job is here saying that God's power is limitless (v. 10) and unpredictable, but his inference is that there is, therefore, no point in trying to argue with God. One might have thought that Job would simply give up his protest at this point, but no, he still continues to put his case to God. Despite God's unknowability, it is all Job can do. He is not a resigned pessimist as we find in the book of Ecclesiastes, where the author has given up the argument with God and simply accepts that God's time for doing things may not be ours. Rather, Job is engaged in a protest against his creator.

God cannot be held to account

As at the start of this chapter, we find the sentiment here that God is not answerable and cannot be constrained by human efforts to pin him down. Job cannot see God, whereas God can see Job, and so even in that God has the upper hand (v. 1). Similarly, when God decides to snatch away (v. 12)—to take someone's livelihood, his family, his possessions, even his life—what can one do to stop him? God cannot be held to account by anyone. We hope that he will look favourably upon his faithful servants, as he seemed to look on Job once. However, that is a hope and not a certainty. We cannot force God to behave as we want him to. No one can call him to account; no one can ask him what he is doing. Job ends with another rhetorical remark: who can question God? Of course the expected answer is 'No one'.

These sentiments give us an overwhelming sense of the power and greatness of God, of which it is good to be reminded from time to time. We all occasionally think that God is only concerned with our small world; it is good to be reminded of his otherness. And yet these sentiments also make us feel small and insignificant and out of touch with the Godhead. We might forget that there is a very personal and caring side of God: he is concerned with each and every one of us, as well as with maintaining a universe. They are two sides of the same coin, but one is being stressed here more than the other.

PRAYER

Lord God, you are mighty and powerful, you created the world that we enjoy as your gift and we are grateful for it. Let us never take your gifts for granted or give you less praise than is your due.

27

ONE CANNOT ARGUE
with GOD *and* WIN

Some people are strong characters who always win an argument, and others are weak and always give in. Most of us are somewhere in between, in that there are some people who make us feel small and helpless in argument, but there are others over whom we exercise a little power. In this passage, Job is feeling the helplessness of trying to argue with God. He picks up the point about God's power. The afflictions that Job is suffering are clearly a result of God's anger, which may be unpredictable and unjust in the light of Job's innocence but is nevertheless a reality. If God is powerful enough to overturn Rahab, his adversary in the primeval battle in creation, what chance has Job in his argument with him? (v. 13). How does he even find the right words with which to begin? This is a contest in which the two sides are very unevenly matched. God is going to win before the match has started. Another rhetorical question asks, 'How can I answer him?' And of course the answer is 'I cannot' (v. 15). Job restates his innocence here—an important starting point which differs from his friends' accusations that Job must have sinned. Job is innocent, of that he is sure, and even though that is true and should give him the strength to argue his case, with God as his opponent and judge at one and the same time, he feels that he has not got a chance.

Would God listen even if he were here?

We have probably all experienced talking to someone about something we find really interesting and getting the sense that the other person is not listening. Even if they are there in body, their mind appears to be elsewhere. Job moves on to this thought about God. Even if he could summon God (and he is not sure that this would work), and even if God answered (which also seems a far-off hope at present), he wouldn't necessarily listen (v. 16). As mentioned earlier, the psalms contain the idea of God hiding his face. Sometimes, when things don't happen as they should, God is accused of this evasion. Maybe he is looking in the opposite direction, as he does have a lot to think about! But Job is saying here that there are no guarantees. Even if God were there, would he listen to a nobody like Job? God is so great that Job's concerns are as nothing to him. Job's sense of littleness and unimportance, as well as his sense of helplessness, come across here. God is all-powerful: he has already inflicted numerous misfortunes on Job and for no apparent reason has inflicted this disease on him. Job blames God for his shortness of breath—a sign of stress—and for his bitterness at his affliction (vv. 17–18).

Strength and the seat of justice

Job sums up the sentiments of this chapter in verse 19. He cannot contend with God because of two things—God's strength and his control over justice. God is so strong that Job cannot even compete in the contest. Similarly, if it is a matter of justice, who can call God to account? No one, because he is the only judge. If he chooses to inflict suffering, there is no one to whom the sufferer can turn. Usually in a legal case the defendant, the one to whom injury has been done, has a separate legal team, as does the prosecutor; and the one who metes out the justice is the impartial judge. We also have the jury as another independent body with no interest in taking sides. In Job's case there is no jury and no judge apart from God himself, who also happens to be prosecuting Job, the defendant. One can't even guarantee to summon him to hear the case, such is his control of all matters of justice. These two attributes of God lead Job to despair of ever having a fair hearing.

PRAYER

Lord God, you have strength and justice on your side. Help us to see these as comforting and protecting attributes rather than being frightened by your power and unpredictability.

28

GOD HAS TURNED *against* JOB

Job's attack on God is well and truly mounted by now. He feels that his innocence is being ignored by God. Perhaps this is rather like telling someone your point of view, arguing your case strongly, and then finding that they take no notice but go on doing what they were going to do anyway. Job feels that God is determined to put him in the wrong. He says that although he is in fact innocent, he will probably be condemning himself in what he says (v. 20): God will find something to pick on. God will 'prove him perverse' despite the fact that he has done nothing. He thus feels that God has turned against him and will put him in the wrong whatever he does. He wonders if he would even be capable of stating his case before God, so overwhelmed does he feel.

Feeling a stranger to oneself

Job's one certainty is that he is blameless. He has to hold on to that certainty to save himself from going mad. He feels so unlike his normal self that he feels a stranger to himself, and loathsome (v. 21). Job starts to get into a very negative, depressed mode at this point. It is sometimes the case, perhaps when we are ill or very depressed about something, that we do not feel 'ourselves' and sometimes others comment on it. This reversal in Job's fortunes and change in his circumstances, coupled with the uncertainty of his relationship with God, which had once been such a security in his life, has made him feel a stranger to himself.

God is to blame

Job gets back to his point about God and his moral government of the world: he destroys blameless and wicked alike (v. 22). If he punishes a blameless man, this must be so. The system of justice in which Job had placed his trust is proved to be a mockery. He turns on God, describing him as mocking at the suffering of the innocent. One thinks here of natural disasters—there seems to be no reason why innocent people are caught up in these tragedies, and no apparent justice in it. The answer is perhaps that disasters happen and it is bad luck if you are in the wrong place at the wrong time; and yet that seems an unsatisfactory answer in the context of belief in a just God. There was a girl from my college who did her degree for three years, took a full part in college life, was popular, intelligent, attractive. She seemed to have everything going for her as she graduated on a summer's day in June. She thought that she would take a year out, and flew to Columbia to begin a great adventure in South America. That night there was an earthquake in the very city where she was staying and her hotel crumbled to the ground under the force. What sense was there in her death? She was in the wrong place at the wrong time. Where was the justice in that?

This thought of Job's is the opposite of the usual one that we find elsewhere in the Bible, which is that God is distraught at the suffering of innocent people. Job is at a particularly low point in his opinion of God. He accuses him, furthermore, of giving the earth over to the wicked and making judges blind to the corruption that is going on (v. 24). This may well be social commentary about the corruption he sees around him, possibly referring to the bribery of judges, a crime commented on throughout the prophets (for example, Amos 5:10–13). Social injustice goes alongside natural disasters. He asks a question: if not God, then who can be blamed?

We all need someone to blame from time to time. If it isn't the government, then maybe it is the Prime Minister, the Bank of England or the Church, or maybe we just blame one another, or blame the cat. Whichever it is, we are quite prone to casting blame away from ourselves and on to others, knowing in our heart of hearts that we ourselves are not blameless either. Job here takes the opportunity of blaming God. God is in charge of justice in the world, so why has it all gone so badly wrong? His cry echoes in the hearts of all who feel that they have suffered unjustly and who have found it hard to hold on to their faith in the light of that suffering. If God is to blame, then why believe in one so cruel and seemingly uncaring? That is the question.

PRAYER

Lord, we need to question you and search our souls
from time to time. Help us to understand and give us faith
that will lead us back to you.

29

TIME FLIES

There is a saying that 'time flies when you are having fun'. However, sometimes it flies past when one is ill or depressed too. Here Job complains that his days are 'swifter than a runner' and pointless at the same time (v. 25). He also likens them to reeds, known for their transience as plants, and like the speed of an eagle swooping on its prey (v. 26). He is using examples from the plant and animal world, which we find a good deal in this book and (as we have already noted) in the Wisdom literature in general. His perception contrasts with the feeling of time moving slowly, for example, at night when one cannot sleep. We find elsewhere Job complaining just this—that time is hanging on him.

The speed with which time flies might lead one to contemplate how life seems to fly by generally. We often say that it doesn't seem long since last Christmas or since our last summer holiday, and it is when we watch children growing up that time really seems to rush away. Time flying is generally seen as a good thing. It means that we are busy and we don't have time on our hands. If there is no meaning in our lives, however, as Job feels, the passage of time can be a frightening thought, as it is to Job right now.

Trying to cheer up

Job goes on to say that he has tried to cheer up, but then he becomes afraid again as the old ideas flood back into his mind (vv. 27–28). This reminds us of times when we wake up in the morning feeling quite cheerful and then suddenly remember that something awful took place the previous day or that there is some bad situation preying on our mind. Sleep has allowed such thoughts to slip away, but then suddenly they are back and we cannot relax. Job remembers again that he will not be considered innocent by God, who will condemn him, it seems, despite his labours.

Interestingly, in the author's parodying mode, Job becomes troubled when he tries to forget his plight, whereas the more usual sentiment is that one is troubled when one tries to forget God (for example, Jeremiah 20:7–9) Normally God is such a strength in time of trouble that it would be frightening to forget him and no longer to have him as a support. However, Job feels that an unjust God is pestering him. He is not worried at God's apparent absence at this point; he is more afraid of forgetting his dreadful situation, of being persuaded out of his stance of innocence by the friends, or simply of being in such a state of weakness that he doesn't have the strength to go on. He has to remember his plight because that is all he has to go on—that is the experience that is driving him to question God at the profoundest level.

What, then, is the point of going on? All is a mockery in the light of the fact that he will not be held innocent. Why work for nothing? Why try to clean himself when God will make him dirty again? (vv. 30–31). The image of washing is an interesting one. It reminds me of Lady Macbeth when she says, 'Out, damned spot' in her sleepwalking dreams, trying to clean her hands of the blood of the murdered king. She rubs her hands over and over, but the stain that is in her mind will never come clean. Job feels that although he is clean, it is God who constantly makes him feel so dirty that even his own clothes will hate him for it (v. 31). The attempt to cheer up has well and truly failed.

God is in control

Job complains yet again at the end of this chapter that God and he cannot meet on equal terms. He makes the point that God is not mortal. He is not, therefore, debating with an equal partner. The idea of one who could mediate between Job and God comes in here (v. 33)—an umpire, as in cricket, or just somebody impartial like a judge or jury. An umpire might look at both sides of the argument, but for Job there is no other side of the argument: God does what he likes. He feels the burden of God's anger. He feels the weight of God's rod and feels fear in his presence (v. 34). There are some people who overawe us and make us feel awkward when speaking in their presence. This is how Job feels in the presence of God. If only he didn't fear, then maybe he could speak more easily and make his case more convincing (v. 35). As it is, however, he feels inferior and so cannot speak out in the way that he would like. He is sure that he is being misunderstood by God: 'I am not what I am thought to be,' he says. He wants to be given another chance, but he knows that to be an impossibility too.

PRAYER

Lord God, help us to make the most of our time on this earth. Help us to use it profitably, to assist others as well as ourselves.

RENEWED STRENGTH

Chapter 10 begins on a note of self-loathing, echoing 9:21b. This time, however, the sentiment leads Job in the direction of fresh impetus to argue with God. When tackling a major difficulty in life, we may often feel times of weakness, of being overwhelmed by the problem, and times of strength when we begin to think that it can be solved or that at least we can try to tackle it. Sometimes the despair sets in late at night, but in the morning life seems a little more manageable. Here Job decides that he is not going to feel too fearful to speak as he did at the end of chapter 9. He will speak out freely. He will tell God not to condemn an innocent man (v. 2). He will ask God 'Why?' He will ask a series of questions about why God is oppressing him, and hence no doubt much of the created world with him, and why the wicked appear to find such favour with God. He is appealing to God's justice and to his role as creator—why 'despise the work of your hands'? (v. 3). It seems pointless to create a world and then punish the very work that you have done. This might be likened to painting a picture and then defacing it yourself or writing a book and burning it in the flames.

Is God human?

It is sometimes hard for us to imagine God. We are told that we were created in his image and according to his likeness. We often speak of him in human terms: in verse 3 of this passage, for example, there is a reference to God's hands forming the world. In fact, we have to speak of him in this way, because we have to use terms of reference with which we can identify. However, we can also recognize that to imagine God as totally human would be to limit him, perhaps in the same way that to limit his system of justice by reference to ours would also be to limit him. Here Job accuses God of being human in the way he looks for sin in Job when none is there. He asks a series of rhetorical questions, asking God whether he has human eyes that see as humans do (v. 4). Of course, he expects the answer 'No'. Job asks if God's days and years are like those of humans (v. 5). This raises a much bigger debate about God's place in time. Here Job is using these questions as an accusation: God must be on a human level if he is taking such an interest in Job's supposed sin. Job finds it hard to believe that God, whose greatness and superiority are known, could stoop down to this base human level that looks for the sin in people. Is his conception of right and wrong the same as ours? Perhaps this is the reason for God's punishment of Job. Is he somehow short of time so that he is rushing to condemn Job before time runs out?

You *know* that I am not guilty

Imagine the frustration of knowing that you have done nothing wrong and yet you are being punished. We might think of those who went to the gallows wrongly accused and lost their lives in a miscarriage of justice. Even being in prison for a crime one did not commit must be a soul-destroying experience. Job must have felt like this. God knows that he is not guilty and yet there is no one who can save Job from God's punishment except God (v. 7). We are back to the triangle of God as Job's prosecutor and judge. Job feels caged in—imprisoned with no escape. And he is innocent! At least in the situation of wrongful imprisonment there might be a chance that an appeal could be made or a retrial could take place. Fresh evidence might be found to clear one's name; one would be likely to have family or friends who could fight on one's behalf. Here, in contrast, Job feels that his friends are useless, that his one true friend, God, has become the enemy and so there is no way out of the situation. God knows that he is innocent, but there is no way out of this punishment at God's own hand—he holds Job in his power.

PRAYER

Lord, we call you loving father and speak of you in human terms.
You sent your Son to live among us. Help us to know you more
intimately and yet not to limit your greatness by our
limited understanding of your nature.

31

GOD *the* CREATOR

Job returns here to the theme of God's having created him only to turn upon him, which seems to Job like a pointless exercise. He explores this argument in speaking to God. Your hands made me, he says, picking up the anthropomorphism used before, and now you turn on me (v. 8). We find the image here of God as a potter, fashioning humans as he might fashion a clay pot (v. 9). This is a common image from the ancient Near East, where we find the gods creating humans out of clay. One tradition sees human beings as being fashioned out of the earth mixed with the blood of a dead god—perhaps an attempt to communicate the unique link with the divine in humanity. The idea of coming from the earth and returning to it is another common image in the Bible (for example, Genesis 3:19). Here Job reminds God that he was fashioned like clay from the earth and is now being turned to dust again. He feels that he is close to death, on the point of destruction, and then he will be nothing but dust. What is the point of that? We then find another image, that of semen pouring out like milk and curdling like cheese, a reference to the creation of each and every human being, with overtones of the creative purposes of God (v. 10). The idea here too is of wasted effort if all is going to come to nothing.

Another image follows to illustrate the next stage of creation. Not only did God metaphorically participate in Job's coming into being, but he helped him to grow, clothing him with skin and flesh and knitting him together with bones and sinews (v. 11). It is not just Job who is being spoken of here, it is the creation of all human beings. All this effort goes into the making of a human being and now it seems to be completely wasted. God's gift of life and then his care of Job—all is a mockery in the light of his suffering. We sometimes feel this sense of futility at the death of a child or a young person. So much effort goes into the giving and nurturing of life, caring for the child, providing education and so on. Is this life to be cut short and not lead to adulthood? Somehow the death of a child seems so much more pointless than the death of an adult. This is not, of course, to deny the great joy that can be experienced in a short life, by child, parents and friends alike.

Hidden purposes

Job contrasts God's earlier care of him with a cruel intent lying hidden in God's heart. God created Job in the womb—he seemed to care—but now it is clear that he did not. Job speaks as if it was God's purpose all along to destroy him in this way (v. 13). Whatever way he had behaved—if he had been wicked or righteous—this was his fate. It is as if God was hiding a secret, giving Job a false sense of security. This sentiment seems to come from the depths of Job's bitterness. He starts to accuse God of underhand purposes, of watching him in an oppressive manner and not forgiving his sin, or of making him feel low even when he is righteous.

I cannot lift my head high

It is often a sign of confidence and pride in a person if they lift their head high. Conversely the mournful person is depicted as having their head in their hands or being stooped under a burden of misery. Here Job says that even if he is righteous (which he believes he is), he cannot lift up his head because of his punishment. He is being wrongfully punished and hence made to feel full of disgrace even when he knows that he is innocent. He feels hunted down by God, as prey is hunted by a lion. He feels battered repeatedly, and argued against continuously and relentlessly. Job uses the images of witnesses ranged against him by God, 'vexation' heaped upon him and fresh troops, as in an army, brought against him. He is just beginning to feel a tentative confidence and then it is shattered by fresh attacks. Job is starting to feel cornered and helpless once again.

There are two types of parody in this passage. The first is of God's watchful eye on human beings, which is normally praised, but which Job finds oppressive. The second parody accuses God of punishing when it is not deserved, whereas normally God is asked to mete out punishment only if it is deserved. For example, in Psalm 7 we find the sentiment that God is a righteous judge and that if the petitioner has sinned he may be punished, or, if he has been righteous, he should be rewarded.

PRAYER

Help us to wonder in your created world, O Lord, to lift
our heads high in your service and to cheer those
who feel downtrodden or misunderstood.

32

WHY WAS I BORN?

Job returns to the sentiments we found in chapter 3, in his opening lament. Why was he born? This is a natural conclusion following the passage on the purposelessness of his creation. Rather than living to endure all this suffering, wouldn't it have been better if he had not been born? (vv. 18–19). Why, he asks God, was he safely delivered from the womb? He wishes he had been stillborn, because if he had died before anyone had seen him, it would have been as if he had never existed. Suddenly the idea of being carried from womb to grave seems an attractive one. Rather like the image I mentioned in the previous reading, of the child who has not had time to have a full life, here the thought is being taken further to remind us of the stillborn child. There is a great sense of waste—all the process of pregnancy and the hope of birth, and then the child does not even have a chance to live, to know what it is like to be cherished and loved by its parents. Job's point is that he would have preferred this short route to death rather than to have had the life that he is suffering now. He is still in the depths of despair.

Leave me alone!

Job reminds God that he doesn't have long on earth: human life is brief in comparison with God's time. Job's life is about to be cut short by death, and he wants to have a brief period of respite before he dies (v. 20). He asks God to leave him alone, contrasting sharply with passages in which he asks God to appear (for example, Job 23:3). Since God is his enemy and judge, he wishes some time away from his presence. Of course this is an impossible hope, like his earlier wish that he might have been stillborn. In a heightened state of grief it is entirely understandable that one might start to hope for impossibilities. When there are many problems bearing down on us, we often feel that we just want to get away from it all. Holidays are often portrayed as the 'getaway' that will enable us to forget our troubles. Many find, however, that troubles aren't so easily shed and that, in fact, having more time as we sit on a sun-drenched beach may lead us to muse even more on our problems, as Job is clearly doing.

Death in store

Job moves on to the thought that all that is in store for him is death (vv. 21–22). He wants a brief respite before he goes to the land of no return. He envisages it as a land of darkness, gloom and chaos, reflecting ideas of the time about Sheol, which (as mentioned earlier) was conceived of as a kind of no-man's land, a place of darkness, a place where there would be no further contact with God. Here Job's gloomy disposition is being reflected in his description of this fate of nothingness. With this thought his second speech ends, and this is the cue for the third friend, Zophar the Naamathite, to chastise Job for his sentiments.

PRAYER

Lord, give us the strength to tackle our problems with your guidance and not to sink into a mire of hopelessness and despair.

33

ZOPHAR'S REBUKE

We now encounter Zophar, the third friend, who does not spend time on niceties but goes straight for the jugular with a rebuke of Job. He begins with rhetorical questions that expect the answer 'No'. He accuses Job of too much talking—of babbling, even. He is using a frequent wisdom motif about the importance of right words and the destructiveness of babbling talk (vv. 2–3; compare Proverbs 13:3; 29:20). He asks, should one as wordy as Job get away with it? And the expected answer from traditional wisdom is 'No'. Should one who babbles so much be vindicated? Of course not. The problem with those who talk too much is that they have the effect of silencing others. 'Is this right?' he asks. He accuses Job of mocking (presumably of mocking the friends). Job needs putting down and Zophar is prepared to do so in a blunt and aggressive manner. He is the most outspoken of the three friends, for he makes no secret of the fact that he perceives Job to be guilty.

The mind of God

A book entitled *A Brief History of Time* was published by scientist Stephen Hawking, containing a discussion of the beginnings of the universe and presenting the latest advances in discovering what caused the universe to appear. On the last page of this book, Hawking states, rather dramatically, that his ultimate aim is 'to know the mind of God'. How far God really comes into the picture in Hawking's worldview is probably another matter, but it reminds us that when we seek to understand everything, it is the mind of the One who knows everything and created everything that we seek to understand, even if we ultimately don't find God in our quest. Zophar cites Job's claims to innocence, and furthermore Job's claim that he is innocent in God's sight as well as his own (v. 4). How can Job dare to know the mind of God? If only God would speak for himself, then Job's guilt would be plain. Zophar feels that it is blasphemous of Job to be maintaining his innocence when it is clear that he is guilty.

The secrets of wisdom

The mind of God contains the secrets of wisdom. If Job knew God's superior wisdom, he would know, says Zophar (who seems ironically to know God's mind himself!), that he is suffering less than his guilt deserves (vv. 5–6). He is not being punished enough for his wickedness. There is a suggestion here that God is in fact being merciful towards Job in not punishing him as much as he should. One wonders what further torments God could have heaped upon Job!

In verse 5, Zophar wishes that God would speak and reveal to Job his greatness as contained in the secrets of his wisdom. God is the ultimate source of all wisdom and clearly human experience can access only a part of that. God reveals some of the secrets of his wisdom in chapters 38—41, when he speaks of his role in creation, but there are always some aspects of God that remain a mystery. Job 28 talks of Wisdom as a secret commodity to which only God knows the way. Human beings may dig as deep as they like to find it, or climb the highest mountain, and it will still be elusive.

Human achievement is a great thing: we see people pushing themselves to the limits of physical endurance in climbing mountains such as Everest, or we see great discoveries being made by researchers such as Hawking about the origins of the universe. As a race, we are full of pride and of optimism that we can achieve all things if we only have the technology. The point made here in Job is that we can go on trying to know many things, but we will never know everything. One wonders whether, if there was nothing left to discover, the human race would virtually come to a standstill. It seems to me that the joy of finding out new information about humanity and the world, of trying new experiments and of unearthing new facts, keeps us interested and motivated and gives our lives purpose. What would it really be like to know about everything? Human beings will never know, for that is the mind of God.

PRAYER

Lord, we now have so much knowledge and understanding of the world you have created, and yet we keep finding more to discover and to know. Help us to understand your mind and your purpose for us, and to continue to wonder at your greatness.

34

WHAT CAN YOU KNOW?

Zophar now returns to some rhetorical questions, this time asking whether Job can know the mind of God (v. 7). There is more than a hint of sarcasm here. Zophar launches into a description of the hiddenness of God's purposes, along much the same lines as Eliphaz took. God's knowledge lies at the limits of human understanding, higher than heaven, deeper than Sheol (v. 8). It is wider than the earth (which was at that time regarded as flat) and broader than the sea. How, then, can Job know God's purposes?

God is just

A fact about which Zophar is sure is that God acts in justice. In Zophar's description, God is infinitely greater than human beings can ever comprehend, but he acts in justice to punish worthlessness and iniquity. Here is a foretaste of what is to come in God's speeches later in the book, although there God's freedom of action is stressed rather than the justice of all his actions. In those speeches, the appeal to God's greatness means that he can do what he likes—a thought that Job uses when he ponders on God's seemingly unjust actions towards him—but in Zophar's argument, God's greatness is a witness to his fairness in matters of right and wrong. Zophar thus limits God to the terms of the doctrine of retribution, and ironically he accuses Job of being narrow in his understanding! God is described here as passing through the world judging the good and the bad. He knows who fits into which category and no one can stop him from punishing justly (vv. 10–11). God is, in a sense, both judge and jury —he has freedom of action in punishment, a fact about which Job complains at some length in his speeches.

Worthlessness and stupidity

God acts in judgment to punish worthless people, often perceiving what human beings cannot perceive. Zophar makes the comment that 'a stupid person will get understanding, when a wild ass is born human' (v. 12). The point is that a stupid man will therefore never get understanding, since what is proposed is impossible. It is a well-known wisdom technique to state two impossibilities alongside one another. Could this be a jibe at Job? Quite probably.

Zophar attacks Job here from two sides, and both angles are an attempt to make him feel that his opinion is not worthwhile. The first attack is to make him recognize his smallness in the presence of God the Almighty. We all feel at times that our own lives are but a second in the life of the universe and, when we travel over continents and islands and look down from a plane at the tiny dots that are houses, we realize that we are just one of very many human beings. Even walking in big cities can give us the sense of being a small rat in a large rat-race. In similar ways, when we reflect on the sphere of God's activity we feel humbled and overawed.

The second attack Zophar makes is to infer that Job is worthless and even stupid. This is where comparison with others who are greater or more successful than we are comes in. There is always someone else that we look up to or admire, whom we envy a little perhaps, who seems to have it all. We all feel worthless and stupid at times—it is human nature to feel so. When we contemplate the greatness of God, which is so much more than that of other human beings, we feel humbled and awed to an even greater extent. We need to build up our own confidence with others and we need to feel God's presence and his confirming power. Zophar's efforts are to make Job feel exactly the opposite!

PRAYER

*Lord, we know that you are free to act as you like
in your greatness. Help us to understand your purposes
where possible, and yet not to restrict you by our
limited attempts to know your will.*

35   JOB 11:13-20

CORRECT BEHAVIOUR

In this last section of his speech, Zophar turns to offering Job practical advice. He certainly thinks that he knows best! We probably all know people who attempt to give us advice. It is often welcomed, but just occasionally it is intrusive into our personal decision-making.

Zophar suggests that Job look towards God, stretching out his hands in supplication (v. 13). This kind of gesture is common in a number of religious traditions—it is a sign of humility, a posture of begging. Zophar thinks that repentance is what is needed because Job has sinned. He tells Job to put 'iniquity' far away from him and not to allow wickedness to live in his tents (v. 14). By this he means that Job must dissociate himself from all that is sinful, both the actions of his own person and of those of his acquaintance. This must be very frustrating for Job to hear, because he knows that there is no 'wickedness in his tents'—and so do we, because we saw Job in the prologue doing everything right. This whole dialogue is set in the time of the patriarchs and so it would have been a possibility that there were those who lived in tents, although the prologue makes reference to the 'houses' of Job's children, and someone of Job's status would probably have lived in a fixed dwelling. If Job repents, says Zophar, then all will be well, he will be able to lift his head up high (a sign of inner confidence) and he will get the security that he needs. There will be no more fear and misery. All will be rectified and soon forgotten.

Repent and all good things come...

You sometimes hear sermons which suggest that if you become a Christian, all good things will come to you. Life will go well, there will be no more suffering, and God will be on your side. Of course, this is a false picture, because becoming a Christian is not a passport to happiness or success, it is simply a message of forgiveness and hope. It is not a magic wand that can be waved over a person's life. If it was, then everyone would become a Christian overnight! Life is more complex than that. Zophar's description of all being made right again if Job repents reminds me of this false message. He presents an attractive picture that might almost have tempted Job to repent despite not having sinned at all! Zophar argues that security, light, happiness, hope, respect, protection and rest—all the things that Job had before, lacks now and longs for—will be his just for the asking, *if* he repents.

The reference to light—the idea that his life will be bright and not dark (v. 17)—recalls Job's desire for darkness in chapter 3. The way of the wise is also sometimes presented as a passport to happiness: follow the path of good deeds and they will be rewarded, says the book of Proverbs (for example, Proverbs 2). The book of Job is a reaction against such a motto. What happens when good is not rewarded and when bad things happen to good people? Then there is a problem.

But the wicked...

The other side of the coin of blessings for the good is punishment for the wicked, and we cannot recall the one without remembering the other. Black-and-white views of the world emphasize the bright blessings of righteousness in comparison to the darkness of hell and damnation. The path of wickedness is described in traditional wisdom literature as a way strewn with thorns. Here Zophar reminds Job of the fate of the wicked: their eyes will fail and they won't be able to find a way out of the trap of wickedness (v. 20). They have no hope for life left—they can only hope to die. It is on this note of warning that Zophar ends his speech. We may have some problems today with seeing other people, or ourselves for that matter, in boxes labelled 'good' and 'wicked'. Few people are entirely good or entirely wicked. Similarly, while we may have clear thoughts about what goodness and wickedness entail, and what living up to our morals requires of us, situations do arise that are not entirely black and white, that take time to clarify and resolve. Sometimes life seems more complicated than the clear moral guidelines of the Bible indicate. We have to adapt our biblical values to modern life, and that is not always an easy thing.

PRAYER

Lord Jesus, we pray for your protection and blessing and for good things, but we recognize that when bad things happen, as they sometimes do, you are alongside us in our suffering.

36 JOB 12:1-6

I KNOW ALL THAT

Zophar has just delivered a lecture on the theory of just retribution and tried to exhort Job to mend his ways. Job answers in a tone that suggests that Zophar is simply telling him what he knows already, and he doesn't want to hear it again (v. 3). The friends may be the representatives of traditional wisdom who will go on adhering to its principles until they die. But Job also knows all these principles and he does not need to be taught them again. The friends make him feel inferior, as if he does not know the very system that he is attacking, and by doing this they belittle his protest. He asks a rhetorical question: 'Who does not know such things as these?' The expected answer is, of course, 'No one—they are widely known.' Job doesn't need Zophar to remind him.

I am a laughing-stock

One of Job's recurrent concerns is about his reputation among others. This is important to all of us: once we lose face publicly it is very difficult for us to rebuild our lives again. We rely throughout our lives on people to recommend us to others, to write us references, to speak about our skills and our reputation to others who may be interested. Job feels here that he has been made a laughing-stock (v. 4). There he was, so upright and self-righteous in a way, with a seeming hotline to the Almighty—and now look at him. The inference that he did not fully understand the doctrine of retribution is a further insult to him. Because of his misfortunes he is no longer being treated with respect. It is simply assumed that his suffering is his fault because he has sinned, and there is no thought among his friends of blaming God. Rather, they look down on Job and ridicule him for this dramatic change of fortune (v. 4).

Sleeping peacefully in one's bed

Job draws a subtle contrast between those who expect trouble because they tempt it—such as thieves and robbers, who might get caught at any time—and those who are 'at ease' and have contempt for misfortune (vv. 5-6). The inference is that he himself used to be 'at ease'—and his friends and those who mock him now are certainly in that category. For the self-righteous, misfortune feels a long way off: they deliberately set themselves on top of a moral pedestal, which is a kind of protection. Misfortune can easily strike the ones whose 'feet are unstable', that is, those who are already treading the rocky path of sin.

Yet for those who tempt fate regularly, and do not pretend to be more than they are, there also is a certain peace of mind. They know that the fall is greater from the top of a pedestal than from the bottom of a rocky slope.

Verse 6 is another complaint against the seeming prosperity of the wicked, picturing them asleep in their beds. Once again, life seems to have turned upside down: why should it be the wicked whose tents are at peace and why should those who provoke God be secure? Even those who worship other gods seem to enjoy this peace of mind that so eludes Job.

PRAYER

Lord God, help us not to belittle others less fortunate than ourselves; help us all to have respect for each other, however unequal life may seem.

37

ASK *the* ANIMALS

This is a curious little passage which suggests that the whole of the created world—the animals, birds, plants and fish—can tell us that God is the One who has created life (vv. 7–8). No person or living thing is ignorant of the fact that he or she owes his or her life to the Creator God. This would be a great affirmation of praise in the usual context. What a great thing that God is the creator of all life, and what a wonderful image of the whole of creation praising him! However, in its present context in the midst of Job's affirmation that God has caused all his suffering, it has a slightly different ring to it. God is the creator, God can do everything, and the inference in the context is perhaps that his actions can be for good or for bad. He has such total control that he can do whatever he likes and this is what the next passage goes on to show. However, at this point, we have what seems to be a straightforward piece of praise to God that could almost have been borrowed from a psalm—although in psalms, nature usually proclaims God's glory (Psalm 98), whereas in this passage nature actually bears witness to God's actions, whether good or bad. Perhaps there is the suggestion of a parody here.

This passage presents a lovely image of animals teaching humans. Animals know that God is their Lord—do humans? There is also the overtone that you only have to look at the wonders of nature to realize that God exists. He exists in the beauty and complexity and diversity of the world and all living things witness to him. Job asks a rhetorical question again: 'Who among all these does not know that the hand of the Lord has done this?' (v. 9). The expected answer is, of course, 'Nobody, not even the tiniest organism on the earth.'

God holds life in his hand

In verse 10, Job expresses the belief that each and every life is in the hand of God. Once again, this does not apply just to humans, but also to animals, birds, plants and fish. Generally the Bible is centred upon human beings, the whole story being about liberation for the people of God. One sometimes wonders what is the place of animals and plants. In the wisdom literature their place is acknowledged. Wisdom takes its starting point from human experience, but it does include the recognition that we are not the only inhabitants on this earth and that we may not be the only ones with the ability to recognize God. Also, the picture of God most prevalent in the wisdom literature is one of God as Creator, which emphasizes that he can be known through the natural world (Job 38). So the picture of God too is less human-centred and much broader than is often seen elsewhere.

Every life and every breath is in God's hand (v. 10). His power is at once overwhelming and awe-inspiring, and also frightening in that God can give and take away life as he chooses.

Is it only the old who are wise?

Job digresses slightly in verses 11–12 with another couple of rhetorical questions, a technique that he uses when he wants to state that something is obvious. 'Does not the ear test words?' he asks (v. 11). Well, of course, if you didn't have ears you could not hear words. You could read them, perhaps—but many people in the ancient world did not read. Rather, they relied on their ears to understand what was spoken to them verbally. The answer, then, is obviously 'Yes': there is no other organ that will 'test words'. 'Does not the palate taste food?' is the second part of the sentiment. Well, of course it does! You could not taste food without one. So Job's words here are designed to state the obvious.

The next line states another seemingly obvious point, but throws it into question. 'Is wisdom with the aged?' (v. 12). Of course it is—the old are wise because they have had longer to become so. Or is it as simple as that? Aren't there some older people who will never be wise, and aren't there some young people who are wise beyond their years? 'Is understanding in length of days?' Well, again, seemingly 'yes' but there is a 'but…'. So this little pair of lines is a clever technique for aligning two issues with the obvious answer 'yes', but the second line raises a question that will lead on to the next idea. Traditional wisdom sayings are used here: verse 12 suggests the answer that wisdom is a matter of discernment, not simply the preserve of a few aged men (which anticipates some of what Elihu, the fourth friend, is going to say in his speeches). The point will become clear in verse 13: true wisdom is with God.

PRAYER

Lord God, the animals and the birds praise you; the plants of the ground and the fish of the sea join in worship of you. Let us rejoice in your created world and in the creatures you have made.

38

GOD IS TO BE PRAISED

The all-powerful nature of God is emphasized here in a passage that seems to be a straightforward hymn of praise to God but, in the second part, changes to become a criticism. To state that God is the fount of wisdom and strength (v. 13) is a well-known sentiment from traditional wisdom as represented in the book of Proverbs (for example, Proverbs 3:5–8). Counsel and understanding are also well-known wisdom attributes. These four attributes are a powerful combination: not many people combine wisdom and strength! Counsel and understanding are attributes very much admired by the wise— they are the qualities of a successful diplomat, politician or administrator, such as some of the wise no doubt became. However, here it is not human wisdom that is being considered, but God's wisdom.

God has the final word

In verses 14–15 Job dwells on the idea of God's strength, and we know from his former sentiments that he sees this as a two-sided matter. Strength is good when used wisely, but fatal when used wrongly. We see this in the modern world when rulers gain power which, if used for the good, can be uniting and beneficial, but, when used for bad, leads to cruelty and despotism. God has the final word because he is ultimate strength. If he chooses to destroy, no one can rebuild (v. 14). The devastation is complete and final and no rebuilding can match the speed of the destruction that is wrought. If God chooses to 'shut someone in', no one can release them. This is perhaps metaphorical—an image used to state the truth that if God has ranged his power against someone, no one can save them. It suggests a bird trapped in a cage: if God has put the bird there and thrown away the key, no one can save it; in fact, even letting it out would do it no good as it will have lost the ability to fend for itself.

The next image is of water—perhaps an overtone of the flood story in Genesis 6 to 9. If God withholds the waters, they dry up (v. 15a). Only God was able to do this after the flood. We might also think of the Red Sea crossing, when God dried up a section of sea-bed to allow the Israelites to walk through (Exodus 14:21–31). The converse of this is when God decides to let the waters go and they flood the land completely, destroying all in their wake (v. 15b).

The images in these two verses make us think of natural disasters. The tornado, earthquake or whirlwind might be the agents of the kind of destruction that could not be rebuilt. The drought or thunderstorm might fulfil the second image of the power of water. The point of these images is to emphasize God's strength, particularly in nature. This forms an interesting contrast to the mention of the animals: there is the beauty and diversity of God's created world on the one hand, and then there is the power and destructiveness of natural disasters on the other—a good and a bad side to everything.

All are in God's hands

Job reiterates the point about God's wisdom and strength in verse 16, but interestingly strength comes first here. Maybe there is a hint that it is God's strength of which Job is most aware in his present condition, rather than his wisdom. While the fact that God is strong and wise is usually a thing to be praised, the inference here is that all are in his hands, good and bad alike, for God to treat as he pleases—and this doesn't always work out in the way that Job, at least, would wish. Job notes that 'the deceived and the deceiver' are God's—he knows all the ways of humans. He holds the lives of both the good and the bad in his hands. The question is, how is he going to treat them? The next part of the passage suggests that God's treatment of people is certainly not according to a fair system of justice.

PRAYER

Lord God, your power stretches to the ends of the earth and you have the wisdom to use that power for good. We pray that effecting the good is your overriding purpose for our world and that we may be used as instruments of that purpose.

GOD BRINGS *the* MIGHTY LOW

Here we find the first signs of the criticism that God might be acting unjustly not only in Job's case (which has been said), but on a global scale. This too could be interpreted in more than one way: maybe God has good reasons for bringing the mighty down. And yet, from a human angle, it does not seem fair. Does it indicate that God is on the side of the less fortunate in society? Or is he simply concerned to counter arrogance where he sees it? Is there any pattern to God's action or is it entirely arbitrary? Job says that God leads counsellors away stripped and makes fools of judges (v. 17). Upright people are brought low. Kings are not exempt—they too find themselves brought low, their fine sashes replaced by waistcloths (v. 18). Priests are stripped of their clothes, and hence their dignity too, and the mighty are overthrown (v. 19). Those who are trusted to speak well are deprived of their speech and the old are no longer wise (v. 20). Princes are the object of contempt and the strong are no longer so (v. 21). Everything is topsy-turvy. What has happened? Job is stating the fact that God is powerful to do all these things—he can and does bring the mighty down. All that is held to be worthwhile by traditional wisdom is scorned and mocked by God if he feels like it.

The emphasis on clothing is interesting. We are all protected by our clothes as we walk about, not simply in the sense that they keep us warm, but perhaps even more significantly because of the privacy they give us. Dignity is stripped from people when their clothes are forcibly removed: this is one of the ways in which prisoners can be humiliated; and the loss of dignity is one of the reasons why we feel vulnerable when wearing only a cape on a hospital trolley as we go in for an operation. Even great men and women are cut down to size when they have no clothes on, says Job. So God can cut down to size those who are considered important in the human world or, perhaps more to the point, feel themselves to be important.

God has power

We now find a reference to God's creative act of uncovering the deep out of darkness—that was a great moment in creation, a thing to be praised (v. 22). Darkness was made by God into light. Maybe the reference is meant simply to stress again God's power. And yet there is an overtone of the question, 'What was the point, if it was just to mock that which he had created?' God raises a whole nation and then destroys it. He makes nations great and then belittles them. There seems to be no moral principle governing the rise and fall of nations. God allows leaders to be stripped of understanding: this, perhaps, is a reference to the illness, or even madness, that overtakes some people when they become old and lose their leadership positions. Leaders and great figures are particularly belittled by the experience of 'wandering in a pathless waste' (v. 24). The way of wisdom is a straight and smooth path, and yet here are these formerly wise people wandering around lost. God, the giver of light, denies them that essential light. They grope in the dark and stagger like drunkards (v. 25). We might see these acts of God as being done almost for sport. Is God laughing at us?

This passage as a whole is a parody of the common hymnic descriptions of God's beneficent power, which are usually, as in Psalm 107, delivered in a tone of praise for God's moral actions. In Psalm 107:39–41, for example, the princes who have oppressed God's people are punished, but the good are not. Here in Job, no purpose in the humiliation of princes is given. The moral justification is absent, giving us another example of the idea of God's power as a danger to humans.

Job is using this critical tone against God because of his anger, feelings of betrayal and sense of loss of all that he has formerly known and believed. It is quite natural for people feeling deep despair and anger to become not just hostile but also openly critical and sarcastic against the one whom they feel is to blame. Such open hostility against God is unusual in the Bible, but in a way it is comforting to find it here in Job, because it helps those of us who feel this kind of anger and cynicism to realize that others have trodden the same path before us—and their emotions are even canonized in the Bible! The Bible is a great compendium of human experience as well as a history of great and saving events, and no part of it is more experientially orientated than the wisdom literature, especially Job.

PRAYER

Lord, we know that nations rise and fall and empires drift away. Help us to see your purpose in these events and help us to try to understand things that may, at first sight, seem senseless and purposeless.

40

I KNOW WHAT I AM
TALKING ABOUT

Job reiterates his knowledge of all that his friends have told him. His eye has seen and his ear has heard all that needs to be known (v. 1). He will not allow his friends to speak down to him and cause him to feel inferior (v. 2). But talking to the friends is pointless when the one that he really wants to talk to is God himself (v. 3). Job cannot argue with the friends because they just tell him what he already knows and they refuse to see his point of view. At least God would get to hear Job's perspective if they were to have an audience together—or so Job thinks. He wishes to go straight to the top and engage with God on the highest level.

The falsity of the friends

Job now launches an attack on his friends. They tell lies; they are useless when it comes to trying to heal Job's wounds. They are verbose: Job wishes that they would simply be quiet and let him suffer in peace (vv. 4–5). It is ironic that at the end of the prologue the friends came and sat in comforting silence with Job. But in the dialogue their role changes and they become too talkative. Job now longs for that previous silence.

There is much on the role of speaking and of silence in the wisdom literature. The silent person is generally praised as being wise— although it is pointed out that if a fool keeps silent, one cannot differentiate him from a silent wise person. The proverbs are against unnecessary talk and gossip (for example, Proverbs 10:13–14 and Proverbs 20:19, 'A gossip reveals secrets; therefore do not associate with a babbler') and find merit in a word spoken at an apt moment and with restraint (for example, Proverbs 10:19, 'When words are many, transgression is not lacking, but the prudent are restrained in speech'). There is also merit in keeping confidences instead of spilling the beans. Keeping silent would be a greater sign of wisdom than all the advice Job's friends are offering (v. 5). Job is pleading with them to listen to his point of view—their ears are closed to his arguments.

Speaking falsely for God

Job now launches into a series of questions which are really accusations of the friends. 'Will you speak falsely for God?' he asks (v. 7), inferring that this is what they are in fact doing. He becomes more personal in his attack, accusing them of speaking deceitfully about God. He suspects their motives: aren't they just trying to keep on God's side and plead his case with their own benefit in view? What will happen when God turns on them? (v. 10). He accuses them of trying to deceive God—maybe they will be successful in doing that. Job is convinced that God will punish them for showing bias or partiality of any kind.

Job is showing some regained confidence in the doctrine of retribution here: surely God will punish those who are false and who witness falsely about him? He asks, 'Will not his majesty terrify you?' (v. 11). The expected answer is, 'Yes, it will.' This is a real attack on the traditional wisdom stance. Job calls their maxims ashes and their defences clay (v. 12)—that is, worthless and transitory. Job feels here that the friends are not being entirely straightforward with him, or even with God. Thus he threatens them with divine punishment when God finds out. We all feel sometimes that people are not being entirely honest with us. Trust is an increasingly precious commodity. Even best friends sometimes let us down. Often, on either side of a friendship, it only takes one bad misunderstanding or event that causes mistrust to put that friendship in serious jeopardy. This seems ironic in the light of the many good times we may have had with that person. Job's friends were presumably once just that—friends—but now he feels that he cannot trust them, and more than that, they are ultimately untrustworthy people.

PRAYER

*Lord help us to witness to your word in truth and honesty
without thought of our own gain.*

41

I HAVE NOTHING TO LOSE

Sometimes people experience such devastation or misfortune that they feel that they cannot sink down any further. They feel that they have nothing to lose in taking risks. This is how Job feels now—he has nothing to lose. He calls for the friends to be silent so that he can speak, and he does not care what the consequences are. He will risk everything, even his life, to argue his case to God (v. 14). He knows that God is powerful to do anything and that he may very well bring about Job's death in the imminent future, so he does not care about anything except pleading his case (v. 15). He does, however, get some small respite from the thought that the godless would not get such an audience with God (v. 16: he is presumably referring to his friends here). A new mood of confidence in arguing his case seems to spring out of the ashes of despair.

Listen to me!

Job keeps reiterating the demand to listen to him (v. 17). It is often the case that we feel we are not being heard, when we are trying to state our case and no one appears to be listening, or, if someone is listening, when they seem to misunderstand what we are saying. There is also the scenario where someone else is doing so much talking that we cannot get a word in edgeways. Job feels both these sentiments. The friends are full of words—they are not listening and certainly not understanding—and God is seemingly absent and appears not to be listening either. All Job wants is a chance to plead his case (v. 18). He wants his words to be heeded, his declaration to ring in all of their ears. Job is using legal language here. He has prepared his case and so he should get a fair hearing. In a moment of optimism, he thinks that he will be vindicated—but maybe this is more of a hope through clenched teeth than a certain hope.

Who will take up the challenge?

In verse 19 Job's attention changes from the friends to God; in fact, in this whole passage it is never entirely clear which he is addressing. It could well be both, since the problem with both God and the friends is ultimately the same: neither party is giving him a fair hearing. Job asks who is going to take up the challenge of contending with him, using legal language and again showing a renewed confidence. Presumably this is another call to God to hear and respond to him. Then Job himself will be quiet because he will have nothing further to say. He will be silent, and then die, knowing that he did his best to plead his innocence. Nothing else matters at this point.

Job is in more combative mood in this passage. Having decided to take the risk of arguing with God, he is now trying to gain God's attention—to force him into the dock, so to speak—in order for God to hear his case. Job is tired of being passive and waiting for his fortunes to change or be explained away by the friends. He now decides to act for himself. The benefit of taking risks in life is that sometimes they pay dividends and we are much happier for having kick-started ourselves into activity. Of course, the down side is that we can lose too. Job has decided that he has nothing to lose in his relationship with God by having a good argument with him. It is crucial, however, that God listens to his cause. It takes two to have an argument! And even if the one we are arguing against is not responding to us verbally, we need at least to know that they are listening to our case. Hence Job's provocative language of challenge: God has got to know exactly what he has to say!

PRAYER

Lord, help us to learn to listen to others and not to be
so absorbed in ourselves and our own lives that we lose that
capacity. Help us in particular to have the time to listen
to those in need, however great or small.

42

TWO REQUESTS

It is clear by now that Job is speaking directly to God. He asks for two things to be granted to him (v. 20), so that he can look God in the eye, so to speak, without feeling that he has to hide from God. The first request is that God withdraw his hand (v. 21). The imagery of the hand of God is interesting: it can be the hand of protection, or the hand of guidance, or the hand that smites, the hand of wrath. Often in the Bible, God's hand upon someone is a sign of blessing, in the manner of a helping hand. Here, however, God's hand lies heavily upon Job's shoulder. Job wishes to be rid of God's weighty hand. He wishes God's attention upon him to be withdrawn. This is a parody of passages where God's concern is a joyous thing, for example, Psalm 27:4 where the psalmist longs to 'live in the house of the Lord all the days of my life, to behold the beauty of the Lord, and to inquire in his temple'. Job's second request in verse 21 is that he may no longer feel so frightened. All his thinking and reasoning has made him aware of the power and terror of God. No longer is God a beneficent figure; instead Job feels that God has turned against him.

Give me a hearing

Sometimes in conversation, we feel that we are talking past the other person—rather like two people speaking at the same time in an argument. There is an orderliness about proper exchange in dialogue where one person speaks and then the other replies. Job asks God to call to him, and then he will answer (v. 22). This would be the natural order of events—that God, the more powerful party, would instigate proceedings and call on Job. Alternatively, Job is prepared to instigate a conversation with God in which he speaks first and God replies to him. Job then questions God, asking him to explain to Job what his sins are (v. 23). He then asks God why he is hiding his face from Job (v. 24)—God appears to be absent. There is a parallelism here: Job first asks God to make him feel that he doesn't have to hide, and then he accuses God of hiding his face. He wants to get away from God's presence on the one hand, but on the other hand he is worried when God appears to have turned away. Job feels that he has become God's enemy. Again, those engaged in strife and argument can feel like this:

it is often only your closest and dearest friends or family members with whom you fight, and there is often the feeling that those who should be your closest supporters have become your enemies.

God has turned against Job

Job feels frightened by God and asks him why he is taking such trouble over a nobody like Job. He feels persecuted. He uses the imagery of a windblown leaf and dry chaff (v. 25): God is so powerful that he could blow a leaf over without even thinking about it, so why does God spend time pursuing the equivalent of a leaf or chaff? Job accuses God of writing bitter accusations against him, and the popular image of God keeping a book of all one's actions, ready for the Day of Judgment, comes to mind. Even the deeds of Job's youth are possibly being listed against him here (v. 26). Job feels hedged in: his legs are in the stocks, he is being watched in everything he does and, in fact, constrained in his movements by God. There is a feeling here of God as 'Big Brother', watching and waiting for Job to put a foot wrong.

The passage ends with a slightly unconnected thought, possibly linked to Job's disease (v. 28). In fact, the reference in verse 27 to a 'bound' being set to the soles of Job's feet may also be a reference to his illness, since in his state he cannot walk far. He feels that his body is wasting away like something rotten, and he uses the image of a moth-eaten garment. This image of garments is an interesting one. As mentioned previously, we all feel protected by our clothes in that they keep us warm and help us to hide our nakedness from the world, but they also give us an opportunity to express something of our personality. We feel that we lose a certain amount of control over our lives if we are unable to cover ourselves adequately and if we are unable to express ourselves by what we wear. If our favourite jumper becomes moth-eaten we feel a sense of frustration and waste. Job feels that sense of helplessness: his body is not whole, and he feels that it is like a moth-eaten garment. Presumably his clothes are hanging from him, infected by his disease and by his situation on the dungheap as well as expressing his poverty and lack of self-esteem.

PRAYER

Lord, hear our prayers and petitions and do not hide your face from us. Help us to feel your protecting power and not to feel hemmed in by your concern for us.

43

The FUNERAL SENTENCES

These verses may be familiar as part of the funeral sentences in the Christian liturgy. They express the condition of humanity—that one certainty in life is death. A man, or 'mortal' as the NRSV translates the Hebrew, born of woman (another certainty), has a relatively short life and has to endure a certain amount of hardship. It is a resigned view of the human condition, and somewhat pessimistic in its characterization of life as short and full of trouble. This is a reference, of course, to Job's own life. We have seen how he feels the brevity of his life and how he is suffering nothing but hardship. Yet, it is also universalized to refer to the human lot in general. A person 'comes up like a flower' (v. 2), a reference to the first bloom of youth or possibly to the growing child reaching adulthood. There are a few years at a peak and then it is all downhill! As a flower comes to maturity and has a moment of beauty, so with human beings; and as a flower inevitably withers and dies, so with human beings also. The moment of beauty is so quick that it flees as quickly as a shadow. There is nothing lasting—change occurs all the time.

Often, when we haven't seen somebody for a while, we see changes in them. We notice grey hairs and wrinkles and an overall impression of increasing age. They themselves, and those with whom they spend their everyday lives, probably haven't noticed, but we all occasionally become aware of the inexorable passage of time. We have the same feeling when we look through old photograph albums, even those recording events that seem quite recent in our minds. We see that we looked different then—thinner or younger, perhaps! As part of the liturgy for the funeral service, this passage makes us aware of our mortality and perhaps leads us to reflect on the need to make the most of life, however fleeting it may be.

Why torment me?

We are back in verse 3 to the theme of God's oppressive watch over humankind, in a more general sense than simply in relation to Job's situation, although his particular case is implicit here. Why does God 'fix his eyes' on a mere mortal whose life is so short and meaningless? Why does God judge Job? He is aching to understand why—hence all these questions. He now asks a rhetorical question (v. 4): 'Who can bring a clean thing out of an unclean?' And this time he actually gives us the answer: 'No one can.' If human beings are sinful, why does God take so much trouble over them? And if Job has sinned, then what good can come of this judgment from God? Nothing, it seems, can change his fate.

Fate versus free will

Job moves on to the idea of God having decided the fates of human beings in advance. God alone knows the number of days that each one of us is to live (v. 5). God has fixed boundaries beyond which people cannot go. We are back to the idea of an oppressive and over-protective God. Why does God limit us in this way? Why can't God just move back, look away and let human beings enjoy what is allotted to them? There are overtones here of the poem about time in Ecclesiastes 3. The sentiment there is that there is a time for everything—a time to be born and a time to die—but that only God knows these times and human beings have no way of knowing them. Thus, to try to understand all this is futile—it is beyond us—and, the author of Ecclesiastes says, we might as well simply try to enjoy life, to eat, drink and be merry, because all we have to look forward to is death.

The reference to labourers in verse 6 is interesting. It suggests that those who have a manual job, which brings them into close contact with nature, have a capacity to enjoy life that those who live on a more intellectual plane, and think too much, do not have. Many people do not spend time worrying about their mortality, they just get on and enjoy themselves; while others spend their lives ridden with such worries and filled with anxiety. The exhortation to enjoy life is an important one. There is a close resemblance between this passage and Job 7:11–21, which is itself a parody of Psalm 8. Psalm 8 praises humanity as God's highest creation, while Job 7 and 14 describe the human condition in negative terms and ask God to leave humans alone.

PRAYER

Lord God, help us to enjoy the days of our brief lives. Give us hope that death is not the final word and that we will return to your protecting arms at the end of our days.

JOB 14:7-12

WHY CAN'T *the* FATE *of* HUMANS BE LIKE THAT *of a* TREE?

All of us have probably felt at some time the frustration of knowing that one day we will die. We do not want to face this fact, and there is a huge industry involved in trying to stay young, stay healthy and live as long as possible. Job here wishes to challenge his fate. He asks, 'Why can't the fate of humans be like that of a tree?' A tree, although it may be cut down, will often shoot again (vv. 7–8). This conjures up the image of a stump of a large tree to which are attached small, seemingly insignificant twigs with green shoots on the end. These are small beginnings but in themselves will, in time, make up a new tree.

One could argue, with reference to human beings, that children are a way of perpetuating at least something of oneself into the future. We have to remember that Job at this stage has lost his family and hence his future investment. Job is simply drawing on the image of a tree to stress to God that our human fate need not be so final. There are examples in nature of a less cruel fate. An old tree root may be very old and dry with a dead stump, and yet, given the right conditions, even this old stump can gain new life. With fresh water and fresh energy, it will bud and eventually put forth branches. The stump imagery is common in the Old Testament to refer to the remnant of Israel: compare Isaiah 6:13, 'The holy seed is its stump.' The remnant of Israel during and after the exile were like this old stump— lacking in life, lacking in numbers, weak and tired—but incredibly the nation survived and grew and grew, new buds shaping up into strong trees. Job asks, 'Why is this not the case with human life in general?'

Death is like a dry lake

Job looks for another image which more accurately describes the human condition, providing a contrast with the tree imagery (v. 10). Unlike the tree that puts forth shoots, mortals die, expire or lie down. They are gone for ever. Similarly, a lake can lose water, gradually dry up and disappear; or a river can suffer a similar fate (v. 11). This kind of loss might be compared to old age—a gradual 'drying up' of the functions of the body so that there is no way back. There is some interesting nature imagery used in this chapter, and in the book as a whole, and it must be remembered that people in the ancient world had a certain closeness with nature that we have perhaps lost. Job uses natural images here to illuminate his view of death. At first he is protesting and asking why death can't be otherwise, but then he shows a certain resignation—recognizing that the human condition has to be this way, despite all his protests.

Death is final

Job comes to the sober realization that death is final and that once human beings have 'lain down' there is no getting up again (v. 12). There is perhaps a suggestion here of the finality of being laid to rest in the ground. Humans will never awake, not even if the end of the world comes. Nothing will ever arouse the dead from their sleep. This passage forms an interesting contrast to traditional Christian belief in an afterlife and seems to indicate that such a belief is not present in the book of Job. There is certainly no idea here of the resurrection of the dead or of any chance of continued existence. Not even the Hebrew idea of Sheol comes into the discussion here.

PRAYER

Lord Jesus, let us be thankful for the resurrection hope that we, as Christians, enjoy. Let us pray for a release from the gloomy thought that death is final, and find instead a reason for us to be hopeful of continued communion with you.

HIDE ME IN SHEOL!

Here we do encounter a reference to Sheol, almost as if, after the gloom of the previous passage, Job has just latched on to a fresh hope. Job is imagining here that he could perhaps be hidden in Sheol for a while and then come back again (v. 13). Sheol was a place where no further communion with God was considered possible, given that the inhabitants were dead, and Job takes this as a sign that at least in Sheol one could get away from God and get some respite from his wrath. We might contrast Psalm 55:6–7, where the psalmist wishes to flee, but not from God, rather from his enemies. Job wishes that he could hide until after God's anger is over and then be remembered by God so that he can be released. Sheol starts to look rather like a prison here: Job wants to serve a term there and then come back to continue his relationship with God. The trouble is, though, that going to Sheol is final—it is a place of no return.

The wider context here is that Job is bewailing his lot—that is, death, to which he feels that he is close—but he doesn't want to die because that will end the discussion with God.

Is there life after death?

In the midst of this set of rather convoluted thoughts, Job asks whether there is any chance that human beings might live again after death (v. 14). This is a somewhat rhetorical question: Job knows that the answer is 'No' and, therefore, that his previous hopes of being hidden in Sheol are simply pointless musings. There is an ongoing discussion among scholars about whether there is any realistic possibility of an afterlife suggested in Job. It certainly seems in this passage that it is wishful thinking on his part.

If only...

Job is good at wishing himself out of his situation and imagining what might have been, or what his relationship with God might be in the future. In any stressful situation we all have moments of denial, of wishing ourselves outside it or far away. Here, though, Job is saying that if only things could be different, he would be prepared to wait and wait for God to release him from his present misery (v. 14). We start to get a feel of his real devotion to God in these sentiments—like a lover saying that he will wait for ever for his loved one. He imagines a more rosy situation between himself and God, in which God would call and he would answer and in which God would really want to be in relationship with Job. If only that were the case, there would be no harassing of Job by God, no counting of his sins. All would be forgiven.

In verse 16 the NRSV inserts the word 'not', to say, 'You would *not* number my steps.' Numbering the steps, however, can be seen as a positive expression of care from God, so Job's wish could be that God would once again keep watch over him. If this were the case, the word 'not' would be unnecessary. On the other hand, it is more in keeping with Job's sentiments that God's constant attention is oppressive. So, on balance, the sentence makes more sense with the 'not' retained. Job is longing here for a more loving God, one who would forgive any transgression and forget it too. This perhaps reminds us of the Christian understanding of forgiveness in which real allowance is made for sins committed and in which no grievance is held, but rather all is forgotten and a new page of the book is turned over. If only God were forgiving like that, says Job. Well, the Christian answer is that God *is* like that, and that his forgiving nature was made manifest in his taking upon himself the burden of sin through his Son, Jesus Christ. By contrast, Job's experience of God, at least at this point, is of an angry and wrathful deity who is causing his formerly pious servant unmitigated grief and pain. It is interesting that, despite this, Job has moments of longing for a good relationship with God and is able to gain strength through such thoughts in the midst of his suffering. We might argue that even in our darkest moments, God is alongside, and that focusing on our relationship with him can only be for good.

PRAYER

Lord, let us not spend too much time dwelling on what might have been, or what might be different, but help us to make the most both of the good and the bad in life, trusting in your unfailing love.

BACK *to* REALITY

The moment of optimism suddenly disappears at the beginning of verse 18. The key word is 'But', indicating a contrast with what has just gone before. Job began to dream himself back into a more ideal relationship with God. But now he realizes that this was nothing but a dream. Just as the elements destroy mountains, just as rocks are removed from their place never to return, just as stones are worn away by water, or floods take large amounts of soil away, so God does all these things to human beings (vv. 18–19). They are destroyed like the mountains, they are removed from their place like rocks, never to return; they are worn away like stones and removed from their place like soil. These images of the power of nature are used to show the relentlessness of the power of God and the inevitability of death. So Job accuses God of destroying human hopes. There is no future for a worn-away section of mountain or a displaced and dispersed rock: like a dry riverbed without water, once something has been changed in this way it cannot be changed back. Job is likening this to death: God has decreed that death is the final word and so his will prevails against any other hope. The smiling faces of human beings are changed to faces of gloom. They are sent away, never to return. Job's deep scepticism and gloomy pessimism return with force in this passage. There is a parody here of hopeful passages in the Psalms, where confidence is expressed that God will rescue his people and deliver them from their enemies—for example, Psalm 28:6–8. Psalm 31, too, contains similar complaints to Job's but ends on a note of trust and hope that Job lacks.

Death is so unfair

We are now given a dark picture of the unfairness of death. Humans die and so they don't know what happens to their children. Their children may come to great honour but they will never know (v. 21). It is a common human feeling to wonder what a dead relative or friend would have thought about our achievements. Would he or she have been proud? Mothers sometimes say to their children that their long-gone grandparents would have been proud of them. It is a source of sadness when people do not go on to see their children's or their children's children's triumphs. Nor are they there to share their sorrows. If their children are 'brought low' they may not be there to offer support in their hour of need. It seems a cruel fate. My grandmother had a poem on her wall entitled 'Mother', which expressed the sentiment that mothers are wonderful—they are the only people who love you unconditionally, who will do all they can for you and who will love you no matter what. The poem ends with the sobering thought, which always made me feel sad as a child, that 'the only bad thing she [your mother] ever does to you is to die and leave you'. Here we are back to the inevitability of death, and one starts to understand what Job means in this passage. It would be so much nicer if people just went on and on.

In death, we are alone

It is a sobering thought that in death we are alone. The reference to pain in verse 22 is perhaps a reference to the anguish of death, which can be a painful and protracted process, and the loneliness of the condition of dying and of death itself. These are issues that are rarely discussed today, even in the pulpit, because they are too depressing to dwell on for long. It is a sign of Job's gloom that he does dwell on these issues. However, perhaps in our culture today, grief has lost the important place that it should have. Mourning our dead is also important, and maybe more discussion of it from time to time would be helpful to many of us.

PRAYER

Let us thank God for all those whom we have loved and who have now died. Let us remember the time we had together and give thanks for all that we shared.

47

WINDY WORDS

All three friends have spoken and Job has replied to each one, as well as complaining to God. Now the three friends start up a second round in the same sequence. Here we encounter Eliphaz responding angrily to Job, accusing him of talking unprofitably, but couching his accusation in the form of a question. Uttering 'windy words' (v. 2) indicates a lack of substance in what one is saying. Eliphaz cites a general principle, phrased as two rhetorical questions. Someone who is 'wise' should know the principle that guarding one's tongue, selecting one's words carefully and knowing when to speak and when to be silent are essential principles of communication, as imparted at some length in the book of Proverbs. The suggestion here is that Job is full of air—full of 'the east wind', uttering words that do no good to anyone. There is some truth in Eliphaz's accusation, as we have seen: Job has been musing on a number of imponderables, creating 'if only' situations to try to avoid the unpleasantness of his ultimate fate.

In an age of communication, we are surrounded with words being spoken at us and being expected of us, both face to face and through the media. Words have power, but too many 'windy' words undermine that power and make a person look foolish. It is always better to say less than more—not to 'shoot one's mouth off', to use a modern phrase. The wise knew the wisdom of silence: a word once spoken could not be withdrawn. We do as well to remember this, when we sometimes speak out of turn and say things in haste or in anger that we later regret.

The fear of God

Wisdom takes its inspiration from the fear of God (v. 4). The quest for wisdom is largely a human concern—watching the world and human relationships and trying to make sense of both—but God is always there at the limits of understanding. In fact, more than this, the Wisdom writers argued that if we put God first, so that he is both the beginning and the end of understanding, and put his morality foremost, then we will live successful and happy lives. In his angry protest, Job is showing a lack of respect for God, rather than an appropriate awe and respect in relation to the Godhead and a realization that his wisdom is far beyond ours (a message that comes across in the speeches of God in Job 38—41).

Eliphaz is here accusing Job of losing the fear of God and, with it, quiet contemplation of the divine. In today's busy world we often have little time to stop and meditate. Just putting aside half an hour in a hectic day is difficult, and the awareness of this difficulty can reinforce a sense of life as tiring and stressful. The wise saw the benefit of quiet contemplation, of taking time out to think and to process one's thoughts. But what Job is doing is the opposite: he certainly has time to think, but his thoughts are running in such a negative and destructive direction that the benefit of meditation is all but lost.

Watch your mouth!

Returning to the theme of communication, Eliphaz points out that Job's sin is dictating what is coming out of his mouth (v. 5). Job is speaking as crafty people speak, trying to twist and turn arguments for his own benefit. Eliphaz now starts to become more personal by stating directly that Job is condemning himself by his very words right now (vv. 5–6). The inference is that even if he was innocent before, as he has always maintained, he is guilty now!

What we say has a huge effect on who we are and how we define ourselves. We often hear the phrase 'Watch your mouth' in reference to swearing and foul language. Swearing is something that the wise would not recommend. They believed in the power of self-control and careful speech at all times.

PRAYER

Help us to know the power of our words and to use them for good;
and help us to hear your voice and your word for us.

DO YOU HAVE ALL *the* ANSWERS?

Eliphaz here asks Job rhetorically, 'Are you the firstborn of the human race?' (v. 7)—that is, was Job there at the beginning of the creation of humanity (recalling Wisdom in Proverbs 8)? Does he know the answer to the riddle of human existence? Eliphaz is sarcastically challenging Job's arrogance. He then asks, again rhetorically, if Job existed before the hills did, because if he was part of the creative process, perhaps he might know some answers. Does Job know God's intentions better than the friends do, and is he the only one to have access to true wisdom? (v. 8) Eliphaz is attacking Job's arrogance again, this time to challenge the idea that Job has all the answers both in relation to God and in relation to the representatives of wisdom, his friends. Job is a lone voice, protesting his innocence and with his own special brand of reasoning with God: it starts to look as if he is putting down traditional wisdom as represented by the friends. Eliphaz asks directly, 'What do you know that we do not know?' (v. 9).

Human beings are all in the same boat when it comes to trying to understand the mysteries of God and the workings of the world. The wisdom quest is a way of trying to deal with such matters. How can Job think that he has all the answers when his answers spring from personal experience and have no grounding in the experience of many generations as embodied in the wisdom tradition? Eliphaz is appealing to the weight of tradition versus one lone voice. He then goes on to state the traditional argument that older people are wiser (v. 10). There was a deep respect for the wisdom of age in biblical times—something we would do well to remember today when we all too readily dismiss elderly people and their opinions. Eliphaz is saying that he and the friends have experiential wisdom on their side. Why will Job not simply be satisfied with traditional 'consolations' and a kind word, rather than lashing out in protest and anger and refusing to be comforted?

The dangers of anger

The wisdom writers were suspicious of anger and of the rash statements and actions into which it could lead people. It defied the principles of coolheadedness and rational behaviour that they advocated.

There are a number of proverbs warning against the angry man: for example, Proverbs 29:22 says, 'One given to anger stirs up strife, and the hothead causes much transgression.' Eliphaz accuses Job of letting his anger run away with him (v. 12). The heart was the seat of the emotions and the eyes reflect the inner emotions. Job's eyes are flashing with anger and his spirit is turned against God so that he speaks nothing but angry and 'windy' words. Eliphaz is pointing out the dangers of anger, which no doubt rings true in our own experience. Many a hurtful word or deed has been inspired by anger, sometimes even leading to crimes being committed. Watch your temper, Eliphaz is saying, and control what comes out of your mouth!

No one is perfect

Eliphaz now moves on to the more general principle that no one is completely sinless and pure, not humans and not even the 'holy ones' of God, presumably divine beings or angels that surround the Godhead (vv. 14–15). The inference is that, if this is the case, how can Job maintain his innocence? The language of cleanness has overtones of the worship context, where clean and unclean were major categories (see Leviticus). The importance of purity is a well-known aspect of Judaism. There is no pure cleanness in human beings—the human condition is sinful since Adam and Eve. Those born of woman cannot be fully righteous because their nature is to sin and be sinful. Only God is perfect, and such perfection does not extend even to his holy ones. It was one of the holy ones who fell and became Satan, and so God is right not to trust them. Even the heavens themselves are not fully 'clean' to God, so how much less Job, who is clearly a sinner! Eliphaz cleverly uses all the arguments at his disposal to try to convince Job that he is arrogant, over-reaching himself, disrespectful of God and, above all, a sinner. He uses strong language here in describing Job as 'abominable' and 'corrupt' (v. 16). Relations are certainly strained at this point—and Eliphaz was supposed to be Job's friend!

PRAYER

Lord, help us not to be arrogant and to think that we have all the answers, but help us too not to lose the ability to think for ourselves and to stand up for justice where we feel that wrong is being perpetrated.

LEARN *from the* TRADITION

It is often said that you have to experience something for yourself to really learn the truth about it. It is all very well learning from other people who have had the experience, and there is no doubt that we all learn from each other, but you can't beat a real experience of love, sorrow, grief, bereavement and so on to teach you how it really feels. This is what has happened for Job. He had accepted traditional answers and used to believe in the same framework of rewards to the faithful and punishment to the wicked. But now his experience of pain, when he knows that he is innocent, has led him to question that framework. The whole wisdom tradition is built on the findings of experience, and on teaching and learning from that experience. Eliphaz is continuing to appeal to this tradition. He asks Job to listen to what he has to say, and to learn from his experience and from that of past sages (vv. 17–18). He refers to the ancestors 'to whom alone the land was given' (v. 19), a rare reference to the historical circumstances of the patriarchs of Israel, who generally do not appear in the wisdom literature (probably because of its very universal stance). These ancestors were the ones to whom the land was given; they were special and marked out, uncontaminated by strangers or foreign ideas. It is these people who have passed down their experience from generation to generation, in which tradition Job and his friends now stand. Is not this wisdom authoritative?

It's not worth being wicked

The traditional view of the fate of the wicked is now described by Eliphaz in frightening and graphic terms. The wicked writhe in pain continuously for years upon end, and they hear terrifying sounds in their ears (vv. 20–21). They may appear to prosper for a time, but their success will be short-lived because destruction is inevitable. They become trapped in a desperate situation from which they cannot escape, like a prisoner destined for execution. They are hungry, anxious for food, and they know that a judgment day is at hand, so they are distressed. Distress and anguish are described as prevailing against the wicked as enemy forces prevail against a king on the verge of a battle. Elements of this description seem to fit Job's own state, which is why the friends think that Job must have sinned, and which is also why Job feels so betrayed.

The price of defiance

We still hold on to a belief that right and wrong can be meted out in certain quantities. There is a kind of unspoken assumption in our culture that if a number of things go wrong, it is about time something went right for a change, and vice versa. When justice is not seen to prevail in this life, it is often stated that in the life to come, on judgment day, all wrongs will be punished and good will be rewarded. It is part of our moral sense as human beings to feel that justice should be done in all cases, and it is an important element of our picture of God that he is seen to reward and punish fairly. However, this pattern does not work according to the rules that we might like to see. Eliphaz is maintaining a strict pattern here, appealing to traditional belief, and yet, for Job, it is a naïve hope. The reason for the punishment of the wicked is clearly given here—because they have defied God (v. 25). We have a description of the wicked stretching out their hands, echoing Job's supplication to God. This, however, is an action of defiance on the part of the wicked: they shake their fists at God rather than putting their hands up in prayer. The wicked are described as stubborn, and the battle imagery is continued with a reference to the wicked running against God with a thick shield. They are described as fat in the face and body—presumably a reference to their over-indulgence, something that was regarded by the wise as undesirable. They are being mocked and ridiculed by Eliphaz in an attempt to get his message across to Job.

This passage shows Eliphaz as having a strong sense of justice, and generally we must regard that as a good thing. We all wish that justice would fill our world, just as love and peace are also ideals for which we should strive. We all know that justice does not prevail all the time and that evil is all too familiar a concept in the world. It is, however, a goal worth fighting for.

PRAYER

Lord, we pray for justice in our world, that we may reward good and punish evil where we can. We look to you, the supreme Judge, for guidance in our task of maintaining a just society and in creating a better and fairer world.

50 JOB 15:28-35

The FATE *of the* WICKED

Eliphaz is now in full flight in his description of the evils that will befall the wicked. Here he proclaims that they will live in desolate cities and in uninhabitable houses that will ultimately become heaps of ruins (v. 28). This suggests that the houses are not well built and deteriorate quickly, and that they are not good to look at, thus making the environment unpleasant. One thinks perhaps of ghettos in cities, or of some of the 1960s and '70s architecture in Britain—including tall tower blocks, which are found in just about every major city in the world. They are badly built and their 'shelf life' is short.

The wicked will not be rich, says Eliphaz, and, if they are, their wealth will not endure (v. 29). The wisdom writers were well aware of the need to have money as security, and they also warned against getting rich quickly (for example, Proverbs 28:22: 'The miser is in a hurry to get rich and does not know that loss is sure to come'). Eliphaz's words echo traditional proverbial material in many places here. He says that the wicked will not strike root in the earth. Their existence will not be lasting because they will not have grown long roots, as a stable plant would (v. 29). Rather, their roots are shallow and easily pulled up—an interesting use of a plant metaphor here, which is taken up later in the passage. We have a reference to the darkness from which the wicked cannot escape, and we are told that fire will dry up their shoots. Any shoots they might put forth (perhaps a reference to offspring) will be destroyed (v. 30). This sounds remarkably like the fate of Job's children in the prologue.

Continuing the plant metaphor, we have a reference to blossom—any blossom the wicked might have will be swept away by the wind. Emptiness is described as their fate, something in which they themselves trust and which will be their reward, paid in full in advance (vv. 31–32). Unlike a plant or tree, their branch will not be green: it will, one assumes, be withered and dry (v. 33).

Comparisons with vine and olive

The general plant or tree metaphor gives way in verse 33 to a more specific reference to the vine and olive tree, both plants local to Israel and the surrounding area. Both are used to provide imagery elsewhere in the Bible, notably Isaiah 5. There, Israel is compared to a vine that is well-tended but yields wild grapes and so is a disappointment to God, who expected better of his people. The picture here in Job 15:33 is of a vine with unripe grapes, which are not good for wine or for eating. Thus the wicked will produce no good, edible thing, but only unripe grapes which will fall to the ground unused and unusable. Like the olive tree, their blossoms will be cast off to no apparent purpose—they will be wasted. The wicked will come to nothing: their offspring will fade, nothing will last and their existence will have been a waste of time, leading to emptiness—a sobering fate indeed!

Shun the company of the godless

Eliphaz's speech ends with the thought that the company of the godless is not worthwhile—it is a barren experience (vv. 34–35). Their bribery and corruption will be punished, their tents consumed by fire. They can do nothing but conspire to do evil and are deceitful to their very being (the heart being the seat of the emotions). They cannot change and nor do they wish to. It is a barren existence for the godless.

This is a very 'fire and brimstone' view of the way that the Almighty punishes wrongdoing, which might be said to leave little room for the Christian view of forgiveness. There is an element here of making one's bed and lying on it: the wicked cannot change the way they are. It is a common idea in the wisdom tradition that one chooses a path and then walks along it, and that the path of the wicked is strewn with thorns and difficulties. Presumably it would then be hard to change paths, although the very fact that the friends are trying to persuade Job to acknowledge his guilt and move on perhaps does suggest that, with true repentance, a way back to God might be found.

There are echoes of accusation in Eliphaz's description of the wicked, although he does not explicitly accuse Job or number him among the sinners. We all have a choice about the kinds of paths that we wish to follow in our lives. Sometimes the path changes at a particular time as we take new directions, sometimes we realize that the path is not as smooth as it might be, and sometimes we forget that our path needs primarily to lead to God as our guide and redeemer.

PRAYER

Lord, help us to follow the path of righteousness and to forgive those who wrong us, guiding them on a fresh path of hope that leads to you.

51 JOB 16:1-11

MISERABLE COMFORTERS!

By now Job is heartily sick of his friends' words and the inference that he is himself suffering the fate of the wicked. He is tired of being preached at by those who were supposed to be friends. There is a deliberate counterpoint here being brought out by the author: just as the patient Job is replaced by an impatient and protesting Job, so quiet, understanding friends have been replaced by badgering adversaries. Job accuses all the friends at this point of being 'miserable comforters'—which, of course, they are. It doesn't do much good to tell someone in a position of great suffering what he already knows but is questioning in a profound and personal way. There is too much lecturing going on!

Verbosity versus words of comfort

Job accuses the friends of spouting 'windy words' (v. 3) and of talking too much, echoing their accusation of him in 8:2 and 15:2. We have all met people who talk too much, whether it is from embarrassment, nervousness, insecurity or the dislike of long silences. We have also probably all met people who can contain their words to such an extent that long silences are not a problem for them—which often makes us so nervous that we are the ones who start jabbering! Job says that he too could talk as much as his friends do, were their roles reversed (v. 4): it is easy to criticize, to appeal to tradition, to have a lot to say on a subject and to shake one's head disapprovingly at others. In chapter 2 the friends bowed their heads in sympathetic mourning alongside Job in acknowledgment of his suffering; now, ironically, they are shaking their heads in disapproval. One can almost hear them tut-tutting!

What a nice change it would be if pleasant and comforting words were spoken instead! It is so true that one can either hurt with wounding words or one can improve a situation with soft and comforting words. These are the choices that we make unthinkingly every day, but it is food for thought. So Job says he could speak encouragingly to his friends rather than against them and he could assuage their pain with his lips if he were in their place and they were the ones suffering (v. 5). This is a backhanded way of saying to the friends that this is what they could be doing. They could be comforting him, as they were meant to, instead of criticizing. How much better he would feel then.

Pain unceasing

Incessant pain is a terrible burden for anybody, whether it be mental or physical pain. Job is suffering both mental torment and physical affliction and so he is experiencing a double dose of pain. Of course, one type of pain often leads to the other—the two are not easily separable. Physical pain often leads to mental depression, and mental pain manifests itself in physical ways too. Job feels trapped by the pain and does not know a way out of it. He wants to speak out and yet when he does so, the pain is still there (v. 6). He thus complains that when he speaks he does not feel any better, nor does he feel less pain when he is silent. He recognizes that the source of his pain is both God and other people.

Job now launches into a tirade against God, waging a protest against his unfair treatment (v. 7). He accuses God of wearing him out. He has no friends. His body is a wreck and he is thin and shrivelled. There is some mixing of third person and second person address here (v. 8) (changed to all third person in the NRSV), which suggests that Job is fluctuating between talking about God and addressing him directly. God has taken everything from him—his energy, his household and his health. He accuses God of tearing him apart, likening God to a wild beast tearing his prey to shreds (v. 9). This parodies psalms which compare the enemies of Israel to wild beasts whilst God is a safe haven, giving humans the will to live and a meaning to life (for example, Psalm 94). Here in verse 10 it is other human beings who are ranged against Job, presumably as a result of God's attack on him. God has cast him into the hands of the wicked and broken him.

Job is also upset at the way others are treating him: his enemies have risen up against him. He is afforded no respect, in complete contrast to his rank in society previously. He is struck on the cheek: he is treated as a wicked person would be by those who are themselves wicked (v. 10). This issue of lack of respect from others is something that weighs heavily with Job, and it is true for all of us that we rely on being treated well by others. The converse is, of course, that we must all treat others with the respect that they deserve.

PRAYER

Lord, we pray for all who suffer and are in any kind of pain, be it mental or physical. Grant them relief from that pain and let a calm trust in your redeeming love replace feelings of stress and anguish.

BROKEN *by* GOD

Job blames God for the way that he has been given over to wicked people, and for his suffering. He recalls the time when he was favoured by God, which is such a contrast to the way things are now. He was 'at ease'—all was right with God and the world—until God began his attack (v. 12). The contrast emphasizes the unexpectedness and violence of God's attack. He accuses God of breaking him in pieces, and of being an archer, his arrows pointing at Job's chest. He uses violent imagery of kidneys being slashed open by God and his gall being poured on the ground (possibly a reference to the effects of his illness). He describes God as a warrior breaching a fortified city (v. 14): Job, then, is the city in whose walls the breaches have been made. Breaching the walls would normally be the final part of a military campaign, denoting victory over the enemy. Similarly, Job is under attack and is overwhelmed by God's might. We are led to ask, how can a human being cope with this and still retain faith in God?

Grief unending and undeserved

Job is in mourning, in sackcloth and ashes, and in grief and despair. He describes sackcloth as having been sewn by him on to his skin (v. 15). This denotes that the sackcloth has become such an integral part of his body that it is inseparable from him. It may suggest that sackcloth has stuck to his open sores so that it becomes a part of his flesh. He feels weak and helpless, all his strength having disappeared. He describes his face as red with weeping (v. 16)—we have all experienced from time to time the soreness of a tear-stained face—and darkness is already settling on his eyes, perhaps a foretaste of death to come, or else a reference to the way one's eyes puff up after crying so that one cannot see clearly. Job asks what he has done to deserve this. He has done no violent acts (unlike God), nor has he had any impure thoughts in his prayers (v. 17). He is an innocent man.

God is my witness

Elsewhere Job has longed for death, but here he does not want to die for he would not then be able to continue his conversation with God. He does not want the earth to cover him. Job is using the language of blood vengeance here. There are images of blood crying out from the earth (v. 18), such as in the story of Cain killing Abel in Genesis 4. The blood of the innocent victim cries out to God from the earth and God makes sure that justice is done. Because he feels a great sense of injustice, Job wishes to stay alive to witness to his innocence. He does not want the earth to cover his blood—and yet if it did, presumably his blood might cry out in protest. Job is like a wanderer, crying in the wilderness. His outcry needs to be heard: he cannot rest until he finds an answer.

Job's witness is God who is in heaven (v. 19). No one else can vouch for his previous model behaviour. Some have seen in these verses the call for a mediator between God and humans, but there is no mediation and that is the problem. In 9:33 Job had lamented that there was no one to whom he might appeal to stand between himself and God. God is the only one who can take up Job's case, and Job begs for this to happen before it is too late. Perhaps the reference to God being in heaven is an expression of the distance Job feels. He is scorned by his friends—they have become enemies (perhaps at God's instigation, 17:4). He feels that God is the only one on his side—or is he? He cries out to God in his distress; his eyes shed tears (v. 20).

Job wants to believe in God's justice, and he wants God to justify him. He calls for just treatment and begs that his rights be recognized (v. 21). He has tried to do right by others, so why is God not doing right by him? Job returns to the unpleasant thought of the inevitability of death (v. 22). He knows that he will die and that he will go to the place of no return. This may happen soon—in a few years, perhaps. He is resigned to his fate, but he doesn't want it to happen before he is ready for it. He begs for justice before it is too late, before he is in the snares of death.

PRAYER

God is our witness. He sees all our actions and hears all our prayers. Let us have faith and trust in him.

JUST LET ME DIE!

Job is at a low ebb and feels that his spirit is broken. He just wants to die. Of course, this is in contrast to passages in which he does not want to die because that would mean he no longer had any discussion with God, or with passages where he feels more optimistic. But at present he feels that he is a broken man and that he has little time left to live. He feels that the grave is ready for him: he is about to give up. It is often said to be the case that people need to have a will to live, otherwise they will bring on their own premature death. It is a curious phenomenon that, often, elderly people who have been in a marriage for many years keep each other going; then, when one dies the other loses the will to live and so dies shortly afterwards. Job has not lost his wife—although she has not been much of a comfort—but he has lost children, possessions, livelihood and respect; and, to top it all, he appears to have lost his good relationship with God. So it is hardly surprising that he feels he does not have much to live for. He feels surrounded too by people who mock him: he has been provoked and teased remorselessly and this is the last straw.

Who will give surety?

Another source of grief to Job is the lack of support that he is getting from both the friends and God. No one will trust him enough to lay down a pledge for him (v. 3). A pledge or an agreement is an affirmation of trust in someone—rather like the pledges made in the marriage service. It gives the other person a sense of worth and a sense of being trusted. Job is saying here that there is no one who will support him, not even God. God will not lay down a pledge, nor will he allow the friends to understand him. God has turned against him just as much as the friends have. In fact, God has deliberately closed the friends' minds (v. 4), it seems, in order to hurt Job further.

The fate of false friends

At the end of this short section we have quoted what seems to be a proverb, perhaps added by the author or even by an editor. It seems slightly out of place here since it is a proverb about the danger of informing on friends with the wrong motives: the result will be that evil deeds will rebound on the evildoer. The particular instance here is in relation to greed, which leads people to betray friends in order to get a share of their property. Not only will such people be punished, but the punishment will even rebound on their children for whom blindness will be the outcome. The proverb has perhaps become attached to this section because of the thought about false friends in the preceding verses—their children will suffer for the friends' callousness—but it is rather loosely connected. It links up better with Eliphaz's words in his last speech about the fate of the wicked, and so it could have become dislocated from that or a similar passage.

PRAYER

Lord, help us not to lose hope. Give us the strength
to pull ourselves out of our difficulties rather than
sinking into deeper despair.

54

I HAVE LOST ALL RESPECT!

Job is back to railing against God, and one of the aspects of his plight that really hurts him is his loss of face among other people. When we reflect on this, we are all aware most of the time of the impression we are giving to others. Whether we like it or not, we have to live in the world and interact with others, even those we do not particularly care for, all the time. We need the support of other people, and our reputation stands or falls on what people think of us and our skills. Job knew what that kind of respect felt like. He was a responsible man within the community, and was respected for it. He was a leader, one who led by the example of his own life and tried to help others. All of this has been made into a sham by his situation. Because of the loss of his children, home and possessions and the affliction of his illness, he has been made to look guilty of sin—freedom from which is the one thing he prided himself on.

Job blames God for this. God knows that he is innocent and yet he has let him become the victim of gossip and ridicule. People are openly talking about him and they even spit in his face (v. 6), such is the contempt in which they now hold him. This has affected him physically, along with his other ailments, so that his eye is dim with grief. When one has been crying for a long spell, one's eyesight does seem to be affected and the eyes become red and puffy (v. 7). This is how I imagine Job feels. His physique has also been affected: his limbs have become less strong than they were. There is no pride left in him, and no strength. He cannot hold his head up high in the community; rather, he is brought low, and not only has he lost the respect of others but he has lost his self-respect too.

The assumption of guilt

Once a reputation is lost, it is very hard to regain. Even if a convicted criminal is later proved innocent, there is a certain stigma still attached to that person, especially if there was some uncertainty over whether justice was being done. It is now assumed by everyone that Job is guilty, and so the upright or the righteous are appalled and the innocent are fired up into action against the godless (v. 8). One can imagine the scene in our own day—everybody with an opinion, many being rather pompous and self-righteous about the situation, few having sympathy with the one suffering. There is a certain strength in being righteous or even considered righteous. It is rather like success, which, people say, builds on success. The righteous, Job says, 'hold to their way': they are on a path on which confidence builds upon confidence (v. 9). These people grow stronger and stronger with each day. When one is feeling weak, it is always hard to face strong people who appear to be able to do everything right and for whom things always go well. This is how Job feels here. It is being assumed that he is guilty; righteous people are looking down on him and regarding him as a sinner—and God is to blame.

No one can see sense

Job feels that all have turned against him. He now considers those righteous people who have given up on him (and the friends are probably included) and decides that they are not sensible. He feels that no one is appreciating his situation and, perhaps more to the point, no one believes his side of the argument. He calls for them to come back so that he can find a sensible person among them, but he knows that they have turned away from him and that no one will take his part.

PRAYER

Lord, we all know the pain of rejection. Give us strength to bounce back from situations that cause us grief, and help us to show understanding to others in pain.

NOTHING *to* LOOK FORWARD *to*

We all need to have things to look forward to or to work towards, whether it be a holiday or a promotion or planning a wedding or achieving a goal. It is part of human nature to look forward, and that happy expectation is a source of renewal after a period of being down. Job here feels that he has now had the best days of his life and that he can no longer plan ahead (v. 11). All the ideas that he had for his life and his future have been broken off suddenly. It is rather like a sudden illness or even a sudden death: we go along making plans as usual, and then a sudden illness might mean that we lose months of work, or a sudden loss might mean that we are unable for a time to get back on to an even keel. As well as our everyday plans, we also all have more long-term desires and needs—these too, Job feels, have been dashed. He had a family, property, respect and his health, and all those have gone. What, then, has he now to look forward to? Nothing.

Darkness and light

Verse 12 is rather obscure: it is not clear who 'they' are. They could be the former scoffers mocking at Job, or the friends themselves. Perhaps Job is not being allowed to sleep and so night is being turned into day. This may be to do with his illness and pain generally, or maybe he is being woken by his taunters. That the light is 'near to the darkness' suggests that there is a fine line between night and day; it might also suggest in this context that Job's life is on such a border-line that he is not far from death. When we think about the passage of day into night, there is a time of dusk where light and darkness meet. And when we think of life and death, there is a time close to death where the border seems very thin.

Down into Sheol

The light/darkness theme is a key image in this section. Sheol, the place of the dead, is characterized as a place of darkness. If Job decides to give up and go to Sheol, the problem is that he will be in perpetual darkness and his hope of vindication will be gone. This passage contrasts with Psalm 139:8, 11 where the psalmist cannot flee from God's presence, even in Sheol. The psalmist's sentiments are in the context of praise at the greatness and omnipresence of God. Job, on the other hand, regards Sheol as a place where God is not.

Imagery of setting up home is used in reference to Sheol: Job would be making his home there and his new parents would be the Pit and the worm (vv. 13–14). Sheol was pictured as being in a vast pit, and it was well known that one's body became infested with worms after death. These objects are here personified as father and mother (or alternatively sister), much as day and night have been personified in Job's speeches before (see ch. 3). Sheol is a place of no hope and no future, and it is described as a place with bars, like a prison. The idea in verse 16 is that once you have descended into the depths of Sheol there is no way back: your way is barred for ever, as in prison.

The trouble with descent into Sheol is that Job would have no hope left there: once he is dead, he is dead. He is weighing up options and although, in one sense, he longs for death as a release from his suffering, overall death and darkness and nothingness and absence of communion with God are not his preferred choice. They don't sound attractive to any of us!

Although traditional Christian ideas of hell are different from those of Sheol (since there is no thought of eternal punishment in Sheol or the fiery furnace, the devil and so on), there is still that sense of nothingness which many today would say is the equivalent of hell. Hell is being without God, being alone, being in the darkness with no hope and no light and nowhere to go, and this is often characterized as the fate of the godless in Christian thought.

PRAYER

Lord, preserve us from untimely death and strengthen our hope in a resurrection life in your name.

SPEAKING & WORDS

It is now the turn of Bildad, the second friend, to speak again, and in this second speech his frustration with Job is more apparent. He returns to the theme of communication and the power of words. He asks Job how long he will hunt for words (v. 2)—that is, how long will he keep trying to express himself in different ways verbally? A dialogue such as this one in Job is, by its nature, very wordy, and as we have seen, considerable verbiage is not what the wise promote. Just as Job accused the friends of windy words, Bildad here accuses Job of ill-considered words: 'Consider,' he says, 'and then we shall speak.' Perhaps Job will come to his senses if he is quiet and ponders the situation rather than railing against God and the world with harsh and angry words. Bildad is thinking of an explosion of words in anger, which, when the angry person calms down, becomes transformed into a more logical argument or more considered set of words. It is always better, we are told, to consider a matter—even to sleep on it—rather than speaking hastily. It is possible to be in proper dialogue only with one who has considered his or her opinions.

Why ridicule us?

The friends are clearly riled by Job's accusation that they are stupid (v. 3). They no doubt pride themselves on their wisdom, and what they have to say has the backing of many generations of experience compared with Job's strange outbursts. They cannot understand why Job is calling them stupid. It is an insult—only cattle are stupid.

This is probably a deliberate technique on Job's part, to insult the friends, to make them feel small and undermined as if their opinion is worthless—and it seems to have worked. However, the friends are prepared to ignore his words, putting them down to his anger and hastiness. Bildad's speech has started with a series of questions to Job, expressing his disbelief at Job's attitude. He sees Job as having overstepped the mark in his anger and complaints: his situation is not as earth-shattering as Job would have us believe. Picking up on Job's own words that God has 'torn him' (16:9), Bildad suggests that it is Job who tears himself in his anger (v. 4). His suffering is self-inflicted.

Who are you?

Rather in the manner of the speeches of God later in the book, Bildad asks Job here who he is to think himself so important. Is Job, as God is, having an influence on creation? 'Shall the earth be forsaken because of you?' he asks. The inference is that Job, in his argument with God, is putting himself at the centre of the universe. He may well be at the centre of his own little world, but God is keeping the universe running in the meantime. The appeal here is to God as creator: he can do as he pleases; he can remove rocks from their place, for example (v. 4). But what about Job—can *he* do that? The question is clearly rhetorical and the expected answer is 'No'. God's order, signified by earth and rock, is not going to be disturbed simply because Job feels sorry for himself.

There is a thought here that we can apply to our own lives, and that is to do with the smallness of our own experience. It is natural to be concerned with ourselves and our families and our activities, but there is a danger that we forget about the size of the world and the sheer number of people in it. We can get caught up in petty local disputes and forget the bigger picture. Furthermore, when we see someone suffering and in a much worse situation than ourselves, it can help us to get our lives in perspective, so that all the little problems we have been worrying about seem small. Bildad is reminding Job here that God is bigger than Job is imagining him. God is not concerned only with Job and his innocence: he is the creator God, and he has power to act as he wills in a way that Job will never have. Thus in his opening words Bildad has tried to put Job firmly in his place, telling him to consider more carefully his words, to stop making hurtful and childish criticisms of his friends, to control his anger which is clearly leading him astray, and to realize his place in the greater scheme of things—not bad for four verses!

PRAYER

Lord, help us to realize that we are not at the centre of the universe and to know your greatness and power, but let us also rejoice in the personal nature of your concern for each and every one of us and value our communion with you.

The DARK LIFE *of the* WICKED

Bildad now picks up the light and darkness theme found in Job's last speech. He speaks in terms of the light of the wicked being extinguished and darkness prevailing. He argues that the flame of their fire does not shine brightly (v. 5), with the inference that this is what is happening to Job. Even the light in the tent of the wicked is a dark light and their lamps are put out. They are thwarted at every turn and denied even the basics of life. Of course this is all metaphorical and not to be taken literally—it is not as if God simply goes around putting lights out. It is that the depth of their sin does not enable the wicked to live life on the same level as others. What appears as light to them is really darkness in comparison to the light enjoyed by the righteous.

This reminds us, perhaps, of the difference between earthly light and heavenly light, the latter of which reputedly shines more brightly than anything we know on earth. Those who have had near-death experiences say that one of the factors is the sense of a very bright light, almost indefinable in terms of light as we know it. This analogy helps us to understand what Bildad is getting at when he describes the dimness of the wicked person's world. He goes on to describe the steps of the wicked as 'shortened' (v. 7): instead of having a proud and long stride, they are nervous and walk cautiously. This could be a reference to old age, but is more likely to carry overtones of the rough path along which the wicked choose to walk—one that is paved with thorns. They scheme and plot and have only themselves to blame when things go wrong.

Trapped

The next section of Bildad's speech dwells on the imagery of pits and traps. Picking up on the last thought of the wicked laying their own traps, Bildad goes on to describe how they are cast into a net by their own feet (v. 8), thus falling into their own traps. They are described as walking into a 'pitfall' or trap. A trap often catches one part of the body which makes the animal or bird or, indeed, human unable to escape (compare Proverbs 1:17). There is also the method of concealing a rope on the path so that a person is trapped when it is pulled up (v. 10). Not only will the wicked be trapped, but they will also be plagued by great terrors on every side—frightened and chased relentlessly. Bildad is building up a picture here of some of our worst fears, in order to scare Job or to bring him to his senses, as well as talking in traditional terms about the fate of the wicked.

Hunger, illness and death

The description of the wicked and their fate does not get any cheerier. Bildad now moves on to the extreme hunger of the wicked, which consumes all their strength and energy, leaving them listless and tired and less able to cope with difficulties (v. 12). Calamity is awaiting them at the first slip or stumble. The next verses could either refer to the disaster of hunger awaiting them, much in line with the previous verse, or could be a reference to consuming disease, which would be an obvious allusion to Job's own desperate situation. A disease will consume their skin—and of course Job's affliction is a skin disease of a very unpleasant kind.

It is not clear exactly what the 'firstborn of Death' refers to (v. 13), but it could be a reference to the way disease starts to consume people even before they are dead, as a kind of anticipation of death. Just as the firstborn child is the harbinger of more children to come, so the 'firstborn of Death' is the harbinger of death itself, in a kind of personification. The wicked are torn away from all that they know or trust (v. 14)—in a desert situation, that would be the tent that represents the security of home—and they are brought to the judgment seat. It is not clear whether the 'king of terrors' is a reference to the Satan as we encountered him in the prologue, or whether again it is a kind of personification referring to extreme terror.

PRAYER

Lord, help us to be calm and not afraid if terrors strew our path.
Help us not to be trapped by our own desires and plans,
and help us to trust in your guiding hand as we walk along
life's path with all its twists and turns.

DESTRUCTION *for the* WICKED

Bildad continues his diatribe about the fate of the wicked. There is a certain repetition of what has gone before, both in his speech and in that of Eliphaz, perhaps indicating that they are both adopting a traditional line. He is expanding the idea of the wicked being torn from their tent, snatched away from their home and all they know. The tent is taken over by others or else fire consumes it (v. 15). Thus all is destroyed of what remained of their home and no memory of them is left. Sulphur was used as a powerful disinfectant which rendered land infertile.

Verse 16 returns to the tree or plant imagery, with the idea that the wicked have no roots: they will dry up through lack of nourishment and likewise their branches will wither. This could be a reference either to the wicked themselves or their offspring: all the foundations laid by the wicked wither away.

No memory

A very important goal for the ancient Hebrews was to preserve their memory after death, whether through having offspring or being remembered by others for great deeds—or both. Thus a lack of memorial was a dreadful fate, and so this is applied to the wicked. Their memory disappears, as does their name (v. 17). They go to the darkness and nothing is left of them in the world. They have no descendants to carry on their name and not even anyone living in their home, presumably because of the destruction of their tents.

We have a very black-and-white picture painted here of the total annihilation of the wicked, and presumably the obverse of that is the preservation of all good things for the righteous. When we try to apply this idea to today's world, it is hard to think of anyone being totally bad—or totally good, for that matter. It seems that people have both qualities, but sometimes there are bad elements to their character that may outweigh the good.

We might ask what the criteria for 'goodness' and 'badness' are. They seem in this context to be the acceptance or rejection of the principles of the moral code of the wise, and behaviour in accordance with or rebellion against these principles, together with the actual evidence of reward or punishment during the lifetime of the person in question. Hence it is assumed that Job is now to be counted among the wicked because his situation seems to indicate it, despite his own protestations.

No one would want such a fate

One of the arguments often posed in favour of capital punishment is that it makes an example of 'wicked' people, and deters others from committing crimes. In the days when criminals were made a public spectacle, this was certainly the motivation behind the practice. People were made to feel that whatever happened they must not suffer such a fate, and so they behaved themselves. Of course, the other side of the coin is that occasionally mistakes were made and the wrong people got punished. However, Bildad ends his speech here by saying that others are appalled at the fate of the wicked—'those of the west' and 'those of the east' denoting the whole known area (v. 20). These people would not want such a fate themselves and the very thought of it fills them with horror. Bildad is inferring that his description should deter anyone from wickedness, and in relation to Job it is designed to frighten him into acknowledgment of his guilt, since he is suffering many of the very punishments that Bildad has described. He ends with a dose of special pleading: 'Surely' this is so (v. 21)—almost begging Job to listen, perhaps even having to remind himself of his argument. This is 'surely' the situation in the dwellings of the ungodly, the fate of those who do not know God. It seems that there were those who did not know God or acknowledge him, and that this was a large part of what it meant to be 'wicked'. Just as the wicked did not know God, so their descendants would not know them: they would not be remembered in the way that we would all like to be remembered, even if only by our nearest and dearest.

PRAYER

Lord, let us preserve our own memories and pass them down to the next generation. Let us preserve memories of you and continue to tell of your love from generation to generation.

HURTFUL WORDS

Job now replies to Bildad. It seems as if Bildad's words have hit home, as Job is clearly stung by them. He does not dismiss them as worthless as he did before; rather, he asks for a reprieve from such tormenting words, which seem to break him (v. 2). By hammering Job with a description of the wicked, Bildad has only increased Job's sense of being attacked by all around him. He feels beaten around the head with words and more words, over and over again, reproached repeatedly for not having acknowledged his sin.

Job begins to argue back, saying that even if it is true that he has erred, it is a personal issue (v. 4). Why should the friends puff themselves up in a self-righteous way and think that they have the right to pass·judgment on him? They do not know what sin he has committed (and nor does Job), so why are they being so tough on him? He notes that they are making his humiliation an argument against him (v. 5). This picks up on the point that Job's desperate situation is taken by the friends as an indication that he has sinned, and they respond by telling Job that he is a sinner in the light of this evidence. They then make this an excuse to criticize and humiliate him, using the evidence of his situation to assume his guilt.

'I am wronged'

Job feels utterly wronged by his friends, who thus torment him and make him feel small. Yet it is made clear by him here that he feels wronged principally by God. He feels trapped, just as the wicked are, but by God (v. 6). God has put Job in the wrong, for if God had treated him fairly he wouldn't be in such a dire situation and the friends would not be criticizing him in this way. God is the one who is supposed to mete out justice fairly, and when he fails to do so, it seems that there is no room for discussion. This is why Job feels so desperate: he is trapped in a 'no win' situation and, like a bird in a net, he is hunted down and caught by God. Whatever Job says, however hard he cries out, God does not listen. He calls for justice but there is none (v. 7). He feels completely let down by the one person in whom he trusted—God.

God has turned nasty

There follows a description of God's activity which is quite different from the usual picture found in the Bible. Job describes God as putting up a wall so that he cannot pass by (v. 8)—his path is blocked. God is accused of putting Job in darkness so that he cannot see where he is going, and he is accused of stripping Job of all his honour and glory. Rather than praising God for the good things that he gives to humanity, Job blames him for the bad things that he does, mainly to Job personally, although with the inference that this kind of behaviour might be more common than people had thought. He is attacking the friends' view that God must always behave in a just manner and always metes out the correct punishments.

Job is like a king whose crown has been stripped from him so that he has lost all standing, respect and status and has become a nobody. He feels broken down on all sides. He is a physical wreck, he is in emotional turmoil, he has lost loved ones and home and even his friends torment him with their arguments. His hope is uprooted like a tree (v. 10). God has become angry with him and is venting his anger in an irrational way. Job is now God's enemy and God is marshalling his troops against him. Job feels surrounded by siegeworks, as if God is encamped around his tent in a hostile manner. There is no rhyme or reason for this behaviour on God's part—it has just happened, and that is the only way Job can understand what has taken place.

To the friends, and even to us, it may seem almost blasphemous for Job to blame God so directly for his misfortune. We could put it down to Job's distorted and over-emotional mind, and yet he is venting feelings that many people in difficult situations of suffering have had. It does sometimes seem that God has turned against us, and perhaps it is good to be able to give vent to such feelings. We cannot know the mind of God or the reasons that he does things (this comes across later in God's own speeches) so perhaps trying to understand is to limit him too much. We may, of course, complain when he does not conform to our rather over-neat view of justice, which, in turn, may lead us to question our own assumptions.

PRAYER

Lord God, your wisdom and justice and truth are all that we have to rely upon. Enable us to know you and to trust in you even when life is rough and everything seems to be against us.

ESTRANGED

Job now expresses his personal feelings about the ways in which his relationships have been affected by his illness and situation. His children are dead, his wife is estranged, and his acquaintances are estranged too (v. 13). His standing in the community is gone and all have distanced themselves from him. His relatives and close friends have failed him (v. 14)—we do not know if the three friends are included under this description. He used to be generous to guests who came to his house, but they have all forgotten him. Even the servants no longer have respect for him (v. 15). He has become a *persona non grata*, an alien, an outcast. We get the impression that everyone is ignoring him. He wants to plead with his servant to talk to him (v. 16), although he would lose all self-respect in so doing; but maybe he doesn't care any more, such is his desperation.

Physically repulsive and pitiful

There have been few references to Job's illness so far, but here he makes it clear that the illness itself has estranged people. His breath has become foul, which is repulsive to his wife, and his own relatives treat him as a loathsome being (v. 17). He is despised even by young children, who talk about him behind his back. He has lost all intimate friends: all appear now to hate him. In fact, he has no loved ones left, no one to take his part and see beyond his miserable state. The situation must be intolerable for Job, with no one to rely on, no family, no friends and ultimately, so it seems, no God. He goes on to describe his physical condition (v. 20): he is so thin that his bones cling to his skin and to his flesh. He is close to death and yet he has escaped death by the skin of his teeth. He is in a wretched state, close to despair.

Even if people think that you have done wrong, they may still be able to pity you. Job calls for pity now (v. 21). The repetition of 'Have pity on me' shows his desperation. God has touched him and put him down—but can't his friends accept his innocence? They have become his enemies. They are as bad as God, pursuing him, making him feel ever worse, not even satisfied with having taken his flesh from his body (that is, his health and well-being). What kind of God is this? And how volatile are human beings—friends one minute, enemies the next?

Written evidence

Many people feel that they would like some written memorial of themselves after their death. We see inscriptions and memorials to people in churches, in halls, in institutions, on park benches. It is part of living on in the community—not just relying on other people to remember you, but having written evidence that you existed. Job now feels that he would have liked his words to be written down (ironically, they are!) so that they will not be forgotten. Then when he has gone, people will read his case. First, he wishes that his words were written in a book and then goes on to the idea of even more permanence—his words being inscribed with iron or lead on a rock. Written evidence is always the most exciting kind for archaeologists when digging up the remains of the past: we only have to think of the great find of the Dead Sea Scrolls at Qumran, where they had been preserved in caves for two thousand years by the dryness and saltiness of the sea air.

Job, then, asks to be able to write his words down so that they last for ever, so that, in case he dies, he will one day be vindicated.

PRAYER

Lord, help us to show pity for those in distress, even when we think that they are to blame for their plight. Help us never to be judgmental or hurtful, especially when we do not know all the facts of a situation, and may those in need know the power of your forgiveness.

MY REDEEMER LIVETH

In this speech Job seems to hit the bottom of his despair and then rise up to a moment of optimism. We might regard him as experiencing a kind of mood swing—a positive moment that relieves the gloom and deep-seated pessimism. This passage has been made famous by Handel's *Messiah*, in which the words 'I know that my Redeemer liveth' are taken to refer to Christ. Many people do not realize that, in fact, they come from the book of Job. Job changes from having longed for a redeemer to mediate between him and God to stating that his redeemer, or mediator, lives. He presumably means here that justice will prevail somehow and that even if God himself seems to have turned nasty, there will be some justice from one who will mediate between him and God. This translates easily into the message of the New Testament that Christ mediates between God and humanity and takes on the sins of the world to close the breach between the earthly and divine realms.

What do the words mean in their context in Job, however? It may be that God and the redeemer are one and the same, rather than there being a third person present. If this is the case, then Job is turning his thoughts more positively to the possibility of eventual vindication by God. This would make most sense, in that God has been the one to whom Job has called throughout for vindication. Perhaps God will restore Job before it is too late.

The afterlife?

This has traditionally been seen as a passage about the afterlife, since it says, 'After my skin has been thus destroyed, then... I shall see God' (v. 26). However, the destruction of Job's skin could simply be referring to Job's illness which, as he said earlier in the speech, leaves him on the boundary between life and death. We have seen elsewhere that he is fearful of death: this is why he wants his words to be written down, in case he dies before vindication. Although he is grasping for a way in which his words might outlast him, he knows in fact that this is an impossibility. God is the only one who can vindicate him, and it has to happen now, before he is gripped by death and unable to continue the conversation with God.

Another crux is the phrase 'in my flesh' (v. 26). This could be translated 'outside my flesh', again meaning after death; but alternatively it could mean 'in my fleshly body', that is, while I am alive. The vision is of a vindication by God, of which Job will be aware. One day he will see God on his side, and that prospect makes his heart faint with wonder.

A warning note

Job closes with another warning to the friends: if they persist in persecuting him, let them beware that they do not also become victims of persecution (vv. 28–29). If they torment him and are proved wrong, there will be judgment in store for them. It is interesting that Job's more positive mood here gives him the energy to have another dig at the friends. However, he seems to be upholding the doctrine of retribution here in reference to them. Perhaps he is hoping that, if vindication comes, then things will return to their normal pattern (which, of course, they eventually do).

PRAYER

Lord, we, as Christians, know that our Redeemer lives.
Help us to affirm that faith and to rejoice in your gift of
your Son to humankind.

IMPELLED *to* RESPOND

It is now Zophar's turn to respond with his second speech, and he opens with a call to 'pay attention' (v. 1). He describes how he has felt impelled to speak out, almost by a force greater than himself. He feels agitated and insulted by what he has heard (vv. 2–3). But more than this, he feels a kind of spiritual impulse to speak (compare Eliphaz in chapter 4). Sometimes we feel so strongly about an issue that we have to speak out. We might feel so uptight that we have sleepless nights and end up increasingly nervous and agitated. We might indeed feel that a power greater than ourselves is impelling us to speak; if so, we can in some way identify with Zophar here. He does not directly address Job, nor does he insult him. He merely asks for the group's attention so that he can have his say.

We might think that Zophar is going to say something radically different from the other friends, but sadly this is not so. It seems that all three friends are incapable of stepping outside traditional descriptions of the fate of the wicked: they are not touching Job's situation of need in the slightest. There is almost the impression of people talking past each other, each with their own agenda, neither party listening to the other.

The joy of the godless will perish

Zophar's main point is that 'the exulting of the wicked is short' and eventually they will get their just deserts (v. 5). It does seem that innocent people (like Job) can be punished, and that, conversely, wicked people seem to thrive. But this view is not allowed in the black-and-white scheme of things, and it is essential for Zophar to state that although things may seem unjust for a while, justice will eventually prevail. He appeals to tradition: these things have been known since time immemorial, he says, even since human beings first inhabited the earth (v. 4). It is rather like our saying that we 'fell out of our cradle knowing that!' Zophar is arguing against Job's appeal to personal experience rather than tradition. The exultation of the wicked is short, he maintains, and any joy that they may appear to have is fleeting. They may seem to be uplifted, high up in society, strong and successful, but their heads are swollen artificially and they will one day go down as far as they were lifted up. This may be a veiled reference to Job's prior success before he was brought low, although it is not explicit and is stated only in general terms. We might compare the stories of Adam and Eve and the Fall (Genesis 2—3) and of the Tower of Babel (Genesis 11), which are both stories of human beings overreaching themselves. In fact, says Zophar, the wicked will perish like their own dung (v. 7)—a very degrading description that conveys the uncleanness of dung. The ancient Hebrews meticulously avoided touching unclean things and being contaminated by excretions of any kind.

They will disappear

In verse 8, we find ourselves back with the idea of having no memorial and a sinking into nothingness. The wicked will disappear so that those who knew them will ask where they are. Just as a dream can disappear from one's mind in an instant, so these people will be out of mind just as quickly. They will not be found because they have been chased away like a vision of the night: now you see me, now you don't! There is an idea here that if others don't see you, you do not exist. At one moment we are in the world, in a state of relationship with it and with the people in it, but as soon as our existence is denied we no longer exist. Eyes that saw the wicked will see them no more and even the places where they were will no longer acknowledge them. Their children will lose any wealth left to them and will have to beg from the poor. The wicked person will be forced to give back his wealth to those from whom he stole it, leaving nothing to hand on to his successors. The wicked person's youth and vigour will disappear (the inference is that this happens prematurely) so that even young and active bones will become dust in the grave. Once more, a rather desperate picture of the fate of the wicked is presented, but without the terrors of Bildad's description.

PRAYER

Lord, impel us to speak out in your name to try to change the world and make it a better place, free from wickedness and self-interest and in tune with your will for us.

63

SWEET & SOUR

In this whole passage we find imagery of food and swallowing. Wickedness tastes sweet in the mouth: otherwise, why would anyone do any actions that were considered wicked (v. 12)? Making money at other people's expense, living ostentatiously, treating others badly, robbing the poor for one's own gain, perpetuating injustice—these are the kind of crimes that have a certain appeal, in that they fulfil the self-seeking aim of 'lining one's own nest' and looking after oneself. This sounds all too familiar to modern ears. But try as the wicked might to hold on to this sweetness—to hide it under their tongues, to try every trick to keep it in their mouths—it will turn sour (v. 14). The food will turn bad in their stomachs as if it were poison, and they will vomit it up (v. 15). When we vomit up food, we have no control over the process, and this is what Zophar is saying here: the wicked have no control over the inevitable punishment that God will ordain. It will happen, whatever they might do.

A poisonous brood

We all know about healthy eating and perhaps, beyond that, about foods that actually make us feel better. We also know about bad food —that is, food that is decayed—and about the unpleasant consequences that it can have for the digestive system. The inference in verse 15 is that the wicked, unknowingly perhaps, are sucking poison, continuing the thought that what appears sweet may not be all it seems. Continuing the theme of poison, the wicked will be poisoned by the tongue of a viper (v. 16). One way or another, they will be 'caught'. They will not be aware of the good things—the plentiful streams of sweet delicacies—rather, they will have a natural propensity for the bad. Although they toil for food, they will not reap its benefits. They will be unable to swallow the fruit of their toil (v. 18), and so all labour will be in vain. There are echoes here of Ecclesiastes, for example, 2:18–23. Although they profit from trading in order to benefit themselves, they will get no enjoyment from it.

Bad behaviour

Finally we are given the reason for these unpleasant experiences: the wicked have behaved badly and transgressed the moral law. They have crushed and abandoned the poor and they have seized the property of others (v. 19). These sins are unforgivable and they will be punished for them—it is as simple as that! This is a very black-and-white view of the world to which we might find it hard to relate today. If only it were that simple. And yet the retributive principle is alive and well in many people's lives and provides a framework for them: do good to others and behave well in life and good things will come to you; be greedy, unkind and unfair and bad things will rebound upon you. I think many people today would agree with that estimate, whether they are Christian or not. There is a strong sense of a human code of behaviour to which we all need to adhere in order to make life bearable and tolerable and, although such ethical codes have strong biblical roots such as in the wisdom and legal traditions of the Old Testament, they exist apart from specific religious affiliation and are also common to other religious traditions. Good behaviour is part of what it is to be a civilized human being; bad behaviour will be collectively punished by those adhering to the good as well as by God, the arbitor of all justice.

PRAYER

Lord, may we do to others as we would have them do to us. With that principle in our hearts and minds, we are living up to your will for us as enshrined in the biblical traditions that we cherish.

GREED

Zophar continues the eating theme with a reference to the disquiet in the bellies of the wicked. They eat, but their food is turned to poison within them and they vomit easily. This can perhaps be understood in modern terms as a veiled reference to some kind of bulimic experience imposed upon the wicked by God. And yet they are greedy to eat and will clear the table of food, such is their greed (v. 20). Because of this overarching greed, their prosperity will be short-lived. Just as they think that they have reached full sufficiency in their lives, it will be removed and they will feel the dissatisfaction of inadequacy. They will feel miserable and full of distress rather than replete and full of food. We all know the feeling of hunger that can make us tetchy and bad-tempered: there is nothing like a good meal to put us in a better frame of mind! The wicked will feel the misery of emptiness from now on because of their excessive greed and complacency in the past.

God's anger

Zophar really starts to get going in the latter part of his speech, which resembles Bildad's more terrifying words in his last speech. He now brings God into the picture. The bellies of the wicked will be filled with God's anger, which is fierce and which will rain down upon the wicked in the quantity that their food used to do (v. 23). God is sending anger to fill the belly, in a reversal of the usual idea that God feeds his people (the manna in the wilderness, for example, in Exodus 16:13–19). Here God is force-feeding the wicked and leading them to a painful end.

God is also portrayed in military terms, as wielding dangerous weapons. The wicked will flee from an iron weapon or a bronze arrow that God will fire in order to run them through (v. 24). Zophar imagines the glittering point of the arrow—glittering, presumably, with blood—which will come out of their insides and reveal their intestines. They will be terrified by this onslaught. It is important in these descriptions that the wicked actually suffer the torment rather than escaping from it through death.

Zophar then returns to a description of the darkness that is waiting for the wicked as their reward. They will be consumed by fire, and so will all that is in their tent (v. 26). This is a picture of total annihilation that will presumably come from heaven: 'a fire fanned by no one' suggests a fire from nowhere that will burn them up.

Heaven and earth will bear witness

In verse 27, heaven and earth are personified as witnesses to the guilt of the wicked and to their judgment. The heavens will reveal their iniquities: there is nothing that God does not see from his seat on high. The earth will rise up against them: that is, those inhabitants of the earth who see injustice done will punish the wicked as they deserve. Their possessions will be carried away on this day of judgment. This, Zophar concludes, is the portion decreed by God for those who have done wrong (v. 29). This is their heritage—far from the one for which they had hoped. Zophar does not directly say that Job is one of the wicked, but the inference is there.

These speeches about the wicked from both Bildad and Zophar have a certain similarity in tone and subject matter, and probably represent traditional diatribes known within the wisdom tradition on the subject, possibly designed to frighten people into submission to the path of wisdom. The representation of greed in verses 20–23 is enough to put us off food indefinitely, but it does indicate that excess in anything is unattractive to others and bad for us. The wicked are seen to do things to excess and to be entirely self-seeking. We might reflect on whether we ever do anything to excess or see others doing so, and whether we might learn something here about moderation.

PRAYER

Lord, help us not to be greedy or to overreach ourselves. Give us a sense of humility and of the power of your love.

BEAR *with* ME!

Job is back for another speech. He begs the friends to listen to his words. One of the problems seems to be that neither party is really listening to the other (vv. 1–2). Because of the traditional tone of their diatribes, there is a sense in which the friends are uttering 'set pieces', which Job feels do not apply to him. Job wants the friends to listen carefully and be consoled by what he has to say. He is almost trying to calm them down after their violent descriptions. He asks them to bear with him and he will speak. Then, when he has had a chance to speak, he says, they can go on mocking him (v. 3): a note of sarcasm is creeping in.

Job's words remind me of the kind of arguments in which the people end up talking at the same time so that neither party hears the other—as seen on some television chat shows, for example. For two people to argue at the same time is a pointless exercise. If only one would listen to the other and let him have his say, then there would be an opportunity for the other to speak in turn. Although in a chat show such arguments may make good television and transmit the explosiveness of a situation, Job is recognizing its pointlessness in this situation. Perhaps the author is communicating here the explosive nature of this dialogue, which is fast turning into a series of speeches with no dialogue at all.

Why shouldn't I protest?

Job argues that his argument is primarily with God. He asks rhetorically, 'Is my complaint addressed to mortals?' (v. 4). The expected answer is 'No'. Then why should he not be impatient if he wants to be? In fact, although there is truth in the statement that his complaint is primarily addressed to God, he is indirectly attacking humans in that he is questioning human principles of wisdom, to which he himself had adhered until all had gone so badly wrong. However, this is his argument and he is trying to justify his desire to complain. Later in the book, this protest appears to be justified by God (42:7), which is an interesting twist in the tail. At this stage in the speeches, though, we get the impression that Job is in the wrong to complain like this, even if we might have some sympathy with him.

A physical wreck

Job seems increasingly preoccupied with his physical condition. It is clearly starting to 'get' to him. He says to the friends, 'Look at me, and be appalled' (v. 5). Although this probably refers to his physical state, it could refer to the words that he is about to speak. People are probably openly showing their distaste of him and his bad breath, laying their hands on their mouths either because of his smell or in order to keep quiet. Job is acknowledging that he notices such actions, which cause him pain in addition to his physical suffering. When he thinks about his physical condition, he himself is appalled and he shudders from head to toe (v. 6). He is in a bad way—and it is all God's fault!

We all feel at times that we are not being listened to, that people are talking past us or arguing with us and not hearing our viewpoint. We also feel justified from time to time in having a good argument ourselves, whether it be with other people or with God. We often get emotions out of our system by doing so, although we should also stop and think about the hurt that may be caused to others by our bad moods. It is very difficult to feel positive when feeling physical pain and mental torment, and this tends to make us less tolerant of others. This in turn may lead other people to avoid us because they are tired of hearing our complaints. Job is describing common human experiences here, even though his suffering is of a rather more intense nature than we might experience ourselves.

PRAYER

Lord, give us the space to be able to vent our feelings of anger and unfairness from time to time. Help us to understand that the whole range of emotions is what makes us human.

The PROSPERITY of the WICKED

We all feel sometimes that less worthy people than ourselves seem to get on in life, to prosper, and to have money, large houses, many children and so on. Some of us try hard to live a moral life and yet never make much progress towards what others would perceive as success. It all seems so unfair. Job is a righteous man—that we have established—and yet he sees the wicked prospering and he asks why. They seem to have the gift of longevity (v. 7), something that was meant to be a reward by God for good behaviour. How is it, then, that they have it and Job does not, since he is close to death? The wicked not only live on, but they are powerful too: old people were respected in ancient Israelite society, not farmed out to nursing homes as all too often happens today. The longer you lived, the more powerful you were likely to be, especially if you had offspring. This is Job's next thought, that in the presence of the older generation the children grow up and become established (v. 8). It is every parent's hope that they will live to see their children established and will know that they are well 'set up'.

Another aspect of security is a safe home (v. 9), something that Job has lost in the calamities. This the wicked have too, and none of the expected punishment from God seems to come near them. Everything happens predictably, in that their bulls breed and their cows calve. It is never *their* animals that have something wrong with them (v. 10)!

This description of the prosperity of the wicked is Job's way of expressing his anguish at the unfairness of it all, and it is somewhat sarcastic. These verses parody passages in the psalms which discuss the prosperity of the righteous (for example, Psalm 37:27–33). Here in Job, the language of prosperity is used but in reference to the wicked. The verses can also be compared to passages describing the prosperity of the wicked—for example, Psalms 10:5–6 and 73:3–9. The difference is that in the psalms their prosperity is generally seen to be short-lived, but here in Job it is long-lived.

They are happy

Perhaps worst of all, notes Job, the wicked are happy. Their youngsters, of whom there are many, go out and sing and dance (v. 11). They are happy and enjoy music. This is a picture of a prosperous community in which the wicked are comfortable, which is expected to go on for ever. There are overtones here of the modern idea of the 'good life', a life that people carve out for themselves. There is a general striving for betterment in society that is to some extent self-motivated and self-perpetuated. All around us today, we see the success and comfort of the wealthy. Perhaps it is not for us to pontificate on whether they are righteous or wicked—that is for God to decide! But Job is complaining that the wicked die happy and peaceful. There is none of the torment for them that he is suffering.

No need for God

The bottom line is that these people have no need of God. They are quite happy without him, and they see their prosperity as self-made. This passage reminds me of an occasion when I was talking about God to a friend of mine, who replied, 'Leave me alone. I am happy as I am, I have no need for God.' I was quite taken aback at the time, unaware until then that God was not a presupposition of my friend's life as he is of mine. It is possible to get to know someone quite well and never really talk about religion. Only when you dare to speak of God do you get to know the true attitudes of others.

The idea that one can be self-sufficient, and that God simply gets in the way and disturbs one's peaceful life, is all too common today. So too the wicked, as described by Job, say to God, 'Leave us alone!' (v. 14), They do not wish to know God—and why should they serve him, as they are doing fine without him anyway? The question of profit comes up in verse 15, as it did at the beginning of the book of Job. Why should I serve God? What am I going to get out of it? So, the wicked say, they will not get anything extra out of being God-fearing. They have 'made it' by themselves; they do not need God.

In verse 16 we see Job's real attitude to all this: the whole way of thinking of the wicked is repugnant to him. This reveals that his description in the previous verses has been tongue-in-cheek, yet it is striking how it resonates with the experience of many of us today. How many people do you know who think that they don't need God?

PRAYER

Lord, help us to recognize our need of you, seeking not our own profit but your redemptive love. Help us to help others to recognize their need also. Amen.

67

HOW OFTEN?

We find four rhetorical questions posed here by Job, all beginning, 'How often...?' (vv. 17–18). The answer is presumably, 'Not often enough for Job's liking!' He would like everything to be as fair as the friends suggest it is, but this never seems to happen. Speaking still of the wicked, he asks, 'How often is their lamp put out?' This is presumably a reference to early death. 'How often does calamity come upon them?' For Job, it comes all too often, but not for the wicked. And what is God doing about it? How often is he distributing pain to them? Again the inference is that God appears to be doing nothing about it. It would be good, thinks Job, if the wicked were blown away like chaff: didn't a storm carry away his beloved children (1:19)? And yet no such storm seems to affect them, not even a light wind. Why is life so unfair? We can feel Job trying to reason it all out but getting nowhere.

Let justice prevail

Job now changes his tack by calling on God to do something. He cites the friends who insist that even if the wicked do not appear to be receiving punishment right now, it will come in the end: the children will suffer for the sins of their parents, for example. 'Let this happen, then!' says Job (v. 19). Or, even better, let the wicked themselves (not just their children) be paid back so that they may know that they have done wrong. For if they never know that they are doing wrong, it's no wonder they think that they don't need God. Let *them* see their numbers dwindling, and let *them* receive God's punishment. If they die a premature death, they will not care what happens to those who are left behind—they will be unaware of it after death (v. 21)—so let them be punished now! Job is now wishing just deserts upon the wicked. We might ask who he thinks he is, to comment on their fate! He is sounding rather self-righteous here, it has to be said.

Death, the great equalizer

Job begins to wonder whether it is God who doesn't understand. Isn't he supposed to be the supreme judge who metes out justice? Why, then, this intense injustice? Does God not really know what he is doing? God needs to realize that the wicked do not care about what comes after death. More radically, God appears to have a limited knowledge of humanity (v. 22). It looks as if Job is reproaching God in this verse, but alternatively his words could be directed at the friends, as a criticism of them for imposing their own rigid doctrine on God.

Job reflects on the fact that one person dies in full prosperity and another dies bitter and twisted, but death comes to both without differentiation (vv. 23–26). He suggests that it is, unjustly, the wicked who are the prosperous ones, at ease and secure, retaining sexual prowess and youthful vigour. It is the righteous, such as Job, who are dying in bitterness of soul. Death comes to all—death is the great equalizer—and the dust and worms cover the bodies of all.

This complaint resembles the thought of the great pessimist in the Bible, Ecclesiastes, who asks what the point of anything is, given that death is the final fate that we all have to suffer (for example, Ecclesiastes 3:20). There is a deep pessimism in Job here. He is despairing of God's so-called justice and sinking further into depression. We might contrast traditional ideas about reward of good and punishment of wickedness (for example, Psalm 1:6) with such a passage as this. These are sobering thoughts about death and are enough to lead anyone into the kind of pessimism Job is experiencing. We might think of others we know who are in a similar situation of depression and despair, and of how we might help them. Job's friends, it seems, have not got the formula right for helping Job. One wonders if their sitting in comforting silence as in 2:13 would not have been a better response for one in a desperate situation.

PRAYER

Lord, help us to recognize that life is not always fair, and to accept it. Help us to rejoice in what we have rather than in what we have not, and to seek to be positive rather than sinking into an unhealthy pessimism and despair.

68

IT'S ALL *a* PLOT *against* ME!

Job appears here still to be talking to God, although he could be talking to the friends or there could be a deliberate *double entendre*. He makes the accusation that a scheme has been hatched by the friends in order to mislead him in their claims about the punishment of the wicked. He is now beginning to wonder if he hasn't had it wrong all along and if, in fact, the wicked were destined to prosper. There is a certain sarcasm here. The friends have maintained that the wicked are destroyed: 'Where is the wicked person's house?' they say. But Job maintains that everyone knows—all who travel widely, anyway—that the wicked are spared (vv. 29–30). There is no punishment for them. They sit tight in their houses and don't have a care in the world.

Who will bring the wicked to account?

Job now asks whose responsibility it is to point out to the wicked the error of their ways (v. 31). If God is not maintaining justice, whose responsibility is it? Who repays them? Nothing seems to be happening. Instead, even when they die someone guards their tomb. Everything is upside-down, and no one seems to care. Even the soil itself is sweet to the wicked, it seems, and nothing is ever done to make them suffer, nor their descendants, nor even the many who have gone before them (v. 33). There is no justice anywhere. Yet again, this is a parody of passages that speak of the honourable fate of the righteous person. Here the sentiments are transferred to the wicked. We might all feel a sense of injustice at the way life is so often unfair for people: inequality is rife, poverty too. We are led to ask why God doesn't balance the riches of the world out more fairly, as well as why he doesn't always seem to rectify the injustices in people's personal lives.

Empty nothings

'Whispering sweet nothings' into someone's ear is a well-known phrase used to describe the expression of affection without specific substance. 'Empty nothings' (v. 34) might be seen in the same way: there is no substance to the words of the friends or to the seeming lack of action by God. The friends' words of comfort are all 'empty nothings'. Their answers are plainly false and have no truth in them at all. Job has just demonstrated this in his description of the prosperity of the wicked. He is at the end of his tether and accuses the friends of downright lying. He is not a happy man!

We have now reached the end of the second cycle of speeches in which all three friends have had a chance to speak and Job has replied to each one. We have seen that the speeches have become gradually more emotional and hard-hitting. The friends' speeches have generally become shorter as Job's have continued to be the same length, which indicates that he is gaining ground over them. There is a certain amount of repetition in the sentiments, and we will see this feature again as we move into the third cycle, which is more fragmentary than the second.

PRAYER

Lord, help us not to feel the pangs of injustice: enable those with power and authority to right wrongs and punish iniquity, so that the world may be a more just place.

69

MORE QUESTIONS

It is now Eliphaz's turn to respond to Job at the beginning of the third cycle of speeches, and he answers Job back with a few rhetorical questions of his own. The gist of his questions is, 'Why should God punish unjustly?' It just doesn't make sense. God doesn't get much from human beings—in a sense he doesn't need them—but he simply chooses to be in relationship with them, The question is, what does God get out of Job's piety? He does not gain from it (v. 3), nor would he gain from punishing Job if he is innocent and has been righteous. 'Is it for your piety that he reproves you?' Eliphaz asks, speaking of God (v. 4). The expected answer is, of course, 'No'. Such a thing would not make sense.

Eliphaz's conclusion is that Job must have done something wrong. He is trying to reason it out but always arrives at the same conclusion. He cannot break outside the confines of his own thinking. How many people do we know who are caught within the boundaries of their own situation and life experiences? This is not necessarily a bad thing: we know what we like, and we like what we know, and there is security in that. However, sometimes it does us good to experience something new and to break outside our own limitations—to push ourselves to achieve a goal, for example, or to meet new friends or take up a new hobby, or to expand our minds by reading or following a new course of study. Eliphaz is trapped in a way of thinking here from which Job himself has moved on.

Great wickedness

Rather than continuing to accuse Job of wrongdoing in abstract terms, Eliphaz decides to spell it out. Job has clearly done wicked deeds (v. 5), and they are now to be enumerated. Eliphaz accuses Job of having exacted pledges (of loyalty, money or goods—it is not made clear) from his family for no obvious reason, and of having stripped the naked of their clothing (v. 6). He has not provided water for the weary traveller or bread for the hungry (v. 7). He has lived a life of prosperity and ease. He has not helped widows or orphans (v. 9). All these good deeds are part of being a righteous person, as expounded in the book of Deuteronomy (for example, Deuteronomy 24:17–18) as well as in the wisdom literature (see Proverbs 15:25). This set of accusations seems odd, since we know from the prologue that Job bent over backwards to do all these things, even on behalf of members of his own family, worrying that they were not pious enough (Job 1:5). Perhaps it is a list of the likely sins he might have committed rather than actual accusations. It anticipates both chapter 29, where Job enumerates his good deeds on behalf of others, and chapter 31, where Job constructs a similar list of sins with the purpose of denying that he ever committed them. He is thus falsely accused. It is a case of the friends' word against his.

Frightening consequences

Eliphaz now spells out the frightening consequences of such wicked behaviour—traps or snares (recalling Bildad's speech in Job 18:8–10) and sudden terror when a situation goes wrong (v. 10). In fact, he is seeing Job suffering the consequences, and extrapolating back from them to the supposed cause. He assumes that Job must have done all these wrong things in order to be punished for them by God. He is upholding the doctrine of retribution, locked inside a certain system and unable to think himself out of it. Job too had believed in that system of just deserts, but his experience has led him to question it.

The threat of the consequences of wicked behaviour also includes darkness, perhaps referring to blindness that may come upon Job, or possibly to endless night. The reference to a flood of water covering Job suggests some kind of cosmic terror, possibly (as earlier) with overtones of the cosmic reversal of creation by God.

Eliphaz is witnessing Job's suffering and deciding that it is the result of sin. Some people still think of suffering as a direct result of sin and there are many dangers in that attitude. For a start, who is anyone else to sit in judgment on another? If a person has sinned, that should be an issue between them and their God. We know that many people suffer who have not apparently sinned and, as Job discovers, there is no necessary connection between the two.

PRAYER

Lord, preserve us from all perils and dangers, and keep us calm in the face of adversity.

GOD IS IN HIS HEAVEN

Eliphaz turns to the thought of God as creator, high above in the heavens, even higher than the stars (v. 12)—images stressing the majesty of God. How does Job dare to cross God and question his knowledge of what goes on? Eliphaz cites Job's accusation that God cannot see through the deep darkness (v. 13) because he is wrapped in clouds and walks on the dome of heaven (a reference to the original division of the firmament in Genesis 1, in which God divided the heavens and the earth and formed order out of the waters of chaos). Eliphaz is citing Job in order to make the opposite point: of course God can see and know all things; just look at his power and majesty! Job's questioning is leading him into paths of wickedness, for he cannot see the truth clearly any more. Nor can he expect to be safe from punishment simply because God is far away.

Reviving wicked ways

Eliphaz accuses Job of going back to old ways trodden by the wicked (v. 15). Of course we know that Job has never been wicked, but Eliphaz is assuming that he must have been, since he is being punished. He thus likens Job to the wicked and asks whether any progress been made after all. There is a saying that 'what goes around comes around'. Ecclesiastes 1:9 makes the same point when it says that there is 'nothing new under the sun'. Some people never learn: they fall back into old ways and the same mistakes are made generation after generation. A contemporary recently said to me, 'Who would have thought that *our* generation would have gone the same way as the last, with divorces and wife-beating and the whole range of social problems?' Somehow there is an idea that 'this time' it will be better—that we might have learnt from the mistakes of our forebears—but this is rarely the case.

Verse 16 makes a rather obscure reference to the generation before the flood, who were of course wiped out by God for their wickedness. The wicked have no need of God: verse 17 is presented as a duel between the wicked and God. In fact, the wicked actively want to be left alone and they do not believe that God can do anything to them. They live a plentiful life. For a moment here, it starts to look as if

Eliphaz is agreeing with Job, but then he brings himself up short. He does not want to consider the wicked. They are repugnant to him (v. 18b).

The laughter of the innocent

Eliphaz's next words smack somewhat of self-righteousness. The idea that the innocent laugh at the misfortune of the wicked (v. 19) is an unpleasant idea to modern ears. And yet, it is perhaps simply to be taken as a statement that there is some point in being one of the righteous. The righteous can take the moral high ground and congratulate themselves on having chosen the correct path from time to time. When the wicked do get their come-uppance, the righteous are there to say, 'I told you so!'

It is good to want to follow the right path and so perhaps influence others by our behaviour, showing them that there is merit in what we are trying to do, such as living a good Christian life, being kind to those in need, turning the other cheek and so on. There is a difficult balance to be found in being genuinely good without becoming self-righteous about following the right path. The danger with the latter is that we become unable to see when we do make mistakes. Rather like Job's friends, we become set in our ways and fail to see that self-righteous behaviour puts other people off following a similar path rather than encouraging them to emulate us. A little humility goes a long way, as the last part of Eliphaz's speech (22:29 in particular) goes on to emphasize.

PRAYER

Help us, Lord, to follow the path of truth and righteousness but not to gloat and become self-righteous.

AGREE *with* GOD—*or with* ME?

Eliphaz calls on Job to agree with God and be at peace (v. 21). But what he is really asking Job to do is to agree with him! Eliphaz argues that once Job is at peace with God, simply acknowledging his misdeeds, all will be well. Job needs to be open to God's instruction and ponder seriously on his words; then restoration will come. The cleansing of Job's unrighteousness will lead to a multitude of good things. All he has to do is to remove the unrighteousness from his tents (meaning from himself and his family). But of course Job doesn't acknowledge that there has been or is any unrighteousness, and we know that to be true. Eliphaz thinks that Job needs to have more respect for God. If he treats God like gold or silver, in the knowledge that God is greater than the finest gold from Ophir (the traditional home of fine gold), then everything will be better (v. 24). We can almost hear the cajoling tone in Eliphaz's voice.

A renewed relationship

Eliphaz expounds what a renewed relationship with God would be like. It would lead Job to delight in God and to lift up his face to God in wonder (probably in the context of prayer, v. 26). Job's prayers would be heard and answered and in return Job would pay his vows of obedience. The book of Proverbs says more than once that a man plans his way and God confirms it (see Proverbs 16:1), and Eliphaz's words here echo that sentiment. Job's decisions will be verified by God; he will know the right steps to take. Again we hear that cajoling tone: these are the benefits of a right relationship with God—peace in one's heart, confidence in one's decisions and confidence in the divine.

Humility

Eliphaz stresses that God is on the side of the humble (v. 29), and he accuses Job of thinking that it is otherwise. The inference here is that Job is demonstrating a certain pride in maintaining his own position—an overweaning one in Eliphaz's eyes, no doubt—and that if Job becomes humble, all will be forgiven. Eliphaz voices the thought that God will save even the guilty if people such as Job are pure. That is, if Job is righteous then he could save others. God purposes deliverance for the righteous and even the righteous can intercede for others (compare 42:7–10).

Humility is certainly a great asset and we saw in the last passage how self-righteous behaviour needs to be tempered with humility. And yet, too much humility is perhaps a bad thing. It can lead to our becoming vulnerable and unable to pursue our own ends. The proverbial literature is well aware of these kinds of contradictions: the right behaviour for one time can be different from the right behaviour for another. There are general truisms, such as the idea that humility is a good thing overall, but nothing is good to excess. Proverbs 15:33 speaks of humility coming before honour, and Proverbs 22:4 mentions that honour is one of the rewards for humility.

With these words about humility, Eliphaz's speech ends. We note that his speech is shorter than previous ones and more to the point. The speeches of the friends get noticeably shorter in this third round, while those of Job remain about the same—another indication, perhaps, that Job is gaining ground while the friends' arguments are tailing off. However, we shall see that there is some muddling of the speeches in the text as we have it. In fact, we need to reshuffle parts of the text so that people are speaking consistently: it doesn't make sense, for example, for Job suddenly to be upholding the traditional position adopted throughout by the friends.

PRAYER

Lord, give us the humility to recognize you and to recognize the needs of others. Yet give us the strength to stand up for ourselves when necessary and not to be ground down by the opinions of others.

GOOD DAYS & BAD DAYS

We all have good and bad days. Sometimes a number of bad days come together but then we can reasonably expect life to pick up again, and it usually does. Job is having a bad day today—his illness is bearing down upon him and he feels particularly dissatisfied (v. 2). As children, we have probably all experienced someone's hand upon our shoulder, its heaviness making us feel small. God's hand is heavily upon Job; the burden of his suffering is weighing Job down. He feels particularly sore and bitter. It seems that the friends' words do not make any difference to him: he is not even bothering to answer the speech of Eliphaz directly. It is clear that now his complaint is firmly against God, the cause of his suffering.

Where are you, God?

Job feels that if he could only find God and confront him, all would be well (v. 3). Sometimes, when we have had a disagreement with someone, it is better to face them. There is something about personal contact that replaces any number of letters, e-mails or telephone calls. Job wishes to find God's dwelling-place and lay his case before him, but even though he is looking for God he cannot find him. This is in contrast to former Job's sentiments, when he felt he couldn't get away from God because of God's all-seeing eye (for example, 6:9). It is a complaint about God's absence, which contrasts with psalms where God's presence leads a person through life (for example, Psalm 23), and also parodies passages that imagine no escape from God (for example, Psalm 139:9–12).

In verse 4, we find the language of the law court used. God is the great judge to whom Job would like to present his arguments and then wait for a just decision. Job has never received God's answer to his complaints, only the replies of the friends who claim to represent God. Job has given up believing a word that the friends say; he now wants a direct confrontation with God. He imagines himself learning from God's answer and understanding it. God's personal word is what he needs to calm himself down and understand what is happening to him.

A just judge

Ironically, Job asks whether God would contend with him in a show of his power, and replies, 'No' (v. 6). Well, of course, that is precisely what God goes on to do when he does finally appear in chapter 38. But this is not what Job is expecting. He is hoping for a sympathetic hearing from God, for a direct reply to his questions and complaints. He imagines that he will be able to reason with God and that because God is a just judge he will be acquitted (v. 7).

We all need to have faith in a system of justice. If that goes wrong, then society becomes chaotic. In lands where the police and the courts are corrupt, there is no justice to be found. This had been the case at times in ancient Israel as described by the prophets. It is an intolerable situation for all, and this is how Job feels in his situation. There is nowhere he can go for justice because the supreme judge has turned nasty. Here, however, he is being more optimistic about the possibility of reasoning with God and getting a fair trial. His emotions about it tend to fluctuate. If only he could find God—but the problem is that he can't. He feels cut off from God, and so he is back to his original position of complaint. He longs most of all for justice. We all long for justice in the world and we cannot force God into making it happen: we can pray for justice and we can try in our own small way to live up to standards of justice that we know to be right.

PRAYER

Lord, help us to feel the power of your presence and let your justice prevail throughout the earth.

73

SEARCHING *for* GOD

Job's mind is now wholly on God: he longs to find him to explain his case, but he cannot find him whichever way he goes, forwards, backwards, left or right (vv. 8–9). Jesus said, 'Search, and you will find' (Matthew 7:7) and Isaiah 55:6 speaks of seeking God while he is available. This might suggest that Job is not looking in the right places. People often say that they would like God in their lives, but they don't know how to find him. How do you know when God is working in your life? This is a difficult question, but many people have a strong sense of God's presence—what some have called an inner voice or spiritual feeling or set of emotions. Somehow, though, Job is seeking God in the wrong way. He feels that he has nowhere to turn since he cannot find him (v. 9).

God will vindicate

Job now reveals that he still ultimately trusts God: he knows that God knows what path he is taking (v. 10). He recognizes that his suffering might be a test from which he will emerge purified like gold (this anticipates sentiments that will come out in Job 32—37 in the speeches of a fourth friend, Elihu). Job recalls all that he has done right in the past: he has kept on the straight and narrow (v. 11). As Proverbs suggests, one can choose the right path by making wise choices, and Job feels that he has done this. He has also kept God's commandments—a reference perhaps to the laws of Israel as in Exodus and Deuteronomy. He has treasured God's words. He is simply confirming here what we as readers already know, that he was upright and blameless and does not deserve this fate. He doesn't know, as we do, that it is a test of his righteousness. It certainly seems a severe one!

Fear of God

Job actually recognizes that God acts as he wishes: because he is alone in making his own decisions, there is no one to argue with him (v. 13). God does what he pleases, and thus however much Job protests, he cannot change his fate. There is a resignation in his words here that is more like the accepting Job of the prologue (2:10).

Because of this 'aloneness' of God, Job says that he is terrified of him (v. 15). God does become more terrifying when he becomes unpredictable. There is something safe about a God who rewards good and punishes evil according to a strict retributive pattern, but when the rules stop working and one is faced with an unpredictable and self-interested God, how does one know where one stands? When Job thinks in this way he is frightened, which is another part of his insecurity in his present situation. He feels that God has made his heart faint and scared him beyond belief (v. 16). He wishes he could disappear in darkness so that he could not be seen by the ever-watchful eye of God.

Sometimes, to ponder on the greatness and power of God is a terrifying thought, as is the idea that God is judging us by our deeds and thoughts. The desire to disappear in this situation is understandable. We can think of God's constant presence as a good thing. He is there as a guide, protector and carer, and in knowing all our thoughts and deeds he can relate to us in a very profound way. This more positive thought is not in Job's mind, however, at this point in his despair.

PRAYER

God, your all-seeing, all-knowing presence is usually a comfort to us and we long for it. Help us not to see it as a burden, as Job did.

GOD'S TIME

The poem in Ecclesiastes 3:1–8 tells us that there is a time for every-thing—for being born, dying, laughing, crying and so on. Human beings, however, can never guess when the right time for all these activities is going to be. God, on the other hand, does know the times at which things happen: he may even plan them. Thus there is a recognition, as here in Job, that God's time is different from human time (v. 1). This gives new meaning to the phrase, 'Doing things in one's own good time'. In fact, Job is asking here why times are 'not kept' by the Almighty, referring presumably to the lack of coincidence of God's timescale with ours. God works in time but is himself outside it; he also chooses when to act.

Job complains similarly that no one understands God's days. Maybe God's days are also different from ours (which might explain the seven 'days' of creation in Genesis 1) and the length of them is unknown to us. Job is complaining that there is a lack of real contact because of the different time-frames. It is rather like telephoning the other side of the world and talking to people in a very different time zone. They are at the end of their day and you are at the beginning of yours. You have that bright new morning 'get on with work' feeling, and they are just winding down at the end of their day, over a quiet glass of wine and a restful meal. It is no wonder such conversations can sometimes be difficult!

The actions of the wicked

If God had set times of judgment on particular days, then the right-eous would find it easy to see that he was punishing wickedness. In the meantime he seems to be somewhat inactive. Here in verses 2–4, we have another description of the bad habits of the wicked (a certain repetition might be noted here). They remove landmarks so that people don't know where they are, or what the boundaries of their own land might be; and they seize other people's property, such as sheep or goats (v. 2). They even deprive the orphan of his donkey and the widow of her ox (v. 3): they have no heart. They are highwaymen, robbing people on the road, and they make poor people fear them

(v. 4). The righteous, then, are suffering at the hands of the wicked and no one seems to do anything about it—especially not God!

Actions have consequences

As a consequence of this harsh treatment by the wicked, the poor walk along slumped, as asses are when they are overworked. They are likened to asses, toiling endlessly and then robbed of the fruits of their toil (vv. 5–6). It is a hard and unfair world out there. Much of this actually, and unfortunately, rings true for us today. We can think of all too many examples of the weak being exploited and the poor robbed of what little they have. Job describes the poor of his day as being left to scavenge food for their young. They end up stealing from the wicked. They are left penniless, naked and alone, soaking wet, clinging to rocks for shelter. It is a sad tale of penury and despair. Where is God in all this suffering? We can think of modern-day parallels: we have all seen homeless people out in all weathers, suffering wet and freezing conditions. In the theological seminary where I once stayed in California, there were a good number of homeless people and the seminary allowed them to shelter in the grounds on particularly cold, wet nights. I remember being woken up one night hearing a man crying out in anguish at his situation. It was a cry of 'Why me?' and it brought Job straight into the present.

PRAYER

Let us pray for any who are in poverty, hunger and need. May we and those that have plenty respond to that need. Send them the nourishment of your love, Lord.

The VICTIMS

The description of the consequences that the actions of the wicked bring continues here. There are wicked people who will snatch a child from its mother's breast, thus making it an orphan, or who will take an infant belonging to a poor person as a pledge, probably for money (v. 9). This is treating children as if they can be bought and sold, and it reminds me of some of the adoption scams one hears about today, in which a child is promised to one couple—sometimes even given to them 'on trial'—and then, when a better financial offer comes along from another couple, the child is 'moved'. The interests of the child are never in the picture. This is clearly wrongful behaviour.

As a result of being exploited by the wicked, the poor go about with few clothes on their bodies, and hungry (v. 10). They have to work, 'and, ironically, they have to carry sheaves of food that they cannot eat. They are employed to press out oil. They are thirsty as they work among the wine presses—another irony (v. 11). There are dying and suffering people crying out for help in the city. The situation is terrible.

Where is God?

Job has just described a situation of great pain and hardship. Where, then, is God in all this? The people cry to God but it appears that he does not pay heed (v. 12). He does not answer their prayer; their lives do not improve. Wasn't God supposed to be on the side of the poor and the oppressed, in accordance with the liberation of his people in the Exodus, and the words of the prophets? Where is he now? He appears to be absent in the face of suffering and pain. This theme of God's absence is found in many of the psalms and laments of the Old Testament (for example, Psalm 13:1; Lamentations 5:20–22). It seems to be legitimate to lament and complain and shout at God from time to time.

Beware of the dark!

In verse 13 the description shifts to the dark deeds of the wicked. It is interesting how wickedness and darkness are so often associated, as are the antitheses—truth and light (compare ch. 3). Those who prefer not to know the light—that is, the paths of righteousness—hide away and veer off that particular path. We find a description of the murderer who rises at dusk to steal around at night unnoticed and to pounce on the poor and the needy. The adulterer also waits for darkness so that he is not seen as he enters a forbidden house (v. 15). He wears a disguise on his face, hoping that no one is looking. Houses are entered, through mud walls that are easily dug through, penetrated and robbed in the dark. By day, the wicked are not to be seen: they are like bats who do not like the light. The night is their time. They wake just as it is getting dark, thus darkness is morning to them. Job describes them as friends of the dark: they love the terrors of night and darkness (v. 17).

Children are often frightened of the dark even within the house. I remember, when young, often wanting a light on the landing at night at home. And as for the darkness outside, particularly on an overcast night when the stars do not light up the sky, or in unlit streets and alleys, the atmosphere of quiet and darkness can be threatening in itself and one imagines that the shadows are criminals hiding behind bushes. Job portrays this kind of atmosphere here. When we are feeling afraid of the dark, we need perhaps to think more positive thoughts of comfort, of the protection that the darkness of night affords and of its peace and quietness, allowing us time to sleep. In the darkness of our innermost thoughts, too, we can find comfort in the thought of God's protecting and loving presence that is all around us and within us.

PRAYER

Lord, pour your light down upon us and help us
not to be afraid of the dark.

The WICKED GET THEIR JUST DESERTS

It is in this section of what is, supposedly, Job's speech that scholars have found evidence to suggest that this third cycle of speeches may have been corrupted in transmission—mixed up during the process of copying and handing on the story. The evidence is mainly that the different individuals, whose positions are quite well known to us by now, start to speak out of character. Verses 18–20 are particularly contradictory in the mouth of Job because the passage speaks of the wicked getting their just deserts, a sharp contrast to Job's description of the prosperity of the wicked in the last cycle. In these verses, the wicked live a short life, their livelihood is 'cursed' and they are avoided by others. Their land is no longer fertile. Their vineyards are empty of grapes so that they have no further need of grape pickers. They have bad luck with weather conditions and they suffer an early death. Just as water is rapidly dried up by heat, so they will be snatched away. They are soon forgotten; even their mother's home will forget them. Death is their portion; even the worm as it devours the body will find it sweet. And so the cycle of wickedness is broken, for once their memory is gone, wickedness will be no more. These words certainly do not resemble any of Job's arguments, and would seem to fit in much better with the sentiments of the friends. Since Bildad's speech in chapter 25 is so short, maybe 24:18–20 should be a part of that speech.

The actions of the wicked

Verse 21 would seem more naturally to fit into the earlier part of Job's speech in this chapter. In 24:1–12 we had a description of the actions of the wicked that harm others, and here in verse 21 the wicked are described as harming the childless woman and doing no good to the widow. Thus they are hurting the downtrodden of society—a low and mean act. This verse, then, is probably attributable to Job. It has been suggested, however, that the actions of the wicked in harming women (v. 21) are the reason why 'the worm forgets them' in verse 20. This may explain the positioning of verse 21 here.

The exaltation of the mighty

In verse 22 the subject matter seems to change from the wicked to the mighty. Those who have been brought low are sometimes lifted up to become strong and powerful. God gives them security by watching their path in the sense of the wisdom tradition—that is, by supporting them along life's way. Then in verse 24 the tone becomes less optimistic: the mighty are exalted for a little while and then are gone. They too are cut off.

Scholars have suggested that verses 22–25 are also to be attributed to one of the friends. But verse 24 sounds more like Job than any of the friends, and verse 25 is a little diatribe that could well form the final verse of Job's speech: 'Who is calling me a liar?' Verses 22–23 could also, in fact, belong to Job: he might simply be describing the seeming security of the mighty before it all goes badly wrong. In that case, it would be only verses 18–20 in this passage that form part of Bildad's speech.

Sometimes when one is in distress it is hard to articulate clearly—the arguments start coming out in the wrong order—and perhaps this is what is happening here to Job. He is not speaking so clearly and is getting confused. Or perhaps the author of the book, or even the scribes who copied it over the centuries, just got muddled over who was saying what, hence the dislocation.

PRAYER

Lord, give us confidence in our arguments with others and help us to articulate our needs clearly. Give us the gift of prayer so that we may prosper in our relationship with you.

GOD'S MAGNIFICENCE

In Bildad's reply we find a description of the might of God: he has dominion and he inspires fear in human beings (25:2), and yet his aim is to make peace in the heavens. This is reminiscent of God's goodness in creation, for after each creative act in Genesis 1 we read that 'God saw that it was good'. He is also powerful, with armies—heavenly and earthly, perhaps—to fight his cause (25:3). He is so all-embracing that his light shines upon all people: his concern is with everyone.

Bildad, like Eliphaz, tries to encourage Job to seek relationship with a just and loving God once more. His words are more upbeat than those of Job. He tries to inspire Job with his description of God, which is almost hymn-like. The majesty and terror of God are described in the same breath.

Can a mortal be righteous?

The next question is a difficult one. 'How can a mortal be righteous before God?' (v. 4). This echoes Eliphaz's words in 4:17 and 5:14–16, and it reminds us of the question at the start of the book, of whether Job was in a relationship with God because of what he could get out of it or purely for the sake of righteousness. The further question is whether anyone can be regarded as righteous before God. Is there such a thing as pure righteousness, or is God alone fully righteous? Are human beings ever going to be able to satisfy God? Human beings are necessarily sinful: they are created, born of woman. There are overtones here of the Fall in Genesis 3 and the idea of original sin. Can human beings be pure in the face of God who is purity itself?

Bildad puts across a rather low opinion of human beings here. He says that even the moon is not fully bright—that is, not as bright as God—and neither are the stars, so how much less can human beings compare with him (v. 5)? God's power over heavenly bodies is stressed here, as in Genesis 1 where God creates the sun, moon and stars. Bildad likens humans to maggots and worms—lowly creatures, crawling on the earth. Is this what humans are in God's sight? Maybe Bildad is trying to cut Job's maintenance of his own innocence down to size, or maybe it is simply an attempt to stress the otherness and might of God.

Bildad's words seem to end rather abruptly at 25:6, and it is often suggested that chapter 26 might belong to his speech, notably verse 5 onwards, which would seem to fit in with his description of God as creator. Other evidence for a dislocation is found at 27:1, where we seem to have the opening to a new speech by Job.

We shall consider 26:5ff. in the next reading. In the meantime, though, we have verses 1–4, which do seem to belong to Job, even though they sound rather optimistic for him.

Helping the helpless?

Job appears here to be addressing his friends, although he could be addressing God. He describes how they have helped one who is powerless. If it is an address to the friends, it would presumably be rather tongue-in-cheek! Job praises them for assisting him in his weakness. Now the irony really sets in: 'You have counselled one who has no wisdom,' he says (v. 3), presumably again referring to himself, who has been 'given much good advice'. He then asks what spirit has helped them to say these words (v. 4), and perhaps the inference is that it might not be God's.

If we take it that Job is addressing God, he could be thanking God for his assistance to him, but that also would presumably be rather tongue-in-cheek at this point. The context of ironic address to the friends seems more likely. Job has not run dry of sarcasm, it seems.

PRAYER

Lord, help us to help others, but help us also to recognize that our help may be misdirected or unappreciated. Enable us to be patient and to try to understand.

GOD'S POWER IN CREATION

The last section of chapter 26 seems somewhat out of place. It is possible that Job would extol the power of God as creator, but the words are equally likely to echo the thought of the friends, or they could be a separate hymn in praise of God's creative power that has found its way into the dialogue here. The stress is on God's might, which makes even the shades of Sheol, the home of the dead, tremble (v. 5). Both Sheol and Abaddon (v. 6) are references to the underworld, traditionally cut off from God but over which God still has dominion.

This description recalls God's creative acts and his power over the natural order. The reference to stretching out Zaphon (the north) over the void (v. 7) could be a reference to the north generally or to the northern reaches of the vault of heaven, or to a mountain in the far north where, in ancient Near Eastern mythology, the gods dwelt (see Isaiah 14:13). Zaphon has perhaps become symbolic of high land and, along with the second half of the verse, might refer to the creation of the earth in the middle of nothingness. We have probably all seen pictures of the earth taken from satellites: we might think of that image here, although, of course, the biblical writers would not have had it in mind.

God binds up the waters in clouds (v. 8). This suggests the flood waters, but here God does not let the clouds spill all their rain. Clouds even cover the moon at the will of God. He sets the limits, drawing a circle on the waters (v. 10)—perhaps a reference to his act of dividing the waters at creation. He also created light and darkness: 'light' in verse 10 could refer to heaven and 'darkness' to Sheol, or perhaps to the earthly realm in general, heaven and earth having been kept separate by God by the making of a firmament (see Genesis 1).

God's power is such that even the pillars of heaven (the mountains supporting heaven) tremble when he is angry (v. 11). He can still the sea: he overcame the chaos monster called Rahab in ancient Near Eastern myth (v. 12). He made the heavens, and he cut down that same serpent of chaos, the piercing and dividing of which was supposed to have created the firmament.

A contrast is drawn between a whisper and the loud sound of thunder (v. 14). We hardly hear a whisper of God and yet his power is so mighty. There is a tension between the strong and mighty God who created the universe and the God who is involved in the lives of each and every one of us. We have to live with that tension all the time in our understanding of God. It is part of his mystery that he can operate on so many different levels at once. The unorthodox note here, though, is that God's creative power is seen as frightening, whereas usually in the psalms and prophets it is to be praised—for example, in Isaiah 40:9–11, where God's greatness in creation is a source of comfort for humanity.

It's all God's fault

At the beginning of chapter 27 we seem to be back with the old Job, complaining again! He is blaming God for taking away his rights (v. 2). He had made a deal with God which has been transgressed, not by him but by God. Each of us has certain human rights, such as freedom of speech, that should not be taken away from us by other human beings. In the same way, we have certain rights in relation to God, such as the right to protest at unfair treatment. Job has maintained his innocence throughout: he is not going to give in now. As long as he is alive, he will hold on to truth. He will not lie: this is against his nature and thus he cannot acknowledge that God is right and he is wrong (v. 4).

Integrity

Job refuses to give in to the friends' persuasions because he is a man of integrity. Two conceptions of God are found here. On the one hand is a picture of a God who has wronged Job, and on the other, a recognition that this is the only God, whom he had previously trusted, with whom he longs to be in communion again and in whose name, ironically, he swears to his integrity. We always admire a person of integrity—someone who keeps promises, supports to the end what they believe is right, practises what they preach and so on. Sometimes, integrity does involve a determination such as that shown by Job. Of course, the other side of the coin is that if the person turns out to be wrong, their seeming integrity just starts to look like pride and stubbornness. However, Job himself believes that he is in the right against everybody—the friends and, most of all, God—and so he is not prepared to give it up. If he did, he would reproach himself, perhaps for ever after.

PRAYER

Lord God, creator of all things, let us hold fast to that which we believe to be good, with an integrity resembling that of Job.

ENEMIES & *the* GODLESS

Verse 7 seems to be somewhat separate from the rest of this section. Job wishes that his enemy may be like the wicked—that is, punished as the wicked would be. The same thought is paralleled in the second half of the verse, but this could be a reference to the friends. We often feel like this about our enemies: we wish they would be punished for hurting us. These are not very charitable thoughts, however.

The next three verses (vv. 8–10) are often thought to have been placed in the wrong mouth. They speak of the hopeless situation of the godless once they have been cut off. This sentiment might belong in the mouth of the friends, although Job could be citing the 'usual' fate of the wicked here. The passage is a series of rhetorical questions presumably expecting the answer 'No'. Will God hear their cry? Will they take delight in the Almighty? The Christian message is that, with true repentance, access to God is always on offer. Here, however, the inference is that the godless have sealed their own fate. These people won't seek God or call upon him to ask for forgiveness even if it is on offer.

In verse 11, Job appears to adopt an instructive mode: 'I will teach you…'. The trouble is that he is claiming to be able to teach about God, and that is much harder than teaching human wisdom, as in the book of Proverbs, which consists of instruction to young men in how to lead a successful life (see especially Proverbs 1—9). Job is teaching about God's actions, and is not concealing anything. Actually, it is not clear whether verse 11 links up with the previous three, and whether it might also belong in the mouth of the friends.

The lost third speech of Zophar?

We might note at this point that there has been no third speech from Zophar. Could verses 8–11 in fact be part of such a speech? It would possibly make sense for verse 11 to link with what went before, in which case it might be Zophar who claims to be teaching Job about God. That would probably fit in well with the arrogance shown by the friends in their claim to know God's thoughts, policy and ways.

Verse 12 is rather obscure. Who is it who has become 'altogether vain'? If these words belong in Job's mouth, they would probably refer to the friends; but if they are part of Zophar's speech, they could be a wider accusation, referring to everyone who has trodden the path of Wisdom. By the time we get to verse 13, it is widely agreed among scholars that we are in Zophar's third speech and that he is maintaining the traditional position that the wicked will get what they deserve, reminiscent of what he has said in chapter 20. It is not a full 'speech', though, since there are not the usual jibes at the beginning and end.

The portion of the wicked

Those who perpetuate injustice will be punished by God. Their many children will all meet death sooner rather than later, either by conflict or through famine or disease. When the wicked die, no one is sorry, not even their widows (v. 15). When a person died of disease at this time, the law denied them a proper burial (compare Jeremiah 22:19), and so there was no funeral at which widows could mourn in the usual way. The reference to pestilence could be a veiled reference to Job's state.

The wise were against the 'get rich quick' mentality: Proverbs 13:11 says, 'Wealth hastily gotten will dwindle.' The wicked appear rich, piling up silver like dust, and clothing like clay (v. 16), but they will lose it all. The innocent will be the ones actually to wear the clothing and divide up the silver. The wicked build seemingly strong homes but they are like nests, likely to be swept away (v. 18). The wicked go to bed with wealth, but it will be gone in an instant: overnight it will disappear (v. 19). This might remind us of a stock market crash, happening in distant parts of the world while we sleep. These threats help to keep the righteous in line: if you are tempted to be wicked, look at the fate that awaits you!

The wicked will not only suffer the loss of all their loved ones and all they possess, but they will be terrified too (v. 20). They will not be able to sleep comfortably and soundly in their beds. Terrors come like a flood or a whirlwind—again, a sudden loss and a very frightening and decisive one. There is a veiled reference here to the fate of Job's children in 1:19, perhaps. The 'clapping' of the wind (v. 23) might refer to the lashing sound that strong wind makes, accompanied by a howling noise and a hissing in the crevices and cracks of a house, but the words can also be taken to refer to the clapping of hands by mourners as a sign of grief, and to contemptuous hissing.

PRAYER

Lord, we often feel dissatisfied that we do not have the wealth of others. Help us to see that it is not the answer to all our problems.

80

MINING *for* HIDDEN TREASURES

We now come to what looks like a separate hymn to Wisdom, although in the context of the book it is in the mouth of Job. The passage is often considered by scholars to be either a later addition to the book by an editor or a separate hymn-like piece added in by the author. The idea is that however deep you dig for wisdom, you are not actually going to find it. The secret of wisdom belongs to God. God used Wisdom in the creation of the world (personified as a female figure in Proverbs 8:22–31), and in that sense she has an indisputable connection with the physical world. But she is not a physical thing to be found and she cannot be fully grasped by human beings in her entirety.

The passage starts with mining imagery. Silver and gold, iron, copper and all precious metals come out of the earth (vv. 1–2). Human beings use all their ingenuity in the quest for precious metal (v. 3). Such things are hidden but can be brought to light, mined and then refined or smelted. Miners are prepared to risk their lives in digging deep in darkness, far away from human habitation (v. 4). People above are ploughing the fields and making bread, while underneath the miners are digging (v. 5). It is worth all the toil, though, for the treasures that are found in the earth—sapphires and gold in abundance (v. 6). There is a note of praise and wonder in this description of the lengths to which humans will go, digging out things that are hidden.

Digging for wisdom

The way of wisdom, like precious metals, is hidden—no bird knows the way to it, not even the beady-eyed falcon (v. 7). The way has not been trodden by wild animals such as lions (v. 8). No one knows the way to wisdom except God. There is a *double entendre* here, with the path to wisdom and the path to the mines both being unknown by birds or beasts. By contrast, human beings have found out what is hidden in the earth. There is praise here for human ingenuity, although, of course, the final message is that, despite such efforts, wisdom remains elusive.

We come back, in verses 9–11, to the imagery of digging. The miners cut the rock, they dig deep caverns in the heart of mountains and they cut out channels. They find all the precious things that there are to find—but still there is no wisdom. They look everywhere, even at the sources of rivers (presumably on high mountains) and at every hidden thing. This wisdom is elusive—or maybe they are on the wrong track.

The passage praises human technological achievement. It is amazing how human beings can access remote and inaccessible places to discover hidden treasure and precious gems. And yet, there is a caveat that wisdom is even greater than this.

The way not known

The second section of the hymn begins with the refrain, 'Where shall wisdom be found?' (v. 12). This reminds us perhaps that in our constant quest for knowledge and understanding, and the huge leaps in understanding that we make all the time in the modern age, once one door is opened another world is revealed. More answers lead to new questions, and there is a sense in which we would cease to be human if we had no questions left to ask. There are limits to human knowledge in every generation. Particular breakthroughs are made from time to time, which advance us to the next stage, but the questions never cease. Although humans know the way to the deepest and darkest parts of the earth, they do not know the way to wisdom. It is not in the earth—in the land of living beings—or in the sea (v. 14). Wisdom is nowhere to be found.

Not only is wisdom not to be found, but it is not to be bought (vv. 15–16). It is incomparable to precious metals and jewels and its price is much higher. We are told that it cannot be bought for gold or silver (the gold of Ophir was particularly prized), nor can it be valued in onyx or sapphire. We sometimes hear the accusation that people are 'bought' for money. Fine jewels and riches are good for a time, but they cannot replace a genuine happiness that transcends material goods. There are things that cannot be bought—love and friendship, for example.

Verses 16–18 give a list of precious jewels—onyx, a gem used for engraving, and sapphire (alternatively lapis lazuli), gold and glass (surprising to find on the list, perhaps, but glass was particularly prized in ancient times) and jewels of fine gold. Coral, crystal, pearls and the chrysolite of Ethiopia (probably yellow rock-crystal, which is a kind of topaz) are also mentioned. All these jewels do not compare with wisdom, the value of which is above price.

PRAYER

Lord, the gift of your love is beyond price. Help us to value it beyond earthly possessions.

81

HIDDEN *from* VIEW

Verse 20 repeats the refrain that we saw in verse 12: 'Where is wisdom to be found?' This indicates a hymn-like, possibly liturgical setting for the poem. Wisdom is hidden—hidden from all living creatures, even from the birds of the air. It is hidden from the places of the dead which are personified here. Abaddon (or Sheol) and Death are described as having no knowledge of wisdom: they have heard only a rumour of it. The 'rumour' may be a reference to the idea that on the threshold of death, humans enjoy a deeper wisdom than they had during their lifetime. It is also supposed to be the case that hearing is the last of the senses to disappear before death.

God knows

Finally the answer comes: only God knows the way to wisdom (v. 23). God is behind everything and he knows everything. He is omniscient as the creator of all things. He is all-knowing and all-seeing. This picks up an idea expressed by Zophar that nothing escapes God's eye (11:11). Here the all-seeing presence of God is something to be praised, in contrast to some of Job's complaints about being unable to get away from God's view.

The next verses give a description of the greatness of God in creation: he orders all creation, giving the wind a maximum force or weight when it blows, to ensure that it does not exceed its boundaries (v. 24). It is an interesting idea that God fixes boundaries which he himself can unfix in his anger if he chooses to, but which he keeps under restraint for most of the time. He gives the sea limits so that the land is not washed away by it. He determines the laws of rainfall and the habits of thunderbolts. The order of creation is in God's hand—reminiscent of the Enlightenment idea of God as the great watchmaker who sets the hands of the clock going and then allows it to run of its own accord, with a little tweaking from time to time. God surveyed creation, set it up and explored it, and in that sense he is actively involved; but he also creates the laws by which it continues. There are overtones here of Proverbs 8:22–31, which describes the setting up of the created order by God through Wisdom, although Wisdom is more overtly personified in Proverbs 8.

Fear of the Lord

Most of the hymn in Job speaks of the impossibility of the wisdom quest and seems in that sense to have a negative tone, although the imagery is rich and the poetry beautiful. In verse 28, this uncertainty is overcome by a positive ending in which the ability of humans to find wisdom, if they trust in God, is expressed. This recalls Proverbs 8, in which Wisdom is accessible to humans if they will follow her path. Here in Job, wisdom is the preserve of God alone and it is only fear of him that will enable access to it. The final verse of the hymn is a crucial bridge between God and humanity: 'the fear of the Lord is wisdom and to depart from evil is understanding'. The important thing is to lead a good life in the service of God and try not to err from his guiding path.

There is a strong suggestion here of the ending of Ecclesiastes, which also concludes, having surveyed possible paths to happiness, that it is best to fear God and keep his commandments (Ecclesiastes 12:13). A deeper understanding of the cosmic order is denied to human beings. The fear of the Lord is true wisdom, which is accompanied by righteous deeds. 'Keep on the straight and narrow, and gradually God's wisdom will be revealed to you' is the message. It almost seems as if we are back to the doctrine of retribution and the words of Job's friends. This hymn, in fact, shows the tension between knowledge of God, which goes only so far from the human side, and those vast areas of knowledge that belong exclusively to God. It is that realm that Job seeks to understand in his suffering, and it is that realm that the friends think they can pin down by limiting God's justice—although they too have moments of realizing, as Job does, that God's justice is greater than ours and is in a far greater context.

PRAYER

Lord, we glory in the wonders of your world, ever more wondrous to us as we seek to understand the mysteries of the created order and as our knowledge progresses.

A WATCHFUL GOD

Job takes up his discourse again, and this is regarded as his final plea to God rather than being one of the speeches in dialogue with the friends. It is the beginning of a long speech that runs from chapter 29 to 31. The dislocation of the third cycle of speeches at the end of the dialogue, whether deliberate or not, has had the effect of breaking down the dialogue pattern. This was already happening because Job was no longer listening to the friends, and now he is concerned only to present his case once and for all to God himself. In this section he recalls the good times when God watched over him and guided his steps. God looked after him and made him feel secure (v. 2). God provided the light to his darkness and Job walked in his ways. He walked in the light enjoyed by the righteous in contrast to the darkness of the wicked (v. 3).

This counters the friends' accusations that Job performed wicked deeds, once again reaffirming his innocence of wrongdoing. Job looks back on the past and on the rightness of his relationship with God. As we go through different stages in life, we often look back with fondness on a particular period of our lives, sometimes with rose-tinted spectacles. This is what Job is doing here: he is remembering a good relationship with God, rather as we might remember fondly a relationship that we had with another person.

The prime of life

We speak of someone being 'in their prime' when they are at the peak of their mental and physical powers. It is not clear nowadays when precisely our prime is. Is it in our 30s, when we are getting established in life and still retain our youthful looks, or is it in our 40s, in mid-career, when we have probably achieved some of our goals? Perhaps, as people are living longer, it is in our 50s, when we are probably getting a higher status in society and feeling that we have put down real roots? Job remembers the time of his good relationship with God as his prime. Often, at the time when we are in our prime, we are not aware of it. Only afterwards do we look back and think, 'That was a good time for me.' This is what Job is doing here. As he looks back, Job remembers the abundance of his relationship with

God. God was with him in everything. God was a real friend and also a part of his family life. Job also remembers with sadness the children that he has lost (v. 5). He could do no wrong then: he had an abundance of good things. Milk and oil (v. 6) are representative of this abundance.

Respect

Job moves on to recalling the position that he had in society. People often comment that on retirement they lose some of the status that they had in society: they move from a responsible position to spending their day at the supermarket. This is how Job feels. He was really somebody once. He was one of the elders who sat at the city gate or in the square (v. 7). Younger men had respect for him and kept a low profile, and other older men stood up in respect (v. 8). Even those with noble blood kept quiet to listen to him and princes also refrained from speaking (vv. 9–10). Whether this was literally so, we might doubt, but the language of nobility and princes communicates the idea that Job really was a respected elder of the city, acknowledged for his wisdom and his righteous deeds. All ears commended what they heard and all eyes approved what they saw of him (v. 11). He was universally loved and respected.

PRAYER

Lord, thank you for the good times. Help us to enjoy them and make the most of them.

HELPING *the* POOR

Now Job's righteous deeds are enumerated by him again: he helped the poor in distress, the orphan, the wretched and the widow. Those at the lower end of society blessed him for his kindness (vv. 12–13). He did all that was expected of him and more—he lived according to the principles of wisdom—so it should have all gone well for him. He acted, as many do today, with concern for others. This is an important Christian principle which is in danger of being forgotten in a less overtly Christian world. Being thoughtful and kind towards other people also makes us feel good about ourselves, and so it works for the benefit of receiver and giver. The question in relation to Job, however, as raised in the prologue, is whether he did such deeds just because of what he 'got out of it' or because he genuinely cared for others. We should likewise examine our own motives when we 'give' to others.

Justice and righteousness are two key concepts in the Old Testament. The prophets repeatedly call for a combination of these two things, which are demanded of human beings by God as part of the covenant relationship (see, for example, Amos 5:24, 'Let justice roll down like waters, and righteousness like an everflowing stream'). Here Job calls on these concepts: righteousness clothed him and justice was like a robe and a turban, so close were they to his heart (v. 14). The point is being made repeatedly that Job couldn't have done more, and that there is no question about his righteousness.

Having the strength to help others

A key part of the Christian message is that we should help others, particularly those in special need. Job did this in pre-Christian times as part of his duties as a wise and responsible person. He helped the blind and lame, he provided for those in need and he helped people he did not know. He genuinely helped others for no gain to himself: he was a selfless man. This is a very different picture of Job, compared with the impression from the dialogue that he was somewhat self-obsessed. It is sad that the change in Job from outward-looking to inward-looking has been so dramatic.

Job describes how helping others and countering injustice made him strong. He countered the unrighteous, frightening the wicked away. In verse 17, we find the image of prey in the mouth of an animal: Job has made the unrighteous drop their case as an animal drops its prey when it is being threatened. The thought of dying in one's nest is rather obscure, but could refer to the preference for dying at home at peace, rather than in some more troubled manner (v. 18). The reference to the phoenix is also somewhat obscure, but it is a mythological bird that has traditionally been associated with longevity, even immortality, and so expresses the idea of a long life, full of days.

We then have an image of roots spreading out so that the tree or plant becomes firm. Job describes his roots spreading out to the waters, with dew on his branches (v. 19). Water is a symbol of life and renewal: the abundance of water indicates his strength and vigour. He was ever strong and fresh to the task, his metaphorical bow ever new in his hand, ready for any challenge (v. 20). He thought that longevity and prosperity were his inheritance and looked forward to a peaceful future. Little did he know... Perhaps there is a lesson here that we shouldn't count our chickens before they are hatched, as the saying goes.

Admiration

Job recalls once again the respect that others had for him (v. 21). This aspect of his loss seems to weigh particularly with him and might suggest that he had a certain vanity. He remembers how people hung on his words and waited for his advice. He was a natural leader, inspiring confidence in others. So powerful were his words that his listeners were stunned into silence. The imagery of water is found again in verse 23: people waited for Job to speak as one might wait for rain after a drought. He was benevolent and smiled on the unfortunate to cheer them up. He was a light in their darkness. He made decisions governing the lives of others; like a king or chieftain he dispensed justice and also provided comfort. This is a very idealistic picture, and it could well be that a hymn about the glory of the righteous has been adapted here to refer to Job's past prosperity, his ethical conduct and God's favour towards him.

PRAYER

Lord, let our deeds be our witness when we meet you face to face
at your heavenly throne. Let justice and righteousness
be our watchwords.

84

DISRESPECT SHOWN *by the* YOUNG

It is often said nowadays that children do not have the same respect for their parents, or for their elders generally, as previous generations had. Our culture tends to value youth and vigour over age and experience. Frailty is condemned rather than being seen as accompanying wisdom.

Job now complains that things are very different from those halcyon days on which he looks back with fondness (v. 1). His situation has changed dramatically so that he is held in contempt by all in society, including those younger or lower down the social scale than he—somewhat of a contrast to gaining the respect of kings and princes. Those who tease him and show him no respect are the children of the wicked, those who do not follow God or pursue paths of righteousness. Job disdained their fathers, so how much more will he scorn the sons. The reference to dogs is an insult: dogs were not kept as pets; they were seen as vicious and dirty. Job would have treated the fathers of these youngsters on the level of dogs, that is, at the bottom of the pile.

The life of the wicked

Job mentions that the wicked are weak, perhaps because of lack of food, and their vigour is gone (v. 2). He is left to associate with the starving and marginalized of society. They live a life of hunger, eating from leaves and bushes (v. 3). They are outcasts from society and people hate them. They are treated as thieves, even though they may not be so. They live an outdoor life, making fires from bushes, reaping what nature allows them.

There is something about the nomadic life that town dwellers find threatening, even today. The wicked are described as living in the open air, something that is well nigh impossible long-term in Britain with its cold weather, but is often seen in warmer climes. They make their home in the gullies of wadis, which is fine until the rains come. They make use of holes in the ground, rocks and bushes. They huddle together for warmth (I recently saw some homeless people do exactly that in central London), and they are essentially outcasts from society, forced to live at a basic level of subsistence.

The taunts of others

Job describes in more depth the acts of disdain heaped upon him by those who now ridicule him for his misfortune with the presupposition, no doubt, that he is a sinner and is getting his just deserts. It is often rather sensational to hear about someone famous, a leader in society in particular, being brought low. Perhaps that is why our newspapers are full of such stories. Job is mocked in song (v. 9): one can imagine tasteless rhymes being chanted at him. He is hated, ignored and spat at (v. 10). The depths to which people will stoop in their disdain of others are incredible; this is a side of human nature that never seems to be cured.

Not only is Job taunted, he is actively pursued and his life made worse by these oppressors (v. 12). He gives the reason: because he has been humbled, it has provided these people with the opportunity to mock. They have cast away their restraint and they have lost their respect. His enemies rise up against him, metaphorically knock him sideways and make plans to ruin him. The imagery of a path is used (v. 13): they break up his path deliberately and block his way. He was walking on a smooth path with an ordered and predictable life, and they have made calamities fall upon him. Job is helpless. No one stops this ill-treatment; no one appears to be on his side.

The wicked pursue him relentlessly. We cannot tell whether this is literally so or whether Job's mind is full of strange imaginings. He sees them rolling through a wide breach, like a wave breaking through a sea wall (v. 14). He is terrorized mercilessly. His honour of former times has disappeared in a gust of wind along with his former prosperity (v. 15). He now blames other people as well as God. 'Society' has become his enemy, just as has God. God, however, has 'loosed Job's bowstring' (v. 11), a reference to untying a cord. This is the opposite of 'girding the loins', which is a sign of strength. It is a reference to Job's perception that God has made him weak.

PRAYER

Lord, let us cultivate respect for all people—for our elders, for our youngers, for rich and for poor, for black and for white—for there are no barriers in your kingdom. Help us also to be compassionate to people in all kinds of situations and need—the homeless, the sick and the poor.

BLAMING GOD

Job is now back to his complaint: his soul is spent. He feels weak from all the grief he has poured out. His days are filled with nothing but affliction; his nights are so painful that he cannot sleep. Just the lack of sleep makes him exhausted. We all know what a strange feeling even just one disturbed night brings: imagine that multiplied many times.

The wicked persecutors were the subject of the last diatribe. In this section, however, 'they' changes to 'he' (v. 18) and it becomes clear that Job's real complaint is against God. He feels that he has been snatched by God and cast into the mire. His bodily disfigurement is such that he has become a physical wreck, like dust and ashes. Of course, he is sitting among ashes, so he must be feeling at one with his surroundings. He has been brought from the highest point to the lowest in one fell swoop. It is God who has ultimately brought this upon him: the 'they' of the last section are merely the human agents responding naturally to Job's now lowly situation.

Blaming God is easy because he is not directly in front of us, answering back. However, as we will see, he does respond in this case. Job accuses God of not hearing his prayer. When Job stands before God, God looks at him rather than doing anything positive to help him (v. 20). Job clearly feels the presence of God, but feels it to be a distant, hostile one. He accuses God of turning cruel (v. 21). We often feel this when a person whom we have loved (and maybe still do), turns on us. Job feels the power of God's mighty hand in a negative way, persecuting him rather than helping him. He feels tossed about on the wind, on the waters as in a storm (v. 22) These metaphors are simply to describe his feelings. Death is the only outcome for Job (v. 23): he feels near to it now since he is physically and mentally so weak.

Everything seems upside-down

Job asks a rhetorical question (v. 24): 'Surely one does not turn against the needy?' The answer 'No' is expected—of course one doesn't. God is perhaps inferred here as the oppressor of the needy. This is all back-to-front: God is supposed to care for the needy, and

Job, as his servant, also did so, emulating God and carrying out God's will. Once the ground rules are changed, no one knows where they stand. Presumably Job is generalizing from his own situation. *He* is now the needy, so where is help from God now?

What Job can't reconcile is that he did everything he should have done: he wept for those who had a hard life, his soul was grieved for the poor (v. 25). He should have been rewarded, but instead he has suffered this terrible plight. He expected light and got darkness (v. 26). This just shows that one cannot always rely on expectations. It is perhaps dangerous to expect blessings before they come our way.

In a bad way

Job returns to the subject of his physical and mental illness (v. 27). Inwardly he is in turmoil and he has nothing but days of affliction. He is gloomy; he cries out. He feels that he is little better than a companion of animals such as jackals or ostriches (v. 29), as he cries and wails like a jackal in the desert, an outcast from society. The ostrich too lives in desolate regions and hides its face in the sand. Job's skin turns black with the leprous disease and falls off him, and he has a burning sensation in his bones (v. 30). He used to play a happy tune, but now his tune is one of mourning and weeping, mingling with the laments of the women who will come and weep when he is dead (v. 31). He is suffering both mental and physical agony—mental in being so despised by others and seemingly by God, and physical in the suffering of his body. God is to blame for both.

PRAYER

Lord, give us peace in our days and throughout the night. Keep us safe in your loving arms and protect us from all who would seek to wrong us and cause chaos in our lives.

MORE QUESTIONS

Job seems to enjoy the technique of asking rhetorical questions. He posits a case: if he had been unfaithful to his wife, what would he expect from God then? The 'covenant with his eyes' is a reference to the marriage vow having bound him to fidelity to his wife, and perhaps he is thinking in the same way of his relationship with God (v. 1). The relationship between God and Israel is certainly portrayed as a marriage elsewhere in the Old Testament and perhaps most famously in the book of the prophet Hosea (for example, ch. 2). With the relationship with his wife in mind, how could he look upon a virgin lustfully? The expected answer is, 'Of course, he couldn't.' Job is now wondering whether, if everything is turned upside-down as it appears to be, his inheritance from God will be different. If the rules are changed, no one knows how to behave. Job then asks a few more rhetorical questions (vv. 2–4). Does not calamity befall the unrighteous? That is what is supposed to happen, but what now? Is God noting Job's actions?

If I did wrong, punish me

It would be all right if Job could see that he had sinned and could pinpoint what he had done wrong. Then he would not mind being punished. He says that if he has been false or deceitful, fine. But he has not, and God is not judging him fairly. If his step had faltered on the path of righteousness or if his eye had strayed, fine. If any blemish is even now upon his hands, let him be punished, let his work benefit another and let Job's food become scarce (vv. 7–8). The inference is, of course, that punishment would be entirely fair in any of these circumstances, but it is not fair to Job, given that he has done none of these things.

In verse 9 Job goes back to the point about his wife. If he had been enticed by another woman and loitered at her door, or neglected (perhaps divorced) his wife or let her be taken by other men, Job would deserve punishment. Infidelity or neglect would be crimes deserving real punishment, such as an all-consuming fire that would burn up everything he owned (v. 12). We do not read the 'But…', yet we hear it. Job is innocent—he has not done anything wrong and this is all upside-down. He has been the most loyal and caring husband.

Concern for others

Job always went out of his way to show concern for others. He is now recalling his treatment of his slaves. Did he ever do anything wrong to them? (v. 13). The answer is 'No'. He always took up their causes and heard them out. If he didn't do these things, then he deserves punishment—but he did, didn't he? We wonder whether Job is almost trying to remind himself of how things were. How did he actually behave? Perhaps it's starting to feel as if these good deeds all happened a long time ago. How will Job respond to God if and when he appears? (v. 14). What will Job say in answer to his enquiries? Job used to know where he stood, but now he is wondering what on earth he will be able to say. He feels overawed by God. After all, God is the creator who made all of us (v. 15). What does one say to one's creator? Job is now realizing his awe of God—a change of attitude, at least for now.

PRAYER

Bless husbands and wives and help them always to seek to please each other and have a loyal concern and support in good times and in bad.

GOING OVER ALL *the* GOOD DEEDS

There is almost a sense here of Job compiling a list. Did he withhold things from the poor? (v. 16). No. Did he treat widows well? Yes. Was he selfish with his food, not giving it to orphans? (v. 17). No. In fact, he took in orphans as his own and guided widows from when he was very young. He always gave clothes to the poor; they were grateful then and blessed Job for his kindness. If he had treated orphans badly in order to impress other people of high rank or authority, that would have been wrong—but he didn't. So what has gone wrong? It is a matter of just deserts. If Job had done any of these neglectful things and treated other people badly, then he would deserve punishment, but on the contrary, he went out of his way to be good to people. If he had gone wrong, he would deserve to have his shoulder-blade or arm drop off (v. 22).

Job did good deeds because he wanted to please God. He was terrified of angering God and incurring calamity upon himself (v. 23). But calamity seems to have happened despite all the good things that he did. He could not have faced the great God even though he had done all that he could that was right. So what is going to happen when he faces God now? That is an unpleasant prospect.

If I have done wrong...

Job's list of the various things that he might have done wrong, for which he could justifiably be punished, continues. The point is that he has done none of these things and is innocent. He has not put his trust in money, or rejoiced at great wealth (v. 24). He has not been proud of his assets. Nor has he been enticed by the sun and the moon (v. 26)—a reference to the worship of sun and moon that was perpetuated by some people at the time. The reference to his heart being enticed by the sun and moon and his mouth kissing his hand (v. 27) is probably to do with rites associated with this kind of astral worship. If he had done these things, he would have been rightly punished by human judges and by God—but he hasn't done them!

The reference to sin within the context of worship is interesting because it is rare. The rest of the list concerns ethical and charitable actions, beyond the strict call of duty. The list does not include heinous crimes. There are fourteen possible sins that Job might have committed in this chapter: it is possibly a set-piece formula, recalling Egyptian mortuary texts in which the deceased affirms his virtue before Osiris and other gods in a list of offences of which he has not been guilty. It is used by the author here in a legal context: Job is laying his case before God in a statement of his integrity, rather like the defendant in a court of law.

The formulaic character of this declaration of innocence continues. If Job has rejoiced at the ruin of those who hated him or rejoiced at the disasters that befell them, then he would be guilty (v. 29). He has not, though—he has done right. He has not sinned with his mouth: he has not cursed others. He has always been generous to strangers, welcoming them into his home (v. 32). Job 'went the extra mile' for people: he did not have to be so generous. If he had concealed his sins or hidden his iniquity, he would have been justifiably punished too. But he didn't!

Afraid of what others might say

If Job had hidden his bad deeds because he was afraid of what others might have said and their possible contempt, then he would have been justifiably punished (v. 33). This is a subtle point—that we are sometimes worried about admitting to something because of what others might think. We all put up a 'front' from time to time, often feeling less than deserving of the praise others heap upon us and the confidence that they have in us. If Job had kept back his transgressions because of what others might have said, or kept silence when he should have spoken out, he would have been punishable.

PRAYER

Lord, give us the courage to speak out when wrongs are being perpetrated and to stand up for what is right. Help us to be generous to strangers and to those less fortunate than ourselves.

Written Evidence

Written evidence is taken more seriously than oral evidence. This is true in a court of law, and it is also true in the world of archaeology, where a written record has more power than oral tradition. Job wishes here that someone would hear him—meaning, no doubt, God (v. 35). He writes down his signature, perhaps to prove in written form that he is making this oath of innocence. Is he not to have a reply? He would like to have received a written accusation from his adversary to say what he has done wrong, but this is wishful thinking again. It is part of his longing to be heard on the one hand and to know the cause of his suffering on the other. He wishes to know, then he could justify himself.

It is the not knowing that is tearing Job apart with anguish. It reminds me of being asked to go and see a teacher, and racking my brain trying to remember what I had done wrong. This is how Job feels. If he had a written indictment, he would carry it around with him so that it became a part of him—on his shoulder or on his head like a crown, as close to his person as clothing or as the accoutrements of status (v. 36). At least then he would know what he had done wrong.

Job imagines that if he had a record of his accusation he could answer it and hold his head up high once more. He would spell out all his innocence to God and would be able to approach God like a prince, in stately fashion (v. 37). He has in fact given his account in all his speeches and in this final plea, but the problem has been that no one appears to be listening. If he faced God head-on, he could respond appropriately.

If I have done any wrong...

This chapter has contained many 'ifs', suggesting that Job has not in fact done any wrong. Here is a further 'if': if his land has cried out against him (that is, if he has maltreated his land) then he would deserve punishment (v. 38). Job shows here that he believes in good treatment of the earth and has striven to carry it out. He has not simply taken from the land without giving something back. We are told that he has not caused the death of the owners of the land—suggesting that not all the land was his. He has not neglected it and let thorns grow instead of wheat and barley. If he had done wrong, fine. But he hasn't!

Job's words are ended

With this, the words of Job end. He has made his plea, and it remains for God to answer him. We can imagine Job finally running out of energy and words, waiting for something to happen.

These last verses would belong more naturally before verses 35–37, which read like an appendix to the section. At the end of Job's oath of innocence (31:5–31), instead of a lament to God, which might be normal in such circumstances, we find Job trying to pin God down with a legal document.

This is not only the end of Job's final plea to God and of his speeches, but it is the end of the dialogue section of the book. In many ways, chapters 29—31 form a closing plea, rather like a summing-up by a lawyer at the end of his defence, and they parallel chapter 3 which is Job's opening plea. We are poised at this point, waiting for the appearance of God, but instead the tension is prolonged by the arrival of a fourth friend, Elihu. Job is poised too, ready for an answer, but we have to wait until chapter 38 for that!

PRAYER

It is hard for us, Lord, when justice does not appear to be done and when good deeds are not rewarded. Help us to understand your ways and accept good and bad from your hand.

The END *of* DIALOGUE

The friends, at the end of their tether, give up on Job. They realize at last that they cannot get through to him. They think that he is self-righteous (v. 1): he cannot admit that he has sinned and is being punished as a result. Just as negotiations break down in world politics once a stalemate has been reached and the only answer is a show of strength in war, so here negotiations have broken down and the friends decide to hold their tongues. They do not wage war on Job, but we can imagine that any vestige of friendship is wearing thin by this stage.

A new 'friend'

The narrative now continues with the introduction of a fourth person who is going to try to reach Job—Elihu, son of Barachel the Buzite, who is of the family of Ram (a good family descended from King David). The first thing we are told about Elihu is that he is angry both at Job, for justifying himself rather than God, and at the friends, because they have not answered the questions satisfactorily despite finding Job in the wrong. Elihu is the typical angry young man who thinks that he has the answers. It is odd that, in the prologue, only three friends come to comfort Job and there is no mention of this fourth person. Nor, perhaps more significantly, is there mention of him in the epilogue, where Job intercedes on behalf of the three friends. This, plus the fact that the style of Elihu's speeches is somewhat verbose and that much of the content is repetitive of what has come before and after, has led many scholars, although not all, to consider that these speeches might be a later addition to the text by an editor. Perhaps the editor was adding his twopenny-worth to the debate. But one scholar, Gordis, has suggested that the editor might be the same person as the author of the dialogue, adding a little extra text later in life, believing that he was improving the book while in fact he was spoiling the movement of the plot. It would have made more sense to have God's speeches at this point, with Job poised for an answer from God. Elihu's speeches can be seen as either slowing down the action or heightening the tension by the delay.

Respect for elders

The reason given for Elihu's reticence in speaking to Job is his youth. He had had respect for his elders, giving the three friends the chance to persuade Job first. However, his anger springs from the fact that, in listening to the debate, he feels that they have failed to provide an adequate answer to Job's plight. He now feels justified in speaking his mind.

We saw earlier how Job bewailed the fact that people no longer respected him as an elder of the community. The three friends, however, are clearly respected by one such as Elihu, for it was out of respect for their views that he did not speak. When we are young—and probably throughout life—we retain respect for those older and more senior than ourselves. We respect their experience, their wisdom and their success. But we hope that they in turn will be responsive to the insights and suggestions of the young and will not become dogmatic in their ideas. The three friends have lost sight of the freshness of approach represented by the youthful Elihu, so he feels justified in interrupting the debate at this point.

PRAYER

Lord, let us listen to the voice of our youth as well as to the voice of the elders of our communities. Help the youth of today to become confident in expressing themselves, speaking their mind and living up to their ideals.

The VOICE *of* YOUTH

This speech begins with Elihu justifying the fact that he wants to speak. He declares his youth in comparison with the friends and says that he was timid because of it (v. 6). It is true that the young often do not have the confidence to state their opinion for fear of being laughed at or thought stupid, particularly in a large crowd or in distinguished academic company. Elihu had respect for those well versed in wisdom, and thought that length of days equalled depth of wisdom.

However, Elihu realizes that it is not age that leads to wisdom, but insight. He expresses it in terms of the spirit of a person as inspired by God. God leads a person to understanding at any stage of their lives (v. 8). The gift of wisdom can be given to an individual. It is true that long experience might lead to wisdom, but how often do we simply make the same mistakes over and over again? It is certainly right to have respect for our elders, but they are not necessarily our betters too, and there is a time and a place for speaking out. Elihu makes the point that it is not only the old who are wise or who understand right and wrong (v. 9): the young do too. In fact, the youthful sense of right and wrong is often even stronger than the viewpoint of those older people who may have had to compromise more as they have trodden life's way.

Give me a chance

Elihu decides to speak out, and asks that the others may listen to him, so that he may express his opinion. He clearly feels embarrassed to ask this, and yet is firm enough in his conviction that he has something to say to venture out and express himself. He first addresses the friends. He had waited on their words and listened carefully, but he did not feel that they answered Job satisfactorily (vv. 11–12). He sees them as giving up on Job with their answer that they have found wisdom but that they must leave Job in God's hands because they cannot persuade him. Elihu is the outsider; it is not against him that Job has argued. He will not repeat the mistakes of the friends by saying what they have said already (v. 14). At least, this is his aim, but as we shall see, he does repeat some of their ideas—almost inevitably, given the subject matter.

Bursting to speak

Sometimes we all have the feeling of bursting to speak. Sometimes we feel so strongly about something that the need to speak wells up inside us and has to come out. This is how Elihu feels: he has so much to say and he has felt constrained. His heart—the seat of his emotions, as they believed at that time—feels like wine with no vent (v. 19). One can imagine a barrel or even a bottle of wine in which the pressure has built up so that the liquid needs to flow out, but instead there is a huge tension within the bottle, pressing against the glass. Elihu lived at a time of wineskins rather than bottles, and the wineskin is ready to burst. He needs to speak to relieve himself quite apart from anyone else (v. 20). He has to speak out—he has decided!

Elihu is concerned to state that he is not taking sides: he has no axe to grind. Neither is he using flattery. He says that he doesn't know how to flatter: he is clearly a straightforward kind of person. If he started flattering, he knows that God would not approve. We all respond to flattery at times. There is a phrase, 'Flattery will get you nowhere', with which Elihu would no doubt agree. But there is also a parody of the phrase, which is, 'Flattery will get you everywhere', which also contains some truth. We are easily swayed by flattery, and we need to recognize it for what it is at times.

PRAYER

Lord, help us not to lose our moral sense of right and wrong,
and inspire us as we tread life's way in all our decision-making.
Give us the words to be able to speak out when we feel that
something is really important and help us to have the
sense of the right time to do so.

LISTEN *to* ME, JOB!

With a certain amount of bravado, Elihu calls on Job to listen to his speech (v. 1). He is concerned to stress his sincerity. He almost talks down to Job as he says, 'Look, I am opening my mouth to speak, using my tongue.' Perhaps Job is a poor specimen of a human being by this stage and he may not even appear to be listening. Elihu is trying hard to grab his attention. He is sincere: his words reflect his inner heart and his lips speak of what is within (v. 3). This is another theme of the wisdom literature—the importance that one's words echo what one knows to be honest and true in one's heart.

Elihu states, again somewhat boldly, that he speaks God's words. God is his inspiration and has breathed his spirit into him to give him life (v. 4). He challenges Job to answer him, almost acting as God's advocate here. He asks Job to set his words in order and to take his stand in front of him. He stresses that he is only human, as Job is, and that both of them are as clay in front of God (v. 6). He comes over as rather self-righteous, nevertheless! Perhaps Job is looking threatened by Elihu, because Elihu tells Job not to fear him. Sometimes when we are feeling down-hearted or weakened, it is not helpful to meet a strong, confident person who gives freely of his or her advice. Sometimes we want to hide away and only see people who are going to sympathize or who will be unthreatening. Elihu says that his pressure will not be heavy on Job—he just wants him to listen (v. 7).

I heard you

Elihu now reveals that he has heard what Job has had to say. He knows that Job claims to be innocent and that he sees God as his enemy (v. 10). He knows that Job feels like the guilty person with his feet in the stocks and that he feels watched and hounded by God (v. 11). He gives a brief resumé of Job's argument, rather as one might do a précis of someone's speech or work. Although he is trying not to be threatening to Job, this in itself must be rather daunting for one suffering as Job is. Elihu reveals that despite having paid attention to Job's words, he does not think that Job is right, and he will explain why.

God is greater

Elihu, like the other friends, argues at this point that God is greater than human beings. 'Why challenge God, then?' he asks. He answers that God speaks in different ways to people, sometimes in a way barely perceptible by human beings (v. 14). This is to prove God's superiority and his elusiveness in the face of Job's plea to be declared innocent and treated as such.

Elihu's depiction of God is similar to that of Eliphaz in 4:12–16. He paints a rather frightening picture of God appearing to people in the night. God speaks through dreams, when people are in a deep sleep upon their beds. He speaks so that they can hear, and he speaks warnings designed to turn them aside from wicked deeds and to keep them from acting with pride. He speaks to them in order to save them from the Pit (that is, Sheol or the land of the dead)—to save them from 'traversing the River', a metaphor for death (v. 18). Having started his speech in a gentle manner, Elihu now moves into a rather terrifying picture which no doubt shakes Job up again. This seems a rather clever technique; perhaps it is deliberate. Elihu suggests that God appears to people in order to deter them from the evil actions they might want to do. God has a hand, therefore, in persuading human beings towards righteousness.

This is a slightly new angle because it suggests that God actively promotes righteous behaviour rather than just urging it. There is a modern scientific theory that everything tends towards chaos if left to its own devices, untended. Here the inference is that God is actively promoting righteousness in people so that the tendency towards wickedness is countered. It is quite a comforting thought that God is actively promoting righteousness, although that possibly makes it more difficult to understand when bad things happen. How can a God who gives righteousness a helping hand, so to speak, allow people like Job to suffer?

PRAYER

Help us to help others and not to threaten them by our presence.
Let our motives be pure and guileless and assist us in avoiding the
need to dominate or advise.

GOD IS IN TOUCH

Elihu continues to confirm the greatness of God and the fact that God speaks in different ways to different people. Some are 'chastened with pain', just as Job is (v. 19). Suffering is seen here as being delivered by God as appropriate to each individual situation. The sufferers are in such continual pain that they lose their appetite. Again, by inference, this refers to Job. Also they suffer from the symptoms of disease: their flesh is wasted away and their bones stick out (v. 21), perhaps reminding us of pictures from Ethiopia and other parts of Africa when we see people suffering famine, such that they are almost literally skin and bone. Elihu states that they are near to death—the Pit being another word for Sheol, the land of underworld and darkness.

A mediator

Elihu picks up on Job's idea of a mediator (v. 23)—possibly an angel who can declare to God that a person is upright and can change God's mind about sending the person to the Pit. This is what Job calls for when he desperately wants a judge between himself and God. Even Satan is a kind of angel (albeit a fallen one) who can influence God, as shown in the wager in chapter 2. Nevertheless, the idea of a mediator is a hopeful one, as it is a picture of someone who would graciously ask God to deliver. The idea of a ransom comes in here (v. 24), which means redeeming or buying the freedom of someone else. Jesus is often regarded by theologians as a ransom for human sin: that is, in his death and crucifixion he took upon himself the weight of human sin and then, in his resurrection, conquered that same sin. He bought our freedom from sin and is thus our redeemer. Job could similarly be ransomed from his sin and get a last-minute reprieve from his fate if he were to be declared righteous.

The result of being restored would be a return to normality. Job's flesh would heal and become smooth, as in his youth. In fact, a return to youthful vigour is hoped for (v. 25). This ransomed person —again, by inference, Job—would pray to God and be accepted by him. He would be joyful in God's presence and his righteousness would be rewarded. The ransomed person would be so happy that he would sing to others of the wonders of his reprieve (v. 27), telling people that even though he perverted what was right, and sinned, he was not paid back. But in Job's terms, that would be like acknowledging that he had sinned and thus being like the wicked, who do not deserve a reprieve such as this, so he would not find this viewpoint acceptable. Elihu is really encouraging Job to acknowledge his sin and be restored, but he is using the language of a reprieve, which is a slight variation on the approach pursued by the other friends.

God gives a second chance

Elihu is concerned to say that God gives people second chances (v. 29). Sometimes people come back from the brink of death, from an illness or accident, and feel that they have been given a second chance. This often has a profound effect on how they wish to use their lives, on what they take for granted, and on how they treat people. Elihu has described how even sinners sometimes get a reprieve, and he is now reiterating this idea. God doesn't just do this once, he does it twice or three times with some people (v. 29). Death is at the doorstep but it doesn't happen. Job's reprieve is that he is still alive.

Elihu now addresses Job directly (v. 31). He had been apparently speaking in abstract terms, but it became increasingly clear that he was referring to Job all along. He now says to Job, 'Listen to me.' Perhaps Job is not clearly listening—perhaps he is still talking. Elihu wants a chance, and he gives Job a chance to talk to him too. He expresses a desire to justify Job before God, just as a mediator might do (v. 32). Maybe Elihu styles himself as that mediator. If Job listens, then he, the young upstart Elihu, will teach him wisdom (v. 33). He tells Job, in no uncertain terms, to pay heed to his wisdom.

PRAYER

Lord, let us feel your presence in our lives, in joy and in sorrow alike. Support us when we are tested by whatever circumstances may arise.

Hear Me Out!

Clearly Elihu is having difficulty being taken seriously. He calls again to everyone to listen to him (v. 2). Those who are in the know should heed him: he has important things to say.

The image of the ear testing words as the palate tastes food (v. 3) is an interesting one and links up with the theme found regularly in Proverbs of the importance of words and communication (for example, Proverbs 18:20–21). We hear many things in our everyday lives, and we sift what we hear and what we remember. We perhaps forget the things that we don't want to hear: 'turning a deaf ear' is a well-known phrase. We are constantly faced with choices, and Elihu urges those who are listening to choose for themselves what is right and good (v. 4). The friends have relied very much on traditional wisdom as it has been passed down, but Elihu calls for people to think for themselves.

Job's case

Elihu cites what Job has said (vv. 5–6), that he is innocent and that God is the one who has robbed him of the justice that should have been his. This shows that at least Elihu had been listening! Job has said that although he is in the right he has been counted as a liar, both by God and by the friends. His guilt has been assumed. He feels that he has an incurable wound festering (probably both on a physical and on a spiritual level), and that it is all wrong because he is being punished although he has done nothing. Now Elihu gives his own opinion: he sees Job as keeping company with scoffers, such is his lack of respect for God. In fact, perhaps continuing the food image, so excessive is Job's scoffing that he is drinking it like water (v. 7). Elihu accuses Job also of keeping company with evildoers, thus stating his opinion that Job is one of them. Job is blind to his own sin, thus he is walking with the wicked (v. 8). Job is once again quoted: he has said there is no point in being God-fearing (v. 9). This aligns him in Elihu's mind with the godless.

God is always just

Elihu calls for all who have sense to hear him. He knows the nature of God—that God cannot be wicked and cannot inflict wrong (v. 10). Justice is at the heart of his nature. He will keep his promise to repay the righteous and wicked according to what they deserve. He will not pervert justice. That would be against his nature. Elihu is clearly well trained in the worldview found in Wisdom literature. He cannot believe that something as fundamental as God's justice could ever be open to question. Thus he opposes Job's premise that God has become unjust: he hasn't, because he cannot become so.

It is imperative that God should be just, because there is no higher power on which to call. Job had called for a judge between himself and God, but that should not be necessary since God is the supreme judge. He is the creator who laid the foundations of the world (v. 13). If he ceased maintaining that creation, all people would perish. We might think of the time when that nearly happened—the period of the flood (see Genesis 6 to 9). Elihu's argument is for the greatness of God: as creator, God has a responsibility to maintain the world according to the order laid down and according to certain principles, notably that of justice. Elihu phrases his comments here as rhetorical questions: of course, no one *gave* God charge over the earth; rather, God is simply in charge (v. 13). He is the one completely in control. If he withdrew his spirit from the world and took the breath of life back, all would cease (v. 14).

As Job believes that God has got it all wrong and that the wicked are prospering while innocents such as himself suffer, Elihu, by contrast, thinks of the wrongness of believing that God could not be just. He calls people to listen yet again (v. 16)—a sign of insecurity, perhaps? If God hates justice, Elihu asks, why is he governing? (v. 17). Only those who are just should govern. Job is wrongly condemning one who is righteous and mighty, one who delivers just punishments even to rulers if they are wicked (v. 18). God treats all equally. He does not prefer the poor, since all people are his creation. This is an important insight, which we would do well to remember if we downgrade others, as we all have a tendency to do at times.

Human beings die swiftly (v. 20). At night they pass away, and this includes mighty and poor alike: we are all equal in death (compare Ecclesiastes 3:20). Elihu is incredulous that anyone would dare to question God in this manner.

PRAYER

Lord, help us to help each other and not to be too judgmental of another's plight. Help us to recognize that you are a God of love as well as of justice, and let us be aware of your life-giving presence.

94

GOD IS ALL-SEEING

It is interesting that the focus of Elihu's speech is on the nature of God, as that is what he believes the friends and Job have failed to appreciate. How Elihu imagines that he has a hotline to the Almighty, we do not know! He says in verses 21–22 that God sees all: he sees all that people are doing, he watches the paths along which they tread, and there is no hiding from God's presence. Evildoers should not believe that their deeds are covered by the darkness. A time will come in the future when all people will be judged according to their deeds, but not yet. God is not afraid to punish: he will shatter the mighty if they have done wrong and set others to rule in their place (v. 24). God knows what they have been up to, and so he strikes them down for their wickedness. They turned aside from the path of following God: they were like the wicked who either ignore God or do not think that they need him (v. 27). They ignored his demands and perpetuated injustice against the poor and unfortunate. God hears the sighs of those afflicted by the mighty and so he punishes (v. 28).

It is interesting that while earlier Elihu had wanted to state that mighty and powerless alike were subject to God's punishment and that there was no partiality to rich rather than poor, here it is the poor and afflicted who gain his attention most. We are more used to this kind of emphasis in the Bible in the prophets and in the New Testament.

Hiding his face

As we have seen, in many places in the Old Testament God is said to be hiding his face. This is a way of stating that God does not appear to be looking at the injustice being perpetuated. It is not an accusation against God that he has forgotten people or wronged them (as Job might think); rather, it is a feeling that God is looking away, that he is busy with other thoughts or activities (v. 29). Elihu makes the point that when God is just being quiet, there is no reason to blame him. When he hides his face, no one has access to him: there is no question of partiality. Whether a nation or simply individuals, none can have access to God when his face is hidden.

The choice of repentance

Elihu now moves on to the idea that one who has been chastised by the punishment of God might be humble enough to say to him, 'I will not offend any more' (v. 31). This person would have the openness to learn, to be taught the errors of his ways. If this is done, God will surely receive this person back (v. 32). Again Elihu poses these thoughts in question form. He asks, 'Has anyone said to God…?' Presumably the expected answer is 'Yes, they have.' And then, 'Will he (God) pay back…?' Presumably the expected answer is 'No' here. A proper repentance, then, will be accepted by God, and it is the rejection of iniquity that will lead to a righting of the relationship. God will not reject a repentant person, because he is just.

We all make choices all the time, every day and in large and small matters. Now Elihu presents Job with the choice that he has: he must decide whether he has knowledge, whether there is more he can learn—whether, in fact, to repent (v. 33). Elihu quotes the wise, who say that Job speaks without knowledge (v. 35). He is inferring here that he agrees with their estimate, but instead of condemning Job outright, he has a more veiled and subtle way of trying to persuade him. The use of this roundabout way of accusing Job, as the friends did when they were being more respectful to Job, is one way in which Elihu achieves this subtle persuasion.

The estimate of the wise seems to be that because Job has questioned God and because he is suffering, he must have sinned, and so he must have chosen to belong to the wicked (v. 36). He perpetuates his sins by this rebellion against God. This is what Elihu particularly disapproves of—Job's attack on God. For Elihu, God is beyond reproach. The more Job speaks against God, the worse his situation becomes (v. 37). He is digging his own pit.

PRAYER

Lord, guide us in our choices and decision-making,
every day of our lives.

95

DARING *to* ANSWER GOD BACK

There is a certain repetition in what Elihu has to say, which is reflected in this passage. He is still concerned about God's justice, and outraged that Job dares to question it. He asks Job whether he should justify himself as 'in the right' before God (v. 2). Elihu finds this an abhorrent thought. He posits a situation where Job might be asking what advantage he has: he is at his lowest ebb and seems to be no better off than if he had sinned (v. 3). But Elihu has an answer to that, which he elaborates in the rest of this passage. Again, the focus is on himself as the one who is providing the answer where others have failed—a slight cockiness of youth emerges. Once again Elihu appeals to the greatness of God: 'Look up at the heavens and the clouds,' he says (v. 5). Of course, in those days, people couldn't see above the clouds as we can today in aeroplanes: the clouds were seen to be at one with the heights of heaven. Elihu asks what Job is expecting to get out of battling against God. If Job has sinned, what will he accomplish? The thought is that he is just worsening his situation by shouting at God. And if Job is righteous, what does God get out of it? Job should be more concerned, perhaps, about how his actions affect others.

Leading by example

This section ends with the thought of the ways in which Job's behaviour affects God (vv. 6–7) and others (v. 8). Regarding God, Elihu asks how Job imagines God might feel when sinned against. Conversely, how does God feel when a person behaves righteously? Regarding others, it is true that our wicked or righteous behaviour (whichever we choose) has a profound effect. If we love others, they respond, but if we hurt them we cause them pain. It is a key point in all religious systems that the way a person acts is an essential aspect of their relationship, first with God and second with other people. At the heart of the Christian message is our relationship with God and the way that we should treat other people—that is, as we ourselves would like to be treated.

A case of oppression

Elihu speaks of a test-case in which people are crying out in anguish because they have been oppressed by the powerful (v. 9). But ironically, no one recognizes the God who gives strength in the midst of anguish and gives wisdom to human beings over all other creatures (vv. 10–11). They are blind to him and do not recognize the great one, the Creator of all. Thus God does not listen to them. The message here is that if people do not recognize God, he will not help them. He doesn't answer people who are proud of perpetuating evil (v. 12). Their cries of anguish are empty because these people are not crying to God (v. 13).

Having cited the test-case, Elihu turns to Job. The reason that Job is not receiving an answer from God is just this—that God does not heed the wicked. Job of course is a God-fearing man, but because of his sins God is not taking heed. Elihu sees Job as having laid his case arrogantly before God, and now waiting for a reply. How misguided Job must be! God is not punishing Job but he is not heeding him because of his sin.

Elihu ends by accusing Job of empty talk and of multiplying words (v. 16). As we have seen, this is a common accusation in the wisdom literature—that people babble on without much substance to what they are saying. I sometimes feel this in the presence of the radio or television: the air-time has to be filled with endless talk. How valuable is it? There is a value in silence and in quietness that we seem to have forgotten in our busy, noisy world.

PRAYER

Lord, help us to set a good example to other people
and witness to our faith through our deeds.

96

GOD IS MIGHTY & JUST

Elihu's confidence seems to reach new heights in this chapter. He claims to be speaking on God's behalf (v. 2) and to have special knowledge from afar (v. 3). He swears that he is telling the truth and that 'one who is perfect in knowledge is with you' (v. 4). Does this claim refer to himself or God? We might assume the latter and that Elihu is God's spokesman, and yet the way it is phrased suggests that Elihu thinks he has all the answers and is speaking the mind of God. He is falling into a worse trap now than the three friends!

Elihu reiterates God's might and justice in dealing with people. God takes no sides; he does not dislike anybody (v. 5). He understands everything and metes out punishment only where it is deserved. He kills off the wicked, but gives the afflicted what they deserve (v. 6). He makes sure that the righteous flourish: they will rule for ever like kings (v. 7). If they are mistakenly imprisoned or caught in affliction, then God tells them what is what (vv. 8–9). If they have sinned or behaved arrogantly, they will know it. Thus, if they are afflicted, there is some good cause.

The suffering of the righteous (Job's position) does not seem to be held out as a possibility here. All has to be black and white because God, in Elihu's view, is working to a straightforward system of justice.

The importance of listening

The wisdom literature stresses the importance of listening as well as the merits of careful speech. In verse 10 the thought is that people should listen to God through instruction—as in the wisdom writings—and also through the law, such as the Ten Commandments (Exodus 20; Deuteronomy 5). These two elements give people the guidelines that they need to lead a righteous life, so they should be carefully heeded. It is all very straightforward for Elihu. If people listen and serve God, then they will lead prosperous and pleasant lives; but if they do not listen they will perish—and they will also die without knowledge, that great prize of wisdom. All of Elihu's comments apply in a veiled way to Job's situation: Job should stop aligning himself with the wicked in questioning God's ways, and instead acknowledge God's discipline.

It is interesting that Elihu feels that godlessness is a worse crime than wickedness. The friends in their speeches spoke of the wicked or the sinner, but because of Elihu's emphasis on the importance of God and the relationship with God, his focus is on the godless. In fact, he makes subtle distinctions between the afflicted who are God-fearing and need God's help (v. 15) and the afflicted who do not recognize God and so are punished (vv. 13–14). The godless cherish anger and do not cry for help to God when they are punished by him: presumably they simply do not acknowledge him. They die young; they are shamed. The godless afflicted are made so deliberately—the chastisement of adversity is designed to make them listen.

Back to Job

Now the veil is lifted and Elihu turns to 'you' (v. 16), presumably Job. God gave Job good things and prosperity, and he is offering those things again. Elihu accuses Job of being obsessed with the case of the wicked, with the question of God's justice, instead of just listening to God and accepting his fate (v. 17). He warns Job not to turn into a scoffer because he is angry at God, and not to be lured off a sensible path (v. 18). He tells Job that crying out will not help; nor will trying to force God's hand (v. 19). Job is foolish to long for the night when people die (v. 20). Elihu accuses Job of turning to iniquity because of his afflictions.

For Elihu, God can do no wrong. He is exalted and powerful and he teaches what is right if only people will listen. He is the wisdom teacher *par excellence*. He makes the rules and is beyond reproach. Who, then, can prescribe what God should do and who can tell God that he has done wrong? The answer to this rhetorical question is surely, 'No one!'

This is a very straightforward picture of God as judge, which is clear and easy to follow, but the point of the book of Job is to say that life is messier than this, that innocent people do suffer and that answers are not quite as easy as they might at first appear. It is sometimes said that as children we tend to have a more black-and-white view of the world, encouraged by our parents, who are keen to simplify and make life straightforward for us, but that as we grow older we increasingly realize the subtleties of difficult situations and ideas. Perhaps Elihu is showing something of the folly of youth here!

PRAYER

Lord, help us to understand your power and justice, but not to become dogmatic in our assurance of that understanding so that we fail to see your greatness.

SINGING HIS PRAISES

Elihu continues his eulogy to God. He reminds all humans, Job included, to extol God's work, and he reminds us that people have always sung praises to God (v. 24). Hymnody is a fundamental part of our worship today, and so it has been for a long time. We have the psalms as witness to the fact that praise was sung from earliest times. We have hymns from the ancient Near East too: for example, the Egyptian 'Hymn to Aten', which extolled the the one god of the sun, is an early witness to monotheistic belief in an ancient culture. Usually the eulogy is about the greatness of God's works—but not so Job's words, it seems.

Elihu says that God's works are manifest for all to see (vv. 25), presumably referring to nature. We can all see the workings of nature and we can all wonder at it. Elihu anticipates the speeches of God here: he is calling Job, as God will, to consider, in an implicit rather than explicit question, whether he understands the ways of God in creation and nature. God's greatness and majesty are emphasized (v. 26). There is the sentiment that God is so entirely 'other' that human beings can say nothing to him. God is so great that we cannot know him: his time is different to our time and his existence is for ever.

Clouds and rain

Verses 27–29 give us a description of rain and clouds. In a pre-scientific age, rain was clearly a source of great wonder. God was seen to draw up the water and then pour it down from the skies, getting human beings thoroughly wet. Elihu asks a rhetorical question: 'Can anyone understand the spreading of the clouds?' Clearly, for the people of that time, the answer was 'No'. Neither did anyone understand where the thunder comes from. We take this knowledge for granted today. There is still much that we don't understand about the natural world, but basic facts such as these are well known.

In verse 31 the social order is closely linked to the purposes of the natural order. It is clearly Elihu's view that human beings are the pinnacle of God's creation and of God's purposes, and it is interesting that he does not mention animals. By contrast, in the speeches of God there is a great stress on the animal world alongside human concerns. Maybe Elihu is demonstrating a more anthropocentric view than is healthy? In modern times, with our increasing understanding of the importance of the whole ecosystem in the flourishing and perpetuation of life, we might prefer God's emphasis to Elihu's here.

Thunder and lightning

There is a wonderful line in the *St Matthew Passion* by J.S. Bach that asks, in rhetorical mode, 'Have lightnings and thunders forgotten their fury?' It is sung first by the bass voices and is, in many ways, one of the most exciting choral parts of the entire oratorio. The thunder and the lightning are personified and they are associated with anger. These elements have traditionally been regarded as manifestations of the power of God (as well as of the Canaanite god Baal). God is seen to scatter lightning, as in a storm, and to be able to send rain gushing into the sea (v. 30). This denotes the scope of his activity as well as his power. By his power he governs peoples and provides food. He has the power in his hands: he can wield the lightning wherever he wants it to strike. It will crash upon the earth all around him, and if he is angry, he uses it freely.

This is a daunting and frightening picture of God, the powerful one. Elihu is presenting here a one-sided picture of God that we might want to question. The power of God is true and real, and yet perhaps it needs to be tempered in our own thinking by more personal aspects of a loving and giving God. Elihu is not concerned with presenting a gentle God, however, because he wishes to frighten Job into submission. We can all present one side of an argument without the other in order to persuade people. However, in the long run, a more balanced view is fairer to both sides.

PRAYER

God, we know your power in nature and on behalf of human beings, but we also know your love. Help us to be unstinting in our songs of praise for your name.

RESPONSE *to* GOD

Elihu is fired up when he thinks about the power of the Almighty. His heart trembles and leaps up (v. 1). When we are excited, we feel this happening inside: the heart beats faster and adrenalin makes us want to leap up and down with joy. Elihu is an enthusiast.

God the creator

Psalm 29 describes God the creator who speaks in the thunder and lightning, and we find the same imagery here in verses 2–5. There is a possible connection here with imagery used of Baal, the Canaanite god of thunder: perhaps the ancient writers transposed that imagery to describe Yahweh. Elihu urges everyone to listen to the thunder, which is God's voice (v. 2). Just as the sound of thunder fills the sky, so does God's word. Similarly, the lightning appears to stretch across the whole world. These are signs of God's power. Despite our present-day knowledge of the causes of these phenomena, we still find many people with superstitions about thunder and lightning: lightning strikes are still commonly regarded as 'acts of God'.

There follows a description of God's creative activity, which is done for its own sake, not for humanity's sake. God makes the snow and rain fall (vv. 6–7). When it rains, animals take shelter (v. 8). He also sends whirlwinds (just what we are going to get in chapter 38!) and cold winds. He freezes the waters, he loads up the clouds with moisture and the clouds scatter lightning (vv. 10–11). Elihu's point is that the elements are in the control of God: they do what he wills. And no one knows why God does these things—whether for correction, or for the land itself, or for love, we do not know (v 13).

The argument that God does whatever he wills is one that Job has used to stress God's arbitrariness. Elihu confirms this characteristic of God, but he delights in it rather than criticizing it. The mysteriousness of nature and God's consequent inscrutability are confirmed.

God knows more than we do

God's greatness means that he is infinitely superior to human beings. God calls the tune: at his command, lightning shines within a cloud (v. 15), and he balances the clouds (v. 16). 'Does Job know how he does it?' asks Elihu. The answer is, 'No, of course he doesn't'. God's knowledge is perfect, and his works are known only to him. Elihu is stressing God's complete 'otherness' and omniscience. Of course, today we do know many of the reasons why things happen in the natural world, of which our forebears had no inkling. Yet, even with our knowledge of the genetic make-up of all life and other such incredible discoveries, we are still a long way from knowing everything. Human beings can do none of these things that God does. When we feel hot in our clothing, it is because God has sent the gentle south wind (v. 17). We cannot 'spread out the skies' (that is, perform creative acts) as God does (v. 18). Mere mortals are as nothing—we even have to be taught what to say to him. We are in the dark compared to God, floundering around.

Elihu says that we cannot even draw up our own case (v. 19), which is a dig at Job, who has presented his case before God. Elihu thinks that Job is making a fool of himself by his actions. Furthermore, God is so great, says Elihu, that one ought to approach him with hesitation and awe. Should God be told that someone wants to speak? he asks, hesitantly (v. 20). We are reminded, perhaps, of people who inspire such awe in us that we feel tongue-tied and awkward in their presence and wish that the ground below our feet would open up.

No one can look on bright light, nor on God, such is his splendour (v. 21). We might think, here, of Ezekiel's vision of God sitting high upon a throne in majesty and might (Ezekiel 1—3). God dwells where human beings cannot even find him. He is great and mighty and, most of all, just. The only thing we can do is fear him: he does not have time for those who are wise in their own eyes only (v. 24).

So Elihu finishes his diatribe and rests his case. His main emphasis in the last six chapters has been on God's power and justice, which he feels that Job has not properly understood. Elihu anticipates much of what God himself will say about his power in the universe, and has an even more dogmatic emphasis on the reward of right and punishment of wrong than the three friends had.

We have heard from too many people who think they know the mind of God. The stage is now set for God to appear and state his own case.

PRAYER

Help us, Lord, to have a proper respect for and fear of you. Let us rejoice in the world that you have made.

OUT *of the* WHIRLWIND

At last God appears and answers Job. This is the climax to the book, which has been somewhat delayed by the chapters of speeches from Elihu but now forms its appropriate conclusion. Job's wish appears to be granted: God has appeared as he requested. As in the dialogue, Job has the opportunity to answer God, although it is interesting that his responses are very short and he is overawed by the experience of God's presence. God appears in a whirlwind (v. 1), a common context for a theophany experience (that is, an experience of the presence of God). God is very much the Creator God here, describing his actions on humanity's behalf purely in natural terms. There is no description of God's actions in history, unlike most parts of the Old Testament (for example, in Isaiah 40 to 55, where the acts of creation and redemption are recalled together). God is no longer hiding his face from Job. He is here, seemingly, to respond to Job's questions, but we will see that he does not do so in a satisfactory manner.

Who is this?

God's first words to Job are a question that sounds like an accusation. Job seems to be scolded: 'Who is this that darkens counsel by words without knowledge?' (v. 2). God could be referring to Elihu here, although reference to Job seems more likely, since the whole debate seems to centre on the two of them. The accusation sounds very much like the sentiments of the friends—that Job is full of words but without understanding. God tells Job to 'gird up his loins' (v. 3), implying that Job needs to muster some strength. There is a suggestion here that Job needs to take his destiny into his own hands instead of blaming God for his misfortune. God declares that he will question Job and will expect some response (v. 3b). Job had many questions, and God is responding to them with ever more questions, many of them rhetorical, as Job's were.

These verses are a parody of passages in which human beings praise God as creator, asking questions out of a sense of wonder (for example, Isaiah 40:12–26). Here the tables are turned and God is asking the questions. The overall message that starts to come across is that God's knowledge and power are greater than those of human beings. This is what Elihu had warned, and now God himself makes it plain to Job.

Where were you?

God asks Job questions that he will never be able to answer because they are impossibilities. 'Where were you when I laid the foundation of the earth?' (v. 4). Was Job there to know the order contained within the creation that God has made? How can Job hope to understand the order of creation if he had no part in the task? Of course, the one who is described as having partaken in the task of creation is Wisdom herself (Proverbs 8). Is this, then, a suggestion that Job has been overreaching himself in his quest to understand? Only she who was beside God at creation would know the answers to such questions. Who is Job to question God, who is the Creator and has been here from eternity, working out his purpose?

There follows a description of the creative acts, which has similarities with both Psalm 104 and Genesis 1 in that it gives an ordering of the actions that led to the making of earth and seas, light and dark—beginning in this passage with the earth. There is a description of God measuring the earth, which is portrayed as a house with foundations and a cornerstone (vv. 5–6). The 'line' is a plumb-line, as one would use to make sure that the walls of a building were straight. The heavenly world is personified: the stars are seen as singing, while the heavenly beings (either lesser gods or angels) shout for joy. The creation of the earth is an occasion for joy and wonder—the kind of wonder, multiplied many times, that we might feel as we gaze on a beautiful natural scene.

PRAYER

*Lord, help us as we increase our knowledge of your world,
to use that knowledge wisely and not to overstep boundaries
or overreach ourselves. Let us rejoice in the world that
you have made and be glad in it.*

The CREATION *of the* SEA

There is something majestic and wonderful about the sea, but something frightening at the same time. There is a power in the sea, especially when storms gather, that is terrifying and that sweeps away all in its path. God is seen here as having not only created the sea but also as having restrained it (v. 8). His power is such that he can do these things. In Genesis 1 we read about the waters of chaos: out of these waters God created earth and sea, but the sea needs to be restrained in order that the earth may prosper and survive. Continuing the building motif, we have a description of God holding the sea in with doors, although some have suggested that this refers to the sand that contains the sea. Verse 8 also likens the waters of the sea to the waters that break at the birth of a child. There may be overtones here of ancient Near Eastern myth, in which the aforementioned chaos monster, once born, needs to be restrained so that it will not destroy the world (compare Psalm 104:9, in which God 'set a boundary that they [the waters] may not pass, so that they might not again cover the earth'). The sheer greatness of God's deeds is highlighted, then, by his creative act in restraining the sea.

Clouds

The personification of the sea continues with the idea of garments and swaddling clothes (v. 9). The clouds are the sea's garment—a reference to the way the clouds hover over the sea, perhaps. Likewise, the darkness is its swaddling band: the action of wrapping a child at birth, for warmth and to control its flailing limbs, is likened here to the first controlling of this potentially dangerous force, the sea.

Boundaries

We return to the idea of boundaries. Bounds and bars and doors are carefully set up to control the sea (v. 10). This may refer indirectly to the rocks and cliffs of the shoreline. We are reminded, perhaps, of the way we have to set boundaries for young children. They need to know the rules in order to learn what is appropriate behaviour and what is not. We all live with boundaries on our behaviour all the time, which are so much a part of us that we don't even think about them.

God decrees the limits of the sea and says, 'You shall only come this far.' The waves are described as proud (v. 11): they will take over if they can. There is a pride that comes with might and power, and that is the nature of the sea. This is a wonderful description of the sea personified, which really conveys to us both the nature of this great force and the majesty of God in creating and confining it.

PRAYER

Lord, you set boundaries on the world. Help us to know our
own boundaries in relation to our attempts to achieve,
and in our dealings with others.

101   JOB 38:12–18

The CREATION of the MORNING

Verse 12 calls us to remember the creation of morning (and, correspondingly, evening). We might compare this to the creation of morning and evening in Genesis 1. God poses a question to Job: has he commanded the morning during his life? (v. 12). Of course the expected answer is 'No'. Only God commands each day into existence. We have to remember that the ancients did not know, as we do now, that both light and darkness are being experienced on different sides of the earth at any one time.

God commands the dawn, personified, to know its place. The stress is on the order of creation in which the elements of everyday life take their place so as to create the regularity of each daybreak. The mention of the dawn reminds us, perhaps, of Job's diatribe in chapter 3, when he curses the dawn of the day of his birth.

The regularity of day and night and of the seasons is something we all take for granted. God's speeches in Job remind us of our need to wonder at the everyday and the familiar, something we all too easily forget to do.

Wickedness overcome

God's listing of his deeds in verses 13 and 15 includes some mention of 'the wicked', but their part is almost incidental given the greatness of the acts of God that are being described. However, it is interesting that the righteous–wicked model is seen to be a part of the structure of the universe: its 'order' is inseparable from the moral order. The creative pattern is linked up, then, with a moral order in which there is no place for the wicked. The principles of retributive justice are upheld in the very created order itself.

The dawn is described in verse 13 as taking hold of the 'skirts of the earth'. The earth is being compared to a tablecloth which is cleansed of its dirt by one who takes hold of the ends and gives it a good shake (v. 13). So the wicked who work at night are shaken out of the earth in the morning as dawn breaks. It is curious how threatening the night can be with its shadows, noises and dark corners, and, by contrast, how bright and pleasant the daytime is, when everything is open and people walk about in relative safety. We are reminded that God is the creator of both.

The description of the earth continues in verse 14: it is 'changed like clay'—presumably a reference to the way clay dries when it is used to seal something—or dyed like a garment. The point is that the earth is changed, as these items are, when the dawn breaks. Light changes all the colours of night, and a brightness pervades the earth. The wicked, however, are robbed of light: they occupy the realm of darkness. They lift up their arms but their arms are swiftly broken (v. 15)—that is, they are cut down quickly, almost as soon as they rise up.

The deep places

A few more rhetorical questions follow. Has Job been where God has been, into the springs of the sea (presumably its sources), or has he walked in the depths of the ocean? (v. 16). We are reminded, perhaps, of divers who do just that! But the idea here is that the answer is 'No': only God can do these things. There is a strong emphasis on the sheer expanse of the earth.

Another boundary is described in verse 17—that between life and death. God has walked the ocean shore and been to the gates of death (v. 17), which bar the entrance to the realm of the dead so that no one can leave. With the reference to 'the expanse of the earth' (v. 18), both depth and breadth have been stressed in this passage. Does Job realize the extent of what he doesn't know?

PRAYER

Lord, we rejoice in your power and your strength and in the mysteries of your creation. We rejoice at the breaking of each new day and give thanks for it.

The QUESTIONS CONTINUE

God's tirade continues with more questions about creation. It is clear that Job does not know any of the things he is being asked; the idea is simply to make him aware of the greatness and otherness of God, along similar lines to Elihu's argument but with less emphasis on God's justice and more on his greatness. The first question is about the way to the dwellings of light and darkness. This might remind us of Job 28, the hymn to Wisdom, which asks where wisdom dwells. These are impossible questions for people of that time: we could perhaps have a stab at the answer today, although the more we find out about light and its origins, the more marvellous and complex the subject becomes. If Job found out where light dwells, he could go to its territory and work out the paths that led there. The image of the path is strong here: knowing the way to something is a means of having control over it. The point is that Job cannot know the way to these natural phenomena. They are the realm of God alone.

Sarcasm

There is a sarcastic note in God's jibe to Job: 'Surely you know' (v. 21). Job is being accused of arrogance in thinking that he knows how God works. Of course Job wasn't born at the time of creation and so he does not know. There is much that he does not know—that is the message. Job is an older man, but not so old as to know about the beginnings of the universe! Is this an attempt at humour? Longevity is a sign of blessing, and Job eventually receives it, but even a life as long as his would be insufficient to have full understanding of God's creative acts.

Secret stores

Verse 22 gives us the image of storehouses where snow and hail are gathered, ready to be used where necessary. This fits in with the idea that the elements are manifestations of God's character—his anger and so on. The snow and hail are stored up ready to use on a day of battle or strife. God is well prepared.

Now comes another question: 'What is the way to the place where the light is distributed?' (v. 24). The place of distribution is distinct from the place where light dwells (v. 19). This again is controlled by God, as is the scattering of the wind. Does Job know where that comes from? The emphasis in these verses is on the wonder of creation and on its intricate workings as set up by God. Job needs reminding, perhaps, of the complexity of the universe, and of his relatively small place in it. He needs to be reminded of how little he really knows and how wondrous the created world is. We are all in danger of forgetting the enormity of the universe. Even with our success in understanding much of its working, we still have some way to go before we can comprehend it all. Are we, like Job, losing the capacity to wonder at creation?

PRAYER

We rejoice in your creation and in your created world, Lord, and we are proud to be a part of it.

RAIN

Questions continue, this time about who is in charge of the way the rain falls into channels (v. 25). We can all call to mind very wet days when the water seems to charge from the sky and immediately channels are cut in the earth that drain the water away. In a hot climate, this process is more noticeable as the dry earth is hardly able to take the water and the flooding can be more dramatic (vv. 26–27). We are reminded here that God is in charge of the process.

Rain comes even in places where no one lives, such as the heart of the desert (v. 26). The idea is to give the vegetation some water and to bring life out of dryness. Perhaps the thought here is that creation is not just for the benefit of humans. It is for all life, and God's actions are for plants and animals as well as human beings in their habitats. The effect of these questions is to express the wonder of God, who does all these deeds that we take for granted.

Dew and water

We are reminded in verse 28 of that early morning freshness when dew forms a covering to all plants and to the grass, giving essential moisture to the earth. God is responsible for that too. There is an interesting use of masculine and feminine images together in verses 28 and 29: God is the 'father' of rain and dew, but the ice comes forth from God's 'womb' too. This would suggest a more gender-inclusive picture of God in the Bible than many have acknowledged. The image of the womb is continued with the idea of giving birth to hoarfrost—the really thick frost that will turn water to hard ice. (This also recalls 38:8 in which the sea is said to burst forth from its womb.)

Reference to the waters in verse 30 recalls the waters divided at creation. The frost turns water hard and even the sea is frozen. The kind of image we might have in our minds here is of the Arctic or Antarctic regions, where the sea is frozen in parts and huge icebergs rise up.

The stars of heaven

The questioning of Job, about whether he can know what God knows in the establishing of the world, continues. Verses 31–32 turn to the constellations and their patterns. Ancient astrologers and astron-omers knew a good deal about these things, which were included in the range of interests of wise men. There is a sense in which this description is a revelation of what was known about the world at that time. The stars and their patterns behave according to certain rules. Does Job know them? Did he establish them? Of course, the answer is 'No'. Job is definitively being put in his place here.

Job is asked whether he can make the clouds spill rain, or decide to start a lightning storm (v. 34–35). The answer is again presumably 'No'! The lightning storms are personified here in their spoken response to God: 'Here we are,' they say. This is rather a nice idea—that the elements respond to God personally when they do his will. There is, of course, no question of the elements disobeying God or questioning his ways, as Job has done.

God turns suddenly from the great to the small. The wisdom that is placed in every person, into the mind and inward parts, is also from him (v. 36). Then he shifts back to the cosmic again: the wisdom to number the clouds is beyond human wisdom; it is the realm of God (v. 37). This speech can be seen as an attack on human wisdom. When it comes to the 'big' questions about order and creation, humans are left behind. Only God, presumably, can 'tilt the water-skins of the heavens'—a reference to the clouds spilling over with water, as a waterskin does when it is filled with water. When there is rain, the dust forms clods that cling together: God causes that to happen too (v. 38). He is in charge—there is no question of that.

PRAYER

Lord, rain is a great gift, bringing life to a parched soil. We give thanks for the water that gives us life. Let us never take these things for granted.

The ANIMAL WORLD

God's sphere of activity includes the animal world, and here we have a description of the lion and the raven, two powerful animals. Can Job hunt prey for the lion? (v. 39). Of course not. Lions naturally hunt, but God is behind their instinctive behaviour. He made it so. Young lions are always hungry. Can Job satisfy their hunger? No, but God has made satisfaction of hunger possible in the way that they hunt, lying in wait and moving effortlessly and noiselessly towards their prey. There is awe at the habits of the lion in this description.

God also provides prey for the ravens (v. 41). Again, the young of the bird are vulnerable, but God provides. The thought here is that the young ravens cry to God and he answers them. The animal world has no problem in recognizing God, unlike many human beings, sadly.

The description of animals continues in chapter 39, still in the form of questions to Job. Job is asked whether he knows the habits of mountain goats (v. 1)—when they give birth, for example. God alone knows the times. He is all-seeing and watches the deer calving. Because deer are by nature easily frightened, this would be difficult for any human being to observe at close hand. God's care for every living creature is being emphasized here: he ensures that calves are in the womb of the deer for the right number of months and then they give birth. God has made this a natural process: the deer crouch to give birth and are delivered of their young.

Young growing up

The young then grow up and leave the nest (v. 4). In the animal world, the leaving of young, and even the rejection of young, by the parents is a common and natural process. I watched my mother cat look after her four kittens with immense care and some good discipline thrown in—but then, when I kept two of the kittens and they grew up, the mother distanced herself and became irritated with the youngsters, as if to say, 'Haven't you left yet?' Of course, there are no cats in the Bible and the creatures described here are wild, not domesticated, but the process is the same. As human beings, we show interest in our young long after they have flown the nest, but in the animal world the distinction between young and mature is more clear-cut.

Wild asses

More questions, this time about wild asses. 'Who has let the wild ass go free?' (v. 5). God, of course. These animals roam the land and God provides for them in their natural habitat. It is the ass's nature to be free and wild, and yet human beings want to tame it and use it for labour in their cities. The wild ass, though, scorns such taming and the authority of human beings. It ranges wide and it searches for greenery all day. This is a rather idealistic picture of God's real intention for asses. The reality probably falls short of the ideal, and yet the ideal is what is being described here in this eulogy to God as creator.

PRAYER

Lord, we give thanks for the animals and for the sheer variety that we find on our small planet.

The WILD OX

We move from wild ass to wild ox. Will the wild ox serve Job? (v. 9).
Of course not—only a tamed one would do that. But for God anything
is possible. The wild ox will not spend the night at Job's crib (images
of Christ's nativity are perhaps conjured up for Christians here). The
wild ox will not labour with ropes attached, making furrows in the
earth, and it will not allow Job to depend on it because of its great
strength (vv. 10–11). These things are all done to tamed oxen, working
on behalf of human beings who channel the ox's strength and make it
labour for them. Wild oxen would not be as reliable as tamed ones:
they would not return and bring grain to the threshing-floor (v. 12).
The point is that the service of humanity was not God's original intention in creating these animals. Wild oxen have a freedom that tamed
ones don't. Similarly, God has freedom to act.

The ostrich

The next example is the ostrich, who again acts according to its own
rules as laid down by God (v. 13). The wings flap—unnecessarily, it
seems, since the ostrich cannot fly, and one reason for that is the lack
of plumage on the wings. It leaves its eggs on the earth and does not
sit on the eggs and care for the young in the way other birds do (v. 14).
It forgets that a foot may crush the eggs as they lie on the earth, or that
a wild animal may trample on them (v. 15). These habits appear cruel
by human standards, but the ostrich is programmed by God to behave
in this way. The thought here is that not all standards have to be
human ones. To believe otherwise is to limit the realm of God's activity. This is perhaps what Job has tried to do—as have the friends, in
their attempts to understand what has happened to him. Perhaps only
Elihu spotted the might of God, but his sense of God's justice limited
him also. The ostrich may well lay eggs that do not come to fruition,
and yet it does not appear to be concerned, unlike humans, who spend
a good deal of time worrying about things over which they have no
control.

We read that God appears to have made the ostrich 'forget wisdom'
(v. 17) and given it 'no share in understanding', but perhaps that refers
to human wisdom and standards. These animals are a law unto them-

selves, and there is a sense of freedom in that. The ostrich spreads its plumes and 'laughs at the horse and its rider' (v. 18): it can outrun them, and it glories in its difference from them.

The horse

There follows a wonderful description of the horse—of its might, its mane, its leaping and snorting (vv. 19–20). Again Job is being asked if he gave the horse all these attributes, and of course the answer is that the giving of attributes is in the realm of God. God makes all the animals, each with a startling individuality, with its own beauty and its own role in life. The pawing of the horse on the ground is described, along with its function in war. It is brave and laughs at fear: it rides courageously into battle (v. 22). It is attacked by quiver, spear and javelin and yet it is undeterred. It gets angry and fierce, frightening its opponents, and when the trumpet sounds it is ready for battle. It even smells the battle from a distance—the thunderous noise and the shouting. It is an inspiration to human beings. Interestingly, this description is of the horse's role in relation to humans, which is rather different from the descriptions of the wild animals whose existence, it was stressed, was not reliant on human activity, and whose true nature was revealed by being in the wild.

The hawk and the eagle

The final descriptions in this chapter are of the hawk and the eagle. The hawk soars high and spreads its wings wide (v. 26). Again, is it Job's wisdom that causes this to happen? Of course not; it is God's. The eagle too—a great and strong bird—rises up and makes a high nest (v. 27). It lives on rocky crags far away from human habitation and in a good position to watch for its prey. It is a bloodthirsty creature, looking to kill prey from a long distance and feeding on bloody corpses where it can. Its young get the taste of blood early on, when they are fed dead meat. It seems to follow its own rules, different from human rules but, again, set up by God to match the nature and needs of the animal and to give it a role in the grand plan of creation.

PRAYER

Lord, we give thanks for the animals that help human beings
in their daily tasks, as well as rejoicing in the
freedom of wild animals.

GOD'S PARTING SHOT

God now provides his summary statement at the end of his first speech: 'Shall a faultfinder contend with the Almighty?' (v. 1). God has given us an impressive display of his might. Does Job dare to contend with that? Job is presumably the 'faultfinder' here, but the question refers more widely to anyone who dares to question God. God taunts Job to respond to him here, reminding us of Job's numerous taunts to God. God has revealed that the universe is a mystery: it was not created just for human use, and so neither it nor its creator can be judged solely by human standards. The natural world reveals God's order, and its pattern and meaning are just discernible by human beings, although its real secrets are with God (compare Job 28).

Job's response

Job begins to answer in verse 3. He realizes that he is a nobody compared to God and his deeds. It seems that God has convinced him in a way that the others failed to do. He is overawed and doesn't know (for the first time!) how to reply. Scholars have made the point that it doesn't really matter what God says, or what Job says in his reply: the main issue is that God has appeared to Job, and the answer lies in the interaction. Job had felt that no one was listening to him or understanding his plight, not even God. Thus, in a sense, whatever God says, the fact of his presence is the key thing for Job. It proves that God was listening all along, and cares enough to take the trouble to answer him. This interaction between God and a questioner is an important aspect of Psalm 73, in which the psalmist goes into the sanctuary of God and then sees things in their proper perspective. He fails to understand the things that trouble him, 'until I went into the sanctuary of God; then I perceived their [the wicked's] end' (Psalm 73:17). God's presence in itself helps Job to clarify his position.

Despite the importance of the presence of God at this moment, however, we have seen that there is substance in what God says, and it seems here to have caused Job to become aware of his insignificance in the grand plan of the universe. Job lays his hand upon his mouth: he is silenced and will speak no more, he says (v. 4). God has not answered Job's questions directly, and in that sense God's speeches are an unsatisfactory response. Yet in Job's reaction there seems to be an acknowledgment that he has in a way been satisfied. Whether that is simply because of God's presence or as a result of what he has said is not made clear. Job is effectively silenced by God. He may be overawed or he may be regretting some of his rasher sentiments—we are not told. This is a very much more restrained Job than we have met in previous chapters. In fact, it is ironic in the light of all his previous 'windy words'.

In verse 5, Job uses the technique of numerical heightening, saying, 'I have spoken once… twice…'. He has spoken once and twice, and will go no further than that—although, ironically, we do find a further response in 42:1–6, which is an expression of repentance. There sometimes comes a point in debate and discussion where one party decides to stop talking. It is usually taken as an acknowledgment that the other side is right, although it could mean that the first person is simply tired of debating. Job's silence probably contains both of these elements, as well as a sense of awe and regret at his outspokenness.

We might raise questions about the profundity of this discussion of innocent suffering in the book of Job. Is it satisfactory for God to stress his power and capabilities without providing rational answers to Job's questions? We might think it is not a very satisfactory answer, to say that God does what he will in his own time and that human beings can have no effect on his action. But it is being acknowledged here that there are things that are greater than we can ever understand, and that those things are the realm of God. And the fact that Job appears to accept God's reply suggests that the author too accepts it, unless his response is regarded as very ironic or tongue-in-cheek.

PRAYER

Lord, guide us in our responses to you and to others.
Give us the courage to speak out where appropriate,
but also to keep quiet as necessary.

GOD'S SECOND SPEECH

God answers Job out of the whirlwind again (v. 6), with a second speech. Many scholars feel that this speech may be a secondary addition to the main text: God has already made his points, and now seems to be 'badgering' Job. Did another author think he would reinforce the points by adding this speech—perhaps the same author that added the Elihu speeches? Such questions are elusive. After Job has 'laid his hand on his mouth', perhaps this second speech is not necessary, but it is substantially different in content from the first speech, focusing on the description of two primeval animals rather than giving a range of images from the animal and natural world. It is repetitive, though, in the sense that God is still stressing his power, which was also the subject matter of the first speech.

How dare he!

As before, God tells Job to gird up his loins like a man (v. 7). He has no time for weakness. He wants to question Job and have him answer. How dare Job put God in the wrong? Does Job wish to condemn God in order to justify himself? (v. 8). This is unbelievable. Who is Job to behave like this? God is attacking Job's arrogance here—that he should think he has all the answers! Isn't it clear that Job has nothing like the strength of God? Who thunders in his anger like God? Who matches him in power? (v. 9). Of course, the implied answer is 'No one'.

This is what to do

In being so negative and critical of Job, God could be seen as little better than the friends. But he now tries to be more constructive. He tells Job to have a little more dignity (v. 10), to get rid of his anger and to abhor the proud (vv. 11–12). The inference is that Job is a little too proud of his former good deeds. God tells him to work towards the demise of the wicked and to seek their death if he can (v. 13). Job is being reminded of the constant need to be vigilant in the light of the forces of pride and wickedness that might overtake him. Is there a hint that Job overstepped the mark before? If he behaves aright, then he will be acknowledged by God (this sounds very much like the sentiments of the friends and Elihu) and God will give him the strength to win victory (v. 14).

Job does not answer God back here, but he might have said that he did attempt to do all these things before disaster struck. God seems to be confirming the laws of retribution, the ideas that had been decisively overturned by Job in the dialogue.

PRAYER

Lord, let our protest and our anger be acceptable to you alongside our joy and our pain.

BEHEMOTH

We now move on to a curious animal description. It has been suggested that the Behemoth (v. 15) is a kind of hippopotamus, but verse 19 identifies it as the monster overcome by God at creation. The point is that God made the animals, just as he made humans. He made this great animal that eats plentifully and that is mightily strong (vv. 16–17). Its tail is stiff like a cedar: muscles and sinews abound. Its bones are hard as bronze and its limbs like iron. It sounds very frightening! Is God trying to scare Job now, or is this simply an extension of the point about God's power? It's probably the latter. This creature is so strong and terrible that only God has the power to vanquish it. Like his conquering of the sea, only God can harness its power.

There is a strong tradition in the Old Testament of God having overcome a chaos monster at creation, out of whose body he created the firmament. This has echoes in Babylonian myth, in which Marduk, the high god, creates the world by the division of the body of Tiamat, the chaos monster. It also suggests elements of Canaanite thought, with Leviathan as the dragon overcome at creation. It is interesting, though that, in Israelite thought, Behemoth is itself created by God rather than being an opposing force in the universe that God has to overcome. There is no dualistic picture of pre-existent evil here. God is in full control of everything, creating the elements that other peoples regarded as gods, and even the enemies of creation are ultimately in his power.

Human beings cannot conquer it

The message is that it is far beyond the reach of human beings to overcome such a creature. Behemoth is described as living with the wild animals, lying under lotus plants, in reeds and in the marsh (v. 21), which does suggest a hippopotamus rather than a mythic primordial beast. It receives shade from the lotus trees and willows (v. 22). It is fearless: even when the river is turbulent it has no worries. It has the strength to overcome the power of the river, even when the currents are strong (v. 23). There is a specific reference here to the Jordan river, flowing through Israel and Jordan, suggesting that the story has been localized for the benefit of its hearers or readers. The question is, 'Can human beings capture this beast with hooks and snares?' (v. 24). Presumably the implied answer is 'No'—this is God's domain.

God's power

The fact that the picture seems to alternate here between a real creature—the hippopotamus—and the chaos monster overcome at creation is a source of confusion to readers. Perhaps the author sees one as symbolic of the other. The main theological point being made is about God's might and power, and human limitations. Similarly, the hippopotamus is a creature of great power that causes more human deaths in Africa today than any other animal. We might reflect on the dangerous aspect of nature, which we can so easily forget if we live in towns and far away from such beasts.

PRAYER

*Lord, protect us from mighty and dangerous creatures
that can kill human beings. We recognize them as a part of your
creation which we should treat with respect, but let us not
fall prey to their violence.*

LEVIATHAN

We now turn to Leviathan, the second candidate for chaos monster, as found in a number of psalms and other references in the Old Testament. Here, however, the link with the chaos monster is not made as explicit. The description seems to fit that of a crocodile, another powerful and dangerous beast. Once again Job is being challenged: can he draw out Leviathan with a fishhook? (v. 1). Of course not. Fishhooks wouldn't be much good for handling crocodiles! What about pressing down its tongue with a cord? Unlikely, since it would probably have your head off if you tried to get as near as its tongue. Equally, trying to pierce nose or jaw would be a futile task (v. 2). The inference is that God could do all these things if he wanted to, because God is in relationship with all animals. Job is asked whether he can draw soft words out of the monster (v. 3). God can relate to animals in a more profound way than we can, perhaps. He can make even the most frightening of creatures into friends. Such an animal will make a covenant with God: it will serve him (v. 4), it will play with him, and he can put it on a leash and take it for a walk (v. 5). We are given images here of domestic life (playing with birds, walking with one's children), as if Leviathan was a family pet, and that is what he is for God, who can control him—but not for Job. None of this can be done by Job or, presumably, by any other human being.

Traders haggling

Crocodile skin is a tradable commodity: in verse 6 God asks whether traders will bargain over it. Nowadays that would certainly happen, and crocodiles are killed for their skin, whether legally or illegally, to decorate shoes and handbags. Here in Job, though, the expected answer is, 'No—traders will not bargain over it or divide it up.' The suggestion is that such a thing cannot happen because a crocodile could not be overcome in this way: Job would not be able to harpoon it or fill its head with spears (v. 7). This conclusion seems odd, because we know that these things are possible—and were even in ancient times. This might suggest that an otherworldly battle between God and the chaos monster is also being envisaged, and that the passage is indeed working on two levels, the literal and the figurative.

Battling with a crocodile

Surely no one who ever had a confrontation with a crocodile and survived would want to venture in that direction again! The creature moves like lightning, and the thought of that huge mouth and all those teeth means that doing battle with it is not an appealing prospect. Just to lay hands on it would be enough to anger it and to endanger one's life (v. 8). There is no hope of capturing it easily.

In verse 9, we have the only concrete suggestion that we might be talking about another form of the chaos monster here, with a reference to the gods who were overwhelmed at the sight of it. The idea is, perhaps, that the high God, Yahweh, was able to overcome the dragon where other lesser gods failed, which might suggest cultural cross-fertilization with ancient Near Eastern ideas again.

No one dares to stir up Leviathan (v. 10): this creature is so fierce that it defies all confrontation. No one dares stand before it—except, presumably, God. Who can confront it and be safe? (v. 11). Of course, the implied answer is, 'Only God can'. This is another display of God's might, but also of his uniqueness. Only he has the power to overcome the chaos dragon or to control its earthly relative, the crocodile. Perhaps in ancient times people had more fear of crocodiles than we do today: there would have been more frequent contact with them if they filled rivers other than the Nile.

It is being made clear in this whole speech that the power of these two beasts is such that only God can tame them. Also, Job is being shown that human beings are not the only orbit of God's concern. God is involved with harnessing creation in a continuous way, constantly maintaining it on a daily basis. This is a different sentiment from that found in the human-centred speeches of Elihu. God's power is beyond human comprehension.

PRAYER

Lord, we acknowledge that the world is bigger than human beings alone, and we rejoice in your creation. Help us to preserve habitats and endangered species.

LOOK AT THOSE LIMBS!

The description of Leviathan becomes more awesome as we move through God's speech. Here, its powerful limbs are mentioned, its great strength and its frame (v. 12). It has a double coat of chainmail—a really thick outer skin—which no one can pierce. No one can strip this animal of its impenetrable outer skin. This sounds like a crocodile's skin, hard and tough. Its face also is impenetrable, and its teeth are terrifying (v. 14). The mouth of a crocodile is, of course, its main weapon, alongside its speed. I am reminded, somewhat frivolously, of the wolf posing as Grandmama in the Red Riding Hood story: what gave 'her' away was the size of her teeth!

A back of chainmail

Verse 15 returns to the image of chainmail: the creature's back is described as being made of shields in rows, or like a seal in its impenetrability. The scales are so close together that no air can come between each section. This aspect of the crocodile seems to be of particular fascination to the author. It is probable that the author knew about animals such as these from personal experience. Otherwise, how could he describe them so closely?

Further attributes of crocodiles

The portrayal of Leviathan, or the crocodile, continues with a description of its breathing, which is like fire (vv. 18–21). First, there are flashes of light when it sneezes, such is the impact, and its eyes are likened to the eyelids of the dawn—somewhat sleepy, perhaps. It breathes out flames, and sparks of fire leap out. Smoke comes out of its nostrils just as it does from a boiling pot or from burning rushes. Its breath is so hot that it would set coals alight. This picture has become more terrifying by the minute, and it seems to have moved away from describing a real animal: it is closer to a description of the mythical dragon.

The concern in verses 22–24 is to stress the strength of this beast. Its neck is strong and terrible. The neck is often the weakest part of an animal, but not this one! Its flesh is in folds because it is so big and fat and strong, and the folds cling together in a manner that is firm and immovable. This recalls the earlier description of the outer skin.

Finally, this creature has a hard heart. This is the first description of something inner rather than outer. Its heart is as hard as stone. Whether this suggests that it is unfeeling is uncertain, but it is clearly strong and courageous without any hint of weakness.

PRAYER

Lord, we both fear and wonder at your created world.
You have a purpose in everything; help us to come
ever closer to understanding it.

The GODS FIGHT IT

Another reference to the gods who cannot prevail against this beast appears in verse 25—overtones again of the creative act and of ancient Near Eastern myth. The gods are afraid when it raises itself up, and when it crashes down with its enormous weight, they are terrified. As we have seen, this reference is perhaps intended to demonstrate the power of Yahweh over lesser gods, and reveals a polytheistic worldview behind the description.

No one can prevail

We are told in this passage that arrows and spears bounce off Leviathan like ninepins being scattered. People try to overcome the monster with swords, which, although they penetrate a little, do not kill it. Spears, darts and javelins are also tried, as are arrows, slings and clubs (v. 26). The creature cannot be overcome by human hand, nor by lesser deities. The inference is that only the mighty God can overcome it, although that is not said explicitly.

It is awesome!

The belly of an animal is often a vulnerable part, but in this creature the underparts are sharp and impossible to overcome. It is huge, spreading itself right across the mud (v. 30). It is hot—presumably with the aforementioned fire in its mouth and smoke in its nostrils—so much so that it even makes the sea boil. It leaves a huge wake behind it when it moves in the water, such that one might think the sea had turned white. This starts to sound like the description of a giant whale, such are the dimensions of this enormous creature. We might think of dragons, or of the Loch Ness monster, if they indeed exist! It is a fearless creature, unlike any other animal on earth. It is king of the beasts. The mention of pride in verse 34 suggests that, because of its might, it has a tendency to arrogance. Could there be a hint of criticism of Job in this suggestion?

This poem is often praised for its descriptive insight and high literary quality. Its content, however is somewhat one-tracked: all that these descriptions convey is the power of God over two excessively powerful beasts. It is thus a reiteration of God's power, which the first speech stressed, as did the speeches of Elihu. Job is being given a torrent of reminders about his weakness in the face of God's might. The content has gone well beyond answering Job's questions about God's justice: there is very little mention of any ethical issue here. There is a sense in which God is showing off—as, perhaps, is the author with his poetic gifts and his undoubted knowledge of animals. This is why scholars have seen God's second speech as 'badgering' Job.

PRAYER

Lord we ask for your protection against all that threatens or endangers us. Give us the blessing of your peace and security from harm.

JOB'S SECOND RESPONSE

At last we encounter Job's repentance. In 40:1–2 he began to make moves in this direction. Now, after a second speech from God, he admits that God's power and purposes are undeniable. He has been well and truly put in his place. There is an air of humility about Job here that contrasts significantly with his protestations earlier on. It is hard for any of us to admit that we might have overstated our case—not that we were necessarily wrong, but that we went about something in the wrong way. It takes a person of character to acknowledge their own limitations and then move on from that point in their lives. This is what Job now has to do. He has been told that he did not have all the answers that he thought he had. In fact, he was even asking the wrong questions. He now has to take a different approach. He was not wrong *per se* and we know that he has not sinned, but he had not appreciated the full might of God.

We might argue that God's tirade is not really a satisfactory answer, and that Job comes out on top in that his arguments are more rational. Scholars have suggested that maybe this is a tongue-in-cheek repentance on Job's part, due to his realization of God's limitations in argument with him. That is not the way it comes across in a straight reading of the book, however.

Job quotes God's first words: 'Who is this that hides counsel without knowledge?' (v. 3). He recognizes that he has questioned beyond the limits of his understanding. He realizes now the full wonder of God's actions in the universe.

Seeing and hearing

Job says an interesting thing in verse 5: he tells God that he had 'heard of you by the hearing of the ear, but now my eye sees you'. This suggests that his understanding of God had previously been by hearsay alone. His actual witnessing of God's presence does seem to have been a more profound experience for him—overriding the fact that God has not really answered his questions. His desire for God to answer him has been exceeded by the profundity of his experience of God.

Often we do not want all our questions answered by God; we wish only to know that he has heard them. Conversely, however, we need to be able to rationalize our faith to a point. It cannot survive if it is based just on emotion or irrationality. Job now despises himself even more for having questioned in the way that he did, and he repents (v. 6). He has, however, been vindicated, in that God has shown that his justice is on a different level to human justice. Thus Job's contention is proved correct, that all human bounds of justice have been broken because of his experience. He does not have a reason for his suffering, but maybe he is coming to understand that there is no reason for it that he will ever comprehend. Understanding is not what matters any more: it is his relationship with God that is, and always has been, at the centre of the debate.

The nature of Job's repentance

Some people have suggested that Job's is a false repentance, a recognition that God has his limitations and that there is no justice in the world after all. Along similar lines, others have wondered whether both of Job's responses are simply an expression of what was expected of him, as in a ritual response of prayer, rather than any genuine repentance. Perhaps he is saying the words of repentance in the situation in which he finds himself, but the words do not come from his heart. These interpretations are perhaps too cynical in the face of what seems to be genuine self-humbling obeisance. Majority opinion sees Job's repentance as genuine and, although there are complaints that Job's repentance spoils the story as he had been such a magisterial figure of protest in the face of undeserved suffering, most take it at face value. Job ultimately proclaims his own limitations in the face of an all-powerful and overwhelming deity whose justice is on another plane than ours.

PRAYER

Lord help us to hear your word and know your presence, and let us look forward to seeing your glory in the world to come.

GOD *against the* FRIENDS

Verse 7 makes the transition to the epilogue, but it is also a pivotal verse for understanding the whole book. The verse seems to vindicate Job for what he has said in contrast to the friends' words. The friends are scolded by God for not having 'spoken of me what is right', as Job has. This is a surprising statement because, all along, the friends seemed to be in the right, maintaining the traditional dogma. Job seemed to be in the wrong in his complaints and in his view of God as his tormentor. Here there is a complete reversal. At last Job is told that he was right to question and that the friends were wrong. This perhaps suggests that it is acceptable to question God's ways, even appearing to put God in the wrong as Job did, rather than uttering platitudes as the friends did. Job has at least learnt something from his experience of suffering: he has grown as a person, while the friends have remained locked into their stock positions.

But then the irony deepens, as we realize that we are now in the realm of the epilogue and Job is about to be rewarded according to the strict doctrine of retribution. Once again he is an innocent man to be rewarded by God with twice as much as he had before. So, in a sense, the friends are proved right! And yet, in his speeches, God has shown that his justice is on another plane. Presumably that means that, while human ideas of justice do prevail at times, at other times they don't. Job was right to question the strict enforcement of such principles and the friends were wrong to think that suffering always meant that the victim had sinned. Job was right to protest, rather than thinking that he knew all the answers as the friends did. In the end Job is vindicated by God. It is beginning to sound like a 'happily ever after' fairytale—or is there just a hint of irony here?

Job's sacrifice

Job is told to make a sacrifice on behalf of them all and to atone for the friends as well as himself (v. 8). This is ironic in the light of Eliphaz's statement in 22:26-30, which suggested that Job would intercede for sinners. All the animosity between Job and the friends is gone, but they are brought low and he is lifted up.

Job is then restored to prosperity in a seeming confirmation of the system of just deserts. The whole dialogue has been spent in overturning that system. How is it that it now seems to be alive and well? We must remember that we are in the epilogue here, and think back to the prologue, which set the scene for the book. Job has passed the test of the prologue with flying colours, and the natural outcome in the epilogue must be his restoration. How else could the book end?

PRAYER

Lord, show us what is right and how we can do 'right' by others, for your name's sake.

COMPANIONSHIP

So, we have the required happy ending. Job's brothers and sisters are mentioned for the first time—so he didn't lose his whole family after all! His wife is not mentioned. The brothers and sisters shower him with gifts, a piece of money and a gold ring from each of them (v. 11). He is once again integrated into his family and into society: his isolation from them was a factor that weighed heavily with him, as we have seen.

We might wonder how we would feel after suffering a great trauma such as Job did, and whether, even with many material goods, we would ever recover mentally. Those who have had experiences of being held hostage or prisoner usually say that the experience had scarred them for the rest of their life.

Doubling of possessions

Job ends up, in true folktale or fairytale style, with twice as many animals as he had before and with a new set of children (vv. 12–13). He is rich—richer than he was before—and he has the blessing of a fresh family. One wonders, though, whether a new family could ever replace the old.

There are some interesting omissions in this section. There is no mention of Job's restoration to health; or of Satan, who has faded right out of the picture although he was the one who inflicted the disease on Job. We are presumably to infer that Job was restored in his body as a part of the restoration of his fortunes, but it is odd that in a passage that has such attention to detail and in all other ways parallels the prologue, this significant factor is not mentioned.

Daughters and longevity

Job has seven sons and three daughters, and we are told the names of the daughters—Jemimah, Keziah and Keren-Happuch—a surprising touch (v. 14). We are told that Job gave them an inheritance as well as their brothers, perhaps to demonstrate his excessive generosity. We are also told of their beauty (v. 15). Finally we hear of Job's longevity, which allowed him to see many generations of children—the Hebrew idea of blessing and of the continuation of a part of oneself after death. He eventually dies happy, 'old and full of days' (v. 17). This is a very different scenario from the bleak pictures of death that have been left behind in the dialogue.

A final word

We have encountered many contrasts in our journey through the book of Job. On the one hand, it talks about a right relationship with God and the happiness that it can bring. This extends to other people and good relationships with them, including our moral behaviour and treatment of others, showing charity to the poor and generosity of spirit to all. This is in contrast to a life racked by pain and fear and darkness, in which God is absent and in which people become tormentors of each other. We, too, have a choice about how to lead our lives and how to influence society for good or bad.

We also have a choice as to how to respond to suffering. Are we going to be like Job the patient, accepting stoically all that comes our way? Or will we be more like Job the protester, waging a battle against God and other people, but gradually coming to a deeper understanding and a calmer acceptance as a result of the trials?

We may never have all the answers: they may be hidden from us, just as ultimate Wisdom is in God's hands. But that doesn't mean giving up the quest to understand and the desire to obtain meaning in life. We should strive to live life to the full and never give up hope in the creator and giver of life, even in our darkest moments.

PRAYER

Lord, we thank you that real-life stories do often have a happy ending. We pray that you may grant us happiness, whatever hardships we may have had to suffer along life's path.

NOTES

NOTES

NOTES

NOTES

JOB

THE PEOPLE'S BIBLE COMMENTARY

VOUCHER SCHEME

The People's Bible Commentary (PBC) provides a range of readable, accessible commentaries that will grow into a library covering the whole Bible.

To help you build your PBC library, we have a voucher scheme that works as follows: a voucher is printed on this page of each People's Bible Commentary volume (as above). These vouchers count towards free copies of other books in the series.

For every four purchases of PBC volumes you are entitled to a further volume FREE.

Please find the coupon for the PBC voucher scheme opposite.

All you need do:

- Cut out the vouchers from the PBCs you have purchased and attach them to the coupon.

- Complete your name and address details, and indicate your choice of free book from the list on page 256.

- Take the coupon to your local Christian bookshop who will exchange it for your free PBC book; or send the coupon straight to BRF who will send you your free book direct. Please allow 28 days for delivery.

Please note that PBC volumes provided under the voucher scheme are subject to availability. If your first choice is not available, you may be sent your second choice of book.

The People's
Bible Commentary

Voucher Scheme Coupon

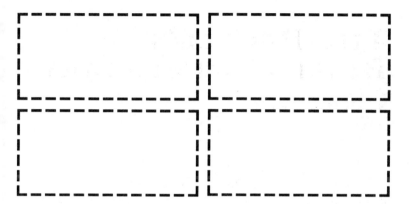

Customer and bookseller should both complete the form
overleaf.

TO BE COMPLETED BY THE CUSTOMER

My choice of free PBC volume is:
(Please indicate a first and second choice;
all volumes are supplied subject to
availability.)

❑ 1 & 2 Samuel
❑ 1 & 2 Kings
❑ Chronicles to Nehemiah
❑ Job
❑ Psalms 1—72
❑ Psalms 73—150
❑ Proverbs
❑ Jeremiah
❑ Ezekiel
❑ Nahum to Malachi
❑ Matthew
❑ Mark
❑ Luke
❑ John
❑ Romans
❑ 1 Corinthians
❑ 2 Corinthians
❑ Galatians and Thessalonians
❑ Ephesians to Colossians
   and Philemon
❑ Timothy, Titus and Hebrews
❑ James to Jude
❑ Revelation

Name: . . . .
Address: . . . .
. . . .
Postcode: . . . .

TO BE COMPLETED BY THE BOOKSELLER

(Please complete the following.
Coupons redeemed will be credited to
your account for the value of the
book(s) supplied as indicated above.
Please note that only coupons correctly
completed with original vouchers will
be accepted for credit.)

Name: . . . .
Address: . . . .
. . . .
Postcode: . . . .
Account Number: . . . .

Completed coupons should be
sent to: BRF, PBC Voucher
Scheme, First Floor, Elsfield Hall,
15–17 Elsfield Way, Oxford
OX2 8FG.

Tel 01865 319700; Fax 01865
319701; e-mail enquiries@brf.org.uk
Registered Charity No. 233280

**THIS OFFER IS AVAILABLE IN THE UK
ONLY**
**PLEASE NOTE: ALL VOUCHERS ATTACHED
TO THE COUPON MUST BE ORIGINAL
COPIES.**